Dangerous Mediations

NEW APPROACHES TO SOUND, MUSIC, AND MEDIA

Series Editors: Carol Vernallis, Holly Rogers, and Lisa Perrott

Forthcoming Titles:

Transmedia Directors edited by Carol Vernallis, Lisa Perrott, and Holly Rogers

Biophilia by Nicola Dibben

David Bowie in Music Video by Lisa Perrott

Animated Music Notation by Cat Hope and Ryan Ross Smith

Resonant Matter by Lutz Koepnick

Assembling Virtual Idols by Nick Prior

Popular Music, Race, and Media since 9/11 by Nabeel Zuberi

Popular Music and Narrativity by Alex Jeffery

Dangerous Mediations

Pop Music in a Philippine Prison Video

ÁINE MANGAOANG

BLOOMSBURY ACADEMIC
NEW YORK • LONDON • OXFORD • NEW DELHI • SYDNEY

BLOOMSBURY ACADEMIC
Bloomsbury Publishing Inc
1385 Broadway, New York, NY 10018, USA
50 Bedford Square, London, WC1B 3DP, UK
29 Earlsfort Terrace, Dublin 2, Ireland

BLOOMSBURY, BLOOMSBURY ACADEMIC and the Diana logo are
trademarks of Bloomsbury Publishing Plc

First published in the United States of America 2019
Paperback edition published 2021

Copyright © Áine Mangaoang, 2019

For legal purposes the Acknowledgements on p. xiii constitute an extension of this copyright page.

Parts of this book appeared in *Torture: Journal on Music in Detention*, 23(2) (2013) and in *Postcolonial Text*, 9(4) (2014).

Cover design by Daniel Benneworth-Gray
Cover image: 'Girl at CPDRC' image by Derek Foott
Photo taken by Áine Mangaoang

All rights reserved. No part of this publication may be reproduced or transmitted in any form or by any means, electronic or mechanical, including photocopying, recording, or any information storage or retrieval system, without prior permission in writing from the publishers.

Bloomsbury Publishing Inc does not have any control over, or responsibility for, any third-party websites referred to or in this book. All internet addresses given in this book were correct at the time of going to press. The author and publisher regret any inconvenience caused if addresses have changed or sites have ceased to exist, but can accept no responsibility for any such changes.

Library of Congress Cataloging-in-Publication Data
Names: Mangaoang, âAine, author.
Title: Dangerous mediations : pop music in a Philippine prison video / âAine Mangaoang.
Description: New York, NY : Bloomsbury Academic, 2019. | Series: New approaches to sound, music, and media | Includes bibliographical references and index.
Identifiers: LCCN 2019008321 (print) | LCCN 2019013007 (ebook) | ISBN 9781501331541 (ePDF) | ISBN 9781501331558 (ePub) | ISBN 9781501331534 (hardback : alk. paper)
Subjects: LCSH: Music in prisons–Philippines. | Popular music–Moral and ethical aspects. | Music videos–Moral and ethical aspects. | Cebu Provincial Detention and Rehabilitation Centre.
Classification: LCC ML3920 (ebook) | LCC ML3920 .M155 2019 (print) | DDC 306.4/8424095995–dc23
LC record available at https://lccn.loc.gov/2019008321

ISBN:	HB:	978-1-5013-3153-4
	PB:	978-1-5013-7838-6
	ePDF:	978-1-5013-3154-1
	eBook:	978-1-5013-3155-8

Series: New Approaches to Sound, Music, and Media

Typeset by Integra Software Services Pvt. Ltd.

To find out more about our authors and books visit www.bloomsbury.com and sign up for our newsletters.

To the dancers
– past and present –
of the Cebu Provincial Detention and Rehabilitation Centre.

CONTENTS

Figures ix
Tables xii
Acknowledgements xiii

Introduction 1

Interlude One   'The *Evil* of the Thriller'   15

1   Seeing sound: Locating music and YouTube's symbiosis 19

Interlude Two   'You're fighting for your life inside a killer, thriller'   41

2   Performing postcolonialism: Filipino history through four-part harmony 45

Interlude Three   Fade to black   71

3   Penal tourists 2.0: The birth of CPDRC's pop programme 75

Interlude Four   'Music is the language of the soul'   91

4   Beats behind bars: Docile bodies and the digital panopticon 95

Interlude Five   Michael Jackson, the undead and the posthumous duet 117

5   Thrilling: Remediating *Thriller* 121

Interlude Six   'It's more fun in the Philippines' 137

6   'Together in electric dreams': Hybridity, nostalgia and imagination in CPDRC 139

Interlude Seven   Thank you for the music 153

7   YouTube's penal spectators 157

Coda 181

Appendix: CPDRC dancing inmates YouTube video uploads by Byron F. Garcia 194
Glossary 197
Notes 199
References 213
Index 229

FIGURES

1.1 Arm in arm, the leading protagonists skip along the concrete yard in byronfgarcia's '"Thriller" (original upload)' 16

2.1 'Better than a trip through the Philippine Islands': brochure front cover of the Philippine Exposition at the World's Fair St. Louis (1904) featuring an unnamed, so-called native Filipino 50

2.2 and 2.3 Crisanto Niere, dancing 'preso', describes why he was chosen as the lead dancer in *Thriller*. Interview in *Dancing for Discipline* 67

2.4 and 2.5 Programmatic control in practice. Photographs from the daily CPDRC dance rehearsals, featuring an inmate wearing a vest bearing the slogan 'I'm Easy To Use And Operate' 69

3.1 Michael Jackson's knowing smile (12.01 minutes) in Michael Jackson's *Thriller* 72

3.2 The final image breaks down into a constellation of black, white and orange at 4.13 minutes into CPDRC's *Thriller* 73

3.3 Gwendolyn Garcia's portrait and profile, featuring choice photographs highlighting the key aspects of her tenure 76

3.4 Still from *The Shawshank Redemption* 79

3.5	Poster produced by Cebu Provincial Capitol advertising the CPDRC Dancing Inmates 'LIVE' performance on 29 May 2010	82
3.6–3.9	Example of four photographs taken by different international tourists and visitors at CPDRC and publicly shared on Instagram	85
4.1–4.3	Scenes of Bilibid prison, in 1930s Manila	93
4.4	Plan of panopticon by Jeremy Bentham	106
5.1	Participants battle it out in the Michael Jackson Dance-Off, Thrill the World	122
5.2	A 'Smooth Criminal' era Michael Jackson fan	122
5.3	A Filipino youth in his red, homemade 'Thriller' jacket	123
5.4	Bassline for 'Thriller'	126
5.5	Bass riff for 'Give It to Me Baby'	126
6.1 and 6.2	The flag-waving interlude from Randy Kofahl's YouTube video of CPDRC's 'Together in Electric Dreams'	140
7.1	A large tarpaulin sign extolling the CPDRC ethos greets you at the entrance/waiting area to the facility	154
7.2	The prison yard transformed into a site of arts and crafts preparation for the upcoming Sinulog costumes	155
7.3	The view of the CPDRC's music room, which overlooks the prison yard	177
8.1	Bootleg DVD featuring *Cebu Dancing Inmates: Gangnam Style* and a pirated copy of American police thriller drama *End of Watch* on sale from a street vendor stall in Marikina, Metro Manila, 20 October 2012	182

8.2	'Do thriller!' commands YouTuber TakingBackFlow; 'ok, will do!' replies byronfgarcia	184
8.3	The Carmelite Sisters of Cebu's Filipino-Hawaiian dance, June 2017	189

TABLES

1.1 Three commonly held perceptions about YouTube 34
1.2 Top 10 most viewed video channels on YouTube 36
1.3 List of the 'most viewed' YouTube videos of all time (as of 30 June 2014) 37
2.1 28 of the 53 Cebuano festivals held annually that prominently feature dance and music 60
7.1 Categories of YouTube comments left by CPDRC's *Thriller* audiences 161
7.2 A sample of CPDRC's *Thriller* YouTube comments expressing being entertained – through an incitement of pleasure, emotion and/or amusement – from watching Garcia's original CPDRC *Thriller* video 171

ACKNOWLEDGEMENTS

Like so many books, this one would not exist without a number of colleagues, friends and family who supported this project from the outset. Thank you Derek Foott, for everything. And a special welcome to little Samuel, who arrived soon after this manuscript was sent to the publishers. My parents Marian and Antonio and sisters Maeve, Deirdre and Marian Antoinette – thanks for your astute insights on all things pop music, psychology, politics and Pinoy karaoke. Special thanks to Sarah and Richard for so many acts of kindness along the way, and to all the extended Mangaoang and Foott families for your constant encouragement as this project stretched over years and across many miles.

The Bloomsbury 'New Approaches to Sound, Music, and Media' series editors Holly Rogers, Carol Vernallis and Lisa Perrott believed in this book from the get-go. I am grateful for your generous comments, conversations and enduring patience throughout the process. Thanks to Leah Babb-Rosenfeld, Katherine de Chant and Amy Martin at Bloomsbury, and Damian Penfold at Integra, who offered important support to bring this book into existence and helped see me through the last mile of the marathon.

This project was sustained with the help of people, institutions and organizations as I worked in between (and sometimes across) four cities and countries. Starting in Ireland a decade ago, an unlikely presentation during my musicology and cultural history Master's at University College Cork started this great ball rolling. *Go raibh míle maith agaibh* to the teachers who taught me so much, and were instrumental in encouraging me to keep at this thing called research: Áine Sheil, Melanie Marshall, Paul Everett, Christopher Morris and Mel Mercier. The seeds of this book were sown as a doctoral thesis awarded by University of Liverpool in 2015. For this I owe a great deal of thanks to Anahid Kassabian, and to my committee, Freya Jarman, Jason Stanyek and Rob Strachan. The Institute of Popular Music 21st Anniversary Scholarship from the University of Liverpool provided me with the funding to pursue a PhD as well as conduct research in the Philippines in 2012–13, and colleagues Sara Cohen, Marion Leonard, Kenneth Smith, Hae-Kyung Um and Mike Jones made my time in Liverpool all the more enjoyable.

At the wise suggestion of Ricky Abad, initial research in the Philippines was made possible through a Visiting Researcher position at the Institute of Philippine Culture, Ateneo de Manila University. I thank Czarina Saloma-Akpedonu and all the staff at the IPC for making my first Filipino *Pasko* so memorable, as well as Ateneo's Rizal Library and the University of the Philippines College of Music Library for their assistance. Thanks to the Cebu Provincial Capitol Archives, the John L. Silva Collection and Elly A. Gooetz for permission to include their images. The Instagram posters included in figures 3.6, 3.8 and 3.9 were contacted for permission, but with no response at the time of going to print. José Buenconsejo, thanks for the warmest welcome to the University of the Philippines and for providing a forum to share my work-in-progress with the great minds at the Department of Music. A rather naive pop musicologist, I quickly learned through this project just how difficult it can be to get into prison to conduct research, how much my presence in the prison created additional work for many individuals, and indeed how very privileged I am to be able to leave when the interviews were over. Permission to visit CPDRC and Cebu Capitol Building was granted by Vice Governor Agnes Magpale, Acting Warden Algier C. Comendador, Acting Warden Bobby Legaspi and CPDRC choreographer Vince Rosales, who allowed me to sit in on dance rehearsals and chat with CPDRC staff and inmates on multiple occasions from 2012–17. Each trip to Cebu was enhanced by the most lively of welcomes from Mo. Mary Aimee Ataviado, Sr. Elia, Sr. Jacinta and all the Carmelite Sisters. *Daghang salamat po* for plying me with *sikwate*, and teaching me how to truly dance the Sinulog. My experiences in Cebuano culture were made all the more fun thanks to insider tips from MC Ren Campanilla, hypeman Genes Tapales and the Cebu Elite Beatboxers United crew.

My colleagues at the University of Oslo's Department of Musicology are the embodiment of encouragement, providing the cosiest environment to research in, and all other manner of assistance necessary to bring this book to completion. Thank you all, especially Stan Hawkins, Raghnild Brøvig-Hanssen, Rolf Inge Godøy, Nanette Nielsen, Peter Edwards, Even Ruud, Hallgjerd Asknes, Kyle Devine and Hans Weisethaunet. The administrative wizardry of Målfrid Hoass, Victoria Tømeraas Berg, Ingrid Bugge Stange and Heidi Bråthan helped ease many practicalities of research.

Beyond these institutional and geographical borders, I am grateful to many thoughtful scholars and friends who have inspired, influenced, and refined many aspects of this book – in particular Tejaswinee Kelkar, Þorbjörg Daphne Hall, Aileen Dillane, John O'Flynn, Griff Rollefson, Tom Western, Anna Papaeti, Jennie Henley, Vincenz Serrano, Ben Harbert, James Butterworth, Emily Baker, Chen-Yu Mag Lin, Leonieke Bolderman, Ragnhild Torvanger Solberg, Kai Arne Hansen, Tore Størvold, Fritz Schenker, Kathrine Barnecutt, Mauwen Luna, Janette and James Rinando, Sarah Burke, Avril O'Sullivan and Maggie White.

Lastly, I owe the most gratitude to the dancers of CPDRC, without whom none of this would be possible. Many of you are not named in these pages, but I hope I have done justice to your experiences. And so it is to the CPDRC inmates – past and present – that this work is dedicated.

Introduction

On 27 June 2009, within ten hours of the breaking news of Michael Jackson's death, prison warden Byron F. Garcia arranged for a music and dance tribute to the King of Pop to be performed by some 1,500 prisoners in front of a live audience of tourists and media corporations in the exercise yard of Cebu Provincial Detention and Rehabilitation Centre (CPDRC) (Garcia 2009a). Neatly dressed in identical bright orange prison jumpsuits with feet moving in matching black and white Chuck Taylor sneakers, the inmates dance to a ten-minute medley of Jackson's hits 'Ben' (1972), 'I'll Be There' (1970) and 'We are the World' (1985) piped through the prison loudspeakers, with such precision and passion that one would be forgiven for thinking one was watching a professional, if slightly unorthodox, Broadway musical.

Such a feat might have gone unnoticed by international media in the turbulent wake of Jackson's death, only for the fact that these prisoners were already YouTube stars who became bona fide internet celebrities following their YouTube 2007 interpretation of Michael Jackson's 1982 epic music video *Thriller* (Garcia 2007a; hereafter referred to as CPDRC's *Thriller*). With over 50 million views to date through the video-sharing platform YouTube, the inmate performers – known as the Dancing Inmates[1] of CPDRC – received attention from an array of mainstream news conglomerates (Al Jazeera, BBC, CNN) and independent bloggers, as videos and photographs of the inmates' dancing appeared throughout the internet, mingling alongside personal messages and professional memos, in email inboxes and on social network pages. Garcia's CPDRC inmates' video-recorded interpretation of *Thriller* takes pride of place in YouTube culture as one of the earliest, and most enduringly popular, viral videos in internet history. As an example of a post-MTV music video, CPDRC's *Thriller* forms part of a growing digital-era practice of covering, sampling and remediating previously recorded music, and these kinds of intensified audiovisual aesthetics have become significant source texts in popular music culture. Connecting existing scholarship on popular music and music video with emerging literature on YouTube, *Dangerous Mediations* is about how scratching the surface of this one, seemingly innocuous, YouTube video can unravel a myriad of questions regarding pop music entertainment, postcolonialism, government policy and prisoner agency. Against this backdrop, I intend for the title *Dangerous Mediations,* to relate to the problematic, precarious and potentially perilous nature of today's media culture's 'YouTube-ification' (Vernallis 2013: 14). To perform a 'dangerous' reading of a media text like CPDRC's *Thriller* is to highlight the significance of historical contexts, ideologies and power relations often not visible at first glance; but without which such mediations would be impossible. By evoking the term 'dangerous', this book suggests that there is indeed a dangerous dynamic to YouTube videos like CPDRC's *Thriller,* with very real consequences for the inmates on the receiving end.

The aim of *Dangerous Mediations,* then, is twofold: one, to offer more recognition and understanding of the complexities of YouTube, as both a site of commercial enterprise and a cultural citizenship; and two, to offer more recognition and understanding of those who find themselves described, or defined, as prisoners. By drawing from the specific yet broad case study of the CPDRC's Dancing Inmates programme, I show how music can serve the moral purpose of creating a more liveable life for those who experience imprisonment, however in doing so reveal the complexities of circulating such work on the cultural yet commercial platform that is YouTube. The following three key themes form the heart of the book's seven chapters, and I listen to these heartbeats as I disentangle the complex issues that CPDRC's *Thriller* brings with it: 1. musical mediations of power and subversion; 2. prison, subjectivity and spectacular entertainment; and 3. music and mediation in postcolonial Philippines.

Musical mediations of power and subversion

Music's function within society and culture always already holds the possibility for danger. The importance of music is far-reaching and not at all limited to understandings in the field of musicology, as philosophers, scientists, medics and therapists alike have written of the many benefits of mankind's exposure to music. In times of war and peace, music is known for promoting physiological and psychological health, maintaining strength and well-being, as well as serving as a form of self-expression and social cohesion. Countless arias, anthems and albums pay homage to music's positive healing powers. In their 1977 ode to music, pop royalty ABBA rhetorically ask us to imagine 'what would life be?' without music. Indeed, as cited in Interlude 7, without music, or specifically for ABBA, without a song or dance, what *are* we?

Philosophers, critics, lawmakers and artists have always argued for the power of sounds and images. Over the past several decades we have seen a major shift in how scholars understand modern power relations in terms of audio/visual sounds and images. Jacques Attali asserts that with music power is born, and also subversion (Attali 1985: 6). Michel Foucault's writings on the power of the panopticon and the confessional demonstrated the intricate relationship between seeing and being seen, hearing and being heard, and how these relations were thoroughly connected to modern concepts of power (Foucault 1977).[2] In the age of new media, where we assume, invariably, that many – but not all – of the world's population have the means to access sound- and image-making media, the boundaries between production, circulation and consumption have become increasingly blurred. Inextricably bound up with instances of visual and sonic power – who sees and who is seen, who hears and who is heard – are questions of politics, colonialisms and postcolonialisms. *Dangerous Mediations* is, fundamentally, centred on the relationship between music, media and power. These 'dangerous mediations' explore the meanings, performances and practices of music as mediated technology and power intersect with the CPDRC's pop-dance performances.

The underlying power of music, its subversive possibilities and its use as a weapon of war are not new phenomena, nor are they especially recent concepts. The Old Testament's account of 'The Battle of Jericho' describes God instructing Joshua to have 'men of war' march around the city of Jericho shouting and blowing trumpets (rams' horns) for seven days. On the seventh day, the walls collapsed, the Israelites charged and destroyed the city, and what follows paints a somewhat harrowing picture, as the narrative describes the killing of every man, woman, child and animal as per God's commands. Whether truth or fable, the historical account of the Battle of Jericho tells us that music's role in places of conflict and its use as a powerful weapon is as old as civilization itself; for indeed, every army in the world has music.

During the last two decades, a need has arisen among scholars to recognize and address the ever-increasing media and literature output surrounding music's role in the areas of detention, violence and trauma. As musicologists, scholars whose fundamental purpose is the study of music, how do we react to such uses of music in contemporary and everyday situations of violence? How do we confront uses of music that are not positive or forces for good, but rather, those that are experienced as 'irritation, manipulation, pain and torture' (Goodman 2010: 17)? In *Torture Journal: Thematic Issue on Music in Detention* (2013), editors Anna Papaeti and M. J. Grant give their reasons for the seeming neglect of this subject by musicologists, starting with the historically rooted belief in the enriching power of music. They write that the:

> presumption that music is an invariably uplifting and ennobling art form is well established and dates back to antiquity. For the Pythagoreans and

the Greek philosopher Aristoxenus of Tarentum, music carried healing powers: while medicine healed the body, music soothed the soul. In the much older Ayurvedic tradition, music was (and is) recognised for its holistic influence on both physical and mental processes. (2013: 1)

For Papaeti and Grant as well as Johnson and Cloonan (2009), the positive function of music that dominates music research can be highlighted in the many 'music as healer, music as refuge' sayings that continue to do the proverbial rounds both online and off.[3] Music has the innate 'seductive power to caress the skin, to immerse, to sooth, beckon, and heal,' Steve Goodman writes, 'to modulate brain waves and massage the release of certain hormones within the body' (2010: 5). Although largely overlooked in academia during the twentieth century for reasons discussed later, this research topic has started to appear in publications over the past decade by an array of scholars including John Morgan O'Connell and Salwa El-Shawan Castelo-Branco's ethnomusicological collection *Music and Conflict* (2010), Susan Fast and Kip Pegley's focus on the paradox of music violence in the *Music, Politics, and Violence* (2012) edited volume, and William Cheng's recent monograph *Just Vibrations: The Purpose of Sounding Good* (2016).

Conceiving of music as a positive and therapeutic force, both in popular and academic discourse, has perhaps meant that music's 'long and equally well-founded association with war, punishment and humiliation across diverse historical periods and cultural and geographical regions' have been comparatively overlooked (Papaeti and Grant 2013: 1). Traditional musicology has had a perhaps implicit and ideological function of legitimizing, valorizing and canonizing certain types of music, particularly those that fall into Western art traditions. An implicit part of this function has been that certain types of music are deemed transcendentally uplifting, valuable and enriching. The consequence of this has occurred in the fields of critical musicology and popular music studies, which in contrast has had an anti-canonizing propensity – or in some cases at least, tried to conceive of a counter-canonizing tendency – that attempts to broaden the array of musicians deemed worthy of scholarly attention. Yet the result of this, particularly in popular music studies' formative years, is that some popular music research has tended to be overly (and/or overtly) celebratory.

With a number of media reports on music and violence in the post-9/11 years as well as more frequent instances of cinematic and televisual representations of music's use as a form of violence and torture,[4] we are faced with such mounting questions as:

> Can music be considered a form of torture? Is it music 'in itself' or the high volume and repetition that transforms it into torture or cruel, inhuman and degrading treatment or punishment? Can the use of music in detention be beneficial for the prisoners, or is it always aligned with an intention to subdue, break, and often ridicule them? (Papaeti and Grant 2013: 1).

We must reconceptualize music – not only as a form of self-expression or socio-culture – but rather, as a weapon, one that can assert power, inflict violence, trauma and cultural imperialism.

Musicological research has recently begun to address such questions, first and foremost by acknowledging that music is not simply a source for power, but power in and of itself (Johnson and Cloonan 2009). Leading the research in music and contemporary warfare is Suzanne Cusick, who combines ethnography, fieldwork and critical theory to provide harrowing but nonetheless critical examples of the United States' use of music as a form of cultural warfare and so-called no-touch torture. Cusick's work highlights in painful detail how Western popular music is intentionally used to humiliate detainees from different cultural backgrounds, and in doing so it not only degrades the human being and the cultural value of the music in question, but more significantly, serves as a component of US symbolic claim to global sovereignty (Cusick 2006: 10). Arguing that although the general premise is that sound can damage human beings, but usually without killing us, Cusick reiterates that the twofold use of music torture is as follows:

> What differentiates the uses of sound or music on the battlefield and the uses of sound or music in the interrogation room is the claimed site of the damage. Theorists of battlefield use emphasise sound's bodily effects, while theorists of the interrogation room focus on the capacity of sound and music to destroy subjectivity. (2006: 5)

The dual use of music, on the frontline and inside prison facilities, speaks to different functions yet ultimately yields the same result – a cruelty that is embodied and thus destroys agency. Cusick's work on music torture sparked vigorous debates on ethics, morals and responsibility within US musicology, and ultimately led to the boards of the American Musicological Society, the Society for American Music and the Society for Ethnomusicology Contemporary passing a joint resolution in March 2008 condemning the use of music for physical or psychological torture. There remains no clear, unambiguous legal framework regarding the use of music in places of detention, and in general the public's response to findings of music's use against detainees in US detention camps remains at best trivial, as Johnson and Cloonan's research detailed (2009: 189–91).[5]

Prison, subjectivity and spectacular entertainment

YouTube videos like CPDRC's *Thriller,* thanks to their power to audiovisually document their subject matter, can record vestiges of contemporary imprisonment in ways that the majority of the population will never witness first-hand. Today, we have come to understand a little of 'the history, forms and functions of modern punishment through images,' as Michelle Brown reminds us (2012: 101). In *Dangerous Mediations*, I build on Brown's assertion and add that much of what we know – or *think* we know – about prisons stems from both visual *and* sonic mediations. Although I address an example of recent mediated prison culture through the lens of surveillance, governmentality theory and the subject, I draw from a range of scholarship written in the past century (and occasionally earlier) to give some historical context to my contemporary arguments on prison performance, spectacular entertainment and digital media.

Throughout *Dangerous Mediations*, government – primarily in relation to the local Cebu administration and by extension, the Philippine government – is used in a broad sense to refer to the 'conduct of conduct' (Foucault 1991), which pertains not only to the state but also to a range of institutions, actions and forms of knowledge. Governmentality here concerns the organized practices of governing others and ourselves in a variety of contexts. Related to Foucault's idea of governmentality, and central to this book, are the ways in which people are constituted as subjects – those inmates who are 'compelled' to dance for us in their prison yard, but also the YouTube audiences who spend hundreds of hours scrolling and clicking through YouTube video after YouTube video. The term 'subject' has, in a Foucauldian sense, dual meaning: 'subject to someone else by control and dependence, and tied to his own identity by a conscience or self-knowledge' (Foucault 1982: 212). Interpreting Foucault, Judith Butler sees subjection as literally meaning the *making* of a subject:

> the principle of regulation according to which a subject is formulated or produced. Such subjection is a kind of power that not only unilaterally *acts on* a given individual as a form of domination, but also *activates* or forms the subject. Hence, subjection is neither simply the domination of a subject nor its production, but designates a certain kind of restriction *in* production, a restriction without which the production of the subject cannot take place, a restriction through which that production takes place. (1997: 84)

Through its operations on subjectivity, power works in subtle ways in modern liberal democracy. Neoliberal discourse, through which the Philippine state governs, is characterized by the market mechanisms for global trade and investment supposed for all nations to thrive equitably. The main points of Philippine state-led neoliberalism include deregulation, privatization of public enterprises, reducing public expenditure for social services by the government, and the change in perceptions of public and community good, to individualism and responsibility of the individual, while fundamentally remaining concerned with the rule of the market. In *Dangerous Mediations*

I am particularly concerned with how people are constituted in such contemporary liberal democracies. I draw on the 'pastoral power' of the Philippine state in overseeing – and supporting the continuation of – the CPDRC music and dance programme. The pastoral power vested in (Christian) churches and related subsidiaries is often linked to modernity, since they appeared more reciprocal than monarchies in their response to the communities and individual quests for personal salvation. We see the state, Foucault argues, positioned as 'a modern matrix of individualisation or a new form of pastoral power' (1982: 783). As I later argue, in CPDRC power has shifted to the Philippine state on the one hand, while on the other the new pastoral power lies in the hands of the YouTube viewing public.

Music and mediation in postcolonial Philippines

The Philippines presents a ripe locus for an investigation on music, media and cultural history. Yet to understand the overwhelmingly favourable reception of the CPDRC performances on YouTube is, on the one hand, to address the age-old assumptions of music's assumed positive function. On the other hand, it simultaneously calls for an investigation into an imagined Philippines that is clearly and eagerly constructed in the videos through a postcolonial project. I argue that colonial stereotypes of the Filipino race as inferior, child-like, feminized, have extended from US imperial operations at the turn of the twentieth century. In part, it is this logic, born of colonialism, racism and gender discrimination, that allowed for CPDRC's YouTube performances to be viewed uncritically, read almost exclusively as entertainment, and celebrated internationally in YouTube comments, newspapers and tourist guidebooks.

Achieving independence from the USA in 1946, followed less than two decades later by a period of martial law (1965–86), the Philippines has overcome centuries of colonial oppression to become a newly industrialized country and one of the fastest growing Asian economies.[6] This cosmopolitan nation with a significant diaspora – approximately 10 per cent of the population of the Philippines live abroad – in addition to a growing youth population (44 per cent of the population is in the 18–24 age bracket) has enabled the Philippines to transform from being the text-messaging capital of the world to the social media, social networking and, most recently, the 'selfiest' capital of the world (Wilson 2014).[7] Old and new media ubiquitously exist side by side in the gleaming malls and back-street karaoke bars of Makati, Baguio and Cebu. The popularity of online social media in the Philippines has been growing steadily over the past decade, from 8.27 million internet users in the Philippines in 2009 to 35.04 million in 2012 before reaching in excess of 54 million by 2016 – over half of the national population.[8]

By 2016, from a total population of 101 million there were 119 million mobile phone subscriptions (117 per cent penetration rate), and 55 per cent of these have a mobile broadband subscription (Garcia 2016). Filipinos spend on average between 3.2 and 5.2 hours online (mobile phone versus desktop and tablet); almost half of that time is spent on social media sites like Facebook (47 per cent) and nearly one-fifth (19 per cent) is spent on video-sharing platforms like YouTube. Social network sites like Facebook – which has been available in the Philippines since 2010 – boasted 47 million active profiles in the Philippines by 2016. The second biggest search engine in the world, it is no accident that YouTube chose the Philippines to launch their first localized Southeast Asian service in October 2011, thereby aggregating the video content – and advertising – that YouTube determine most relevant for Filipino audiences. Partnering with Filipino media companies including ABS-CBN, GMA Network, and music labels like VIVA Records, PinoyTuner, Vicor Records and Star Records, the move to a localized site enabled Philippine-based creators who enjoyed millions of views to earn revenue from advertising placements. Such was the popularity of the localized Filipino YouTube service that by 2016, the Philippine government's YouTube channel (the Philippines' Presidential Broadcast Staff Channel or the RTVM Malacañang) was ranked as the second most active world leader on YouTube by virtue of uploading over 8,200 videos and 290 playlists (Burson-Marsteller 2016).

From the bottom-up and top-down, digital technology and social media are fundamental ways for Filipinos to stay connected with their communities, both in the Philippines and the large diaspora of Overseas Filipino Workers (OFW) scattered throughout the world. Scholarship focused on the Philippines and/in social media are in comparatively short supply given its popularity and proliferation in the Philippines. Notable exceptions include Deirdre McKay's work on social media in Filipino social networking and across the Filipino diaspora (2007; 2016), and a recent burst in sociology-oriented publications on social media, ethics and digital humanitarianism (Cabanes and Acedera 2012; David, Ong and Legara 2016; Madianou, Longboan and Ong 2015; Ong 2017). However, discussions of music and social media in a Philippine context are far more scarce, as are studies on contemporary Philippine popular music practices. Frederick (Fritz) Schenker's PhD dissertation *Empire of Syncopation: Music, Race, and Labour in Colonial Asia's Jazz Age* (2016) offers an insightful reading of the music and musical relationships between the Philippines and USA in the early twentieth century. Monika Schoop's recent monograph *Independent Music and Digital Technology in the Philippines* is a breakthrough, marking the only major academic (ethno)musicological and social media study of Metro Manila (2017). A further exception is Christi-Anne Castro's essay on subjectivity and hybridity in the case of Charice Pempengco and Arnel Pineda (2010). The compelling nexus between the Philippines, Filipinos and Filipino culture, with contemporary music and media practice, makes the Philippines an apt site to investigate the intersections of music, new media and mediation.

A note on method

Dangerous Mediations comprehends the CPDRC phenomenon by considering the many facets that resulted in the international popularity of their video and the after-effects of these. This required an alternation of ethno/musicological methods including textual and discourse analysis of the online, audiovisual works during my doctoral study in Liverpool and postdoctoral research in Oslo, as well as field visits to Cebu for conversations with CPDRC staff, inmates and government officials between September 2012 and June 2017. Interviews with inmates were only permitted to be conducted in the presence of CPDRC staff, and interviews with staff were held with government officials who were present. After much consideration, I chose not to include transcripts of interviews with the inmates I spoke with, but I do make reference to points made during interviews with CPDRC staff. This distinction is purposeful, and attempts to take into account critical issues of agency and ethics that such different kinds of interviews present. This conflation of methods – fluctuating between the online and offline – provides an interdisciplinary, holistic approach to assist understanding of the intimately interconnected conventions of music as rehabilitation, nation and postcolonial culture. Accordingly, this work draws from the perspectives of textual and contextual analysis, popular musicology, new media studies and intertextuality to trace the impact of a new audiovisual work – CPDRC's *Thriller*, the legacy of a historic music video, Michael Jackson's *Thriller* – and recontextualizes these works by putting the Filipino Dancing Inmates of CPDRC at the heart of this book.

My research, therefore, differs to many other YouTube, DIY music videos, music and cultural history projects as I utilize both a textual and contextual approach to examine the aesthetic, cultural, ideological and industrial implications of this powerful, independently produced YouTube video. There are limitations to research like mine that deals with a single, localized case study rather than a broad investigation into the use of music in multiple places of detention. However, this single case study offers much insight into the world of new and complex audiovisual textures and cultures. The theoretical ramifications of this case study are many: as we will see, the audiovisual, digital swirl of CPDRC's *Thriller* facilitates a form of social control, as much for the inmates captured as for the 'free' audience surveilling their performances from both near and far.

The CPDRC performances – experienced online and off – enlist audience responses akin to that from the spectacles of punishment going back to the medieval period, serving to reinforce 'us' and 'them' differences. CPDRC's *Thriller* offers a critical challenge for all readers to redirect the colonial gaze, the prison gaze and the YouTube gaze to the historic forces that gave rise to these situations. And as I argue throughout these pages, not only do the implications of this case study bear relevance to a great deal of YouTube videos, but more specifically, the ramifications are pertinent to our engagement with contemporary popular music practice, new audiovisual media and online participatory culture.

Troubling statistics: The perils of researching YouTube

As this book is, in part, an investigation of a specific YouTube practice embedded in a particular time and place, on occasion it required the use of figures collected by YouTube or by various music institutions that might often be, at best, somewhat biased. The inclusion of such statistics is not without its methodological problems. Still, such statistics reproduced in this book are considered constructive, when understood with a certain critical awareness, as providing a starting point with illustrative purposes – as part of a wider discourse. At points throughout *Dangerous Mediations*, view-counts, chart sales and other statistical data are reproduced regarding key music and video works, primarily because it seemed necessary to ascertain the YouTube view count of the CPDRC's *Thriller* video that forms the heart of this study. For the sake of clarity, I report the number of views on the original posting of CPDRC's *Thriller* – Byron F. Garcia's uploaded video only – knowingly leaving aside the hundreds, and potentially thousands of digitally replicated as well as alternative, remixed or more recent live versions of CPDRC's *Thriller* available on YouTube. For example, a search in YouTube for 'cpdrc thriller' on 12 June 2014 produces about 6,170 video results. The top results include the '"Thriller" (original upload)' video by Byron F. Garcia, followed by various versions of CPDRC's *Thriller* performances taken by fans, visitors to the facility and/or prison officials in 2009, 2008 and 2011. Additional results include CPDRC's *Thriller* in a YouTube-curated video mix that includes such other famous viral videos as the 'Evolution of Dance' video, 'Charlie bit my finger' and 'JK Wedding Entrance Dance'. Apart from the impossibility of collating every single mirrored and remixed version of CPDRC's *Thriller* that exists and monitoring their fluctuating status, such a task is beyond the scope of my research – yet it is nevertheless important to help understand the implications of studying such ever-shifting, complex, multifaceted texts. One must acknowledge the sheer multitude of replicas and remediations that YouTube's circulation affords, and put in place necessary limitations on the scope of approaching any study of YouTube videos.

Dangerous Mediations' structure and approach

The seven chapters that follow are structured around understanding CPDRC's *Thriller* through the relationship between musical mediations of power and subversion; prison, subjectivity and spectacular entertainment; and music and mediation in postcolonial Philippines. Each chapter is preceded by a reflexive interlude, interwoven in between the chapters as a gesture towards *katakata*: the Filipino art of didactic storytelling.[9] Collectively, the interludes detail assorted thematic narratives from external and internal perspectives, drawing explicit attention to specific moments of import that function as linchpins to discussions in the subsequent chapters. Each interlude has a practical function, at times describing moments from YouTube videos or fieldwork in a manner not possible in the chapters themselves. Moreover, they act as a shared starting point for the reader.

The chapters zigzag across what can only seem to be exceedingly disjunctive categories: from music videos and YouTube; a retelling of Philippine postcolonial history through music and dance; sound and punishment, hybridity and nostalgia; to YouTube, spectatorship and remediating Michael Jackson. All of this aims to achieve two things: first, to situate CPDRC's *Thriller* in the wider context of such historical concepts and moments; second, to reveal, little by little, the many and varied environments that were required to create a video like CPDRC's *Thriller*, as well as lay bare the *mechanisms* required for it to go viral. Despite the vast array of issues presented in each of the chapters, together they work to show how a seemingly innocuous YouTube video draws on established histories, which, if ignored, can indeed be dangerous.

The significance of YouTube's interface is crucial in understanding this video, and so I begin Chapter 1 by addressing digital culture and the changing status of the music video within today's music industries. Throughout this chapter, I put forward new ideas on music and YouTube's (largely overlooked) symbiotic relationship in order to expose how CPDRC's *Thriller* emerged from this very particular user-generated, audiovisual environment. Central to *Dangerous Mediations* is the notion that the apparent success of CPDRC's *Thriller* relies not only on its position on YouTube's website, but also on a web of colonial histories and postcolonial discourses. To that end, Chapter 2 makes the obligatory leap from online to offline, mapping Philippine postcolonial history through mediations of music and dance. By doing this, I develop a correlation between issues raised from the colonial, historical, musical moments from the Philippine Exposition at the St. Louis World Fair (1904) with the audiovisual, digitized representations of the CPDRC inmates on YouTube.

Following on from this, Chapter 3 investigates the origins of CPDRC's *Thriller* from the ground up, introducing the main Cebuano political players behind the viral video – the powerful Garcia family. I unearth the prison's politicized transformation into a hybridized form of popular music heritage, problematizing the matter of CPDRC's emergence as a popular prison tourism destination. Chapter 4 advances the specific issues of music and/ in a Philippine prison raised in Chapter 3, and situates CPDRC's music and dance practice within the wider – and more subversive – practice of using music in places of detention. Drawing from contemporary and historical accounts of discipline, punishment and surveillance from around the world, I argue that CPDRC's YouTube foothold creates a kind of digital panopticon where inmates are policed and surveilled by a global public.

In Chapter 5, I take a slightly sideways but necessary glance to address CPDRC's *Thriller* from the perspective of Michael Jackson's oeuvre and global impact. Given the lasting legacy of *Thriller*, I provide a close, intertextual reading of the King of Pop's original *Thriller* in order to illuminate the ancestral line of CPDRC's homage and better understand it as part of a wealth of YouTube *Thriller* remediations that followed. Chapter 6 returns to the Philippines to discuss the place of hybridity, nostalgia and imagination in CPDRC's performances. Here I put forward the idea of CPDRC's *Thriller* acting as a form of spreadable media in and of itself, by addressing some of the many multimedia offspring CPDRC's *Thriller* has inspired. I return to issues of the postcolonial performance raised in Chapter 2, and consider the place of neocolonial ideology embedded in their actions. Moving on from this, Chapter 7 follows by studying CPDRC's global, online audience as penal spectators. Taking advantage of YouTube's communicative structure that enables and encourages audiences to interact with the video in question, my analysis of the YouTube comments left under CPDRC's *Thriller* video extends the interrelation between CPDRC's reception and ideas of music and/as national pride, and cultural citizenship. The Coda and Postscript return to the idea of CPDRC's *Thriller* as a 'dangerous mediation', and offer some final reflections on the ways digital and analogue audiovisual worlds collide and intermingle through this video. I journey back to CPDRC amid fresh human rights abuse allegations in the current Philippine political climate, and find more dancing behind bars from perhaps the most unlikely of places.

Together these pages offer several things. The following chapters underpin the fundamental point of *Dangerous Mediations*; that is, to perform a potentially 'dangerous' reading of audiovisual mediations like CPDRC's *Thriller* is to render visible historical and contemporary connections, and colonial legacies that would otherwise remain invisible. Through a textual and contextual analysis of CPDRC's *Thriller*, *Dangerous Mediations* demonstrates that the use of popular music in contemporary culture is plural, varying across locations, in audiences and in meaning. As this single case study illustrates, punishment practices and music experiences can be subject to the same levels of mediation as any other aspect of modern life.

By zooming in to one viral video, *Dangerous Mediations* explores the vastly uncharted relationship between music and YouTube, which in the age of ubiquitous media is fundamental to all aspects of contemporary music practice – its appreciation, construction, collection and dissemination. Lastly, *Dangerous Mediations* draws attention to the many musicians and performers whose work is widely overlooked, despite the fact that such performers – the prisoner, the amateur, the Filipino, the subaltern – create real, tangible work that is voraciously consumed, but often not valued, in our 'audiovisual swirl' (Vernallis 2013). Such performers and performances are frequently written out of (popular) music history, an oversight that is dangerous as it silences the labour of a great many people. Though my initial discovery of this YouTube video was purely accidental, my decision to focus on this text – on the music and dance practice of detained individuals in the Philippines – is nothing but deliberate, and indeed, provocative. Cebu, the site of my focus, lies not in the West but in the (Far) East. And the musical, and mediated lives of prisoners – particularly those in non-Western countries – remain for the most part, acutely underrepresented in scholarship. *Dangerous Mediation* argues, then, that such performers constitute an active – and actively contested – population of popular performers. If we care to look *and* listen, we find that music is central to much of today's mediated works. And so it is with music that this book begins.

INTERLUDE ONE

'The *Evil* of the Thriller'

Framed by beguiling, jumpy, hyperlinked images and their intriguing titles, with the click of a play button the '"Thriller" (original upload)' video begins to the sound of a repeated synthesized groove synched to the image of a couple walking gaily, arm-in-arm across grey concrete slabs (Figure 1.1). Filmed from behind and high above the couple's forward gait, the camera's eye maintains its high position throughout, establishing its authoritarian gaze. We cannot see their faces. Instead, we watch them move forward with a discernable synchronized spring in their step – left together, right together, arms swinging in time to the amplified, synthesized groove. The figure on the right, sporting a dark-haired crew cut and average build, wears a bright orange jumpsuit emblazoned with a large letter 'P' on the back of his t-shirt and left trouser leg. In contrast, the feminine figure on the left wears her brown hair in a ponytail, against tanned, bare shoulders in a baby pink low-back, halter top paired with light-blue jeans and high-heeled shoes.

From the beginning we see that the couple are not alone in their concrete jungle. Another dark-haired crew-cut head with orange jumpsuit shoulders briefly edges into the opening frame, but quickly the camera pulls away, preferring instead to focus, for now, on the couple as they move in unison, following their movements from above, markedly distant and apart. Three seconds into the video, and the opening credits pronounce 'CPDRC inmates practice ... Thriller', and we see the couple continue their forward trajectory, skipping along what is now understood to be a prison yard. Alongside the

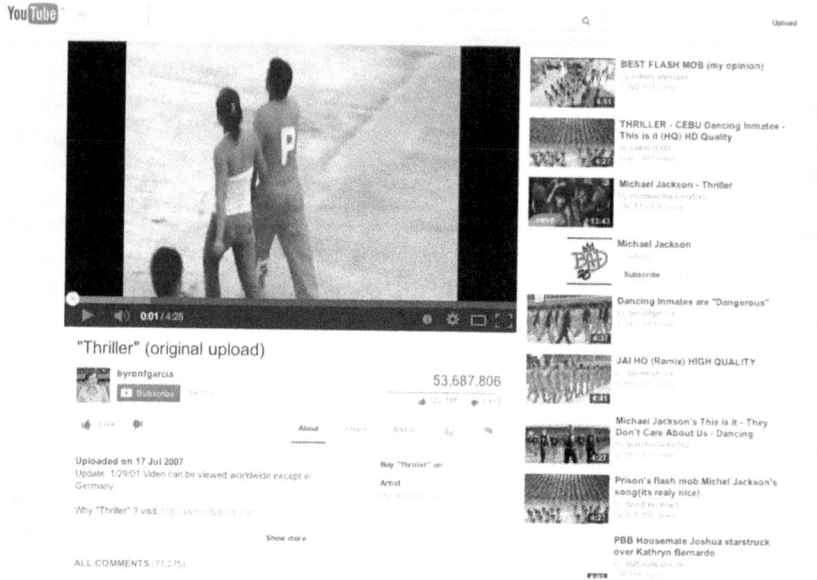

FIGURE 1.1 *Arm in arm, the leading protagonists skip along the concrete yard in byronfgarcia's '"Thriller" (original upload)'. YouTube, 17 July 2007.*

opening title credits, the opening ten seconds are sufficient to signal the video as a remixed, remediated version of Michael Jackson's short film *Thriller* through its audiovisual markers alone.[1] Framed by my old, thirteen-inch laptop computer screen, the video itself takes up just over a quarter of this space – the rest jumps to life with recommended videos and seemingly endless hyperlink options.

The multifaceted visual aesthetics of this YouTube screen are echoed aurally: the soundtrack's tinny sound is a complex reconstruction of several audio factors. The initial, CPDRC performance consisted of playing *Thriller* across the prison's amplifiers – speakers primarily tasked with conveying verbal instructions and not necessarily musical recordings. These speakers are projected across the prison's open-air yard, losing much of the low-end bass in the process. Add to this environmental sounds (neighbourhood traffic, barking dogs, crowing roosters) and the fact that the video is a recording of a lower-quality sound that is re-recorded on a low-quality camera microphone means the resulting audio parameter in CPDRC's YouTube video is significantly sonically altered from Jackson's *Thriller*. In addition to the obvious shifts in visual aesthetics from Jackson's to CPDRC's *Thrillers*, the audio undergoes similarly drastic levels of remediation in CPDRC's. By the time CPDRC's *Thriller* reaches our variable ears via YouTube – through laptop speakers, headphones, smartphones or other means – it is already limited to the mid- and higher-range frequencies. So although we may recognize the soundtrack as Michael Jackson's *Thriller*, it is changed, and in its remediation it *sounds* very different.

To those already familiar with the 1982 *Thriller*, the leading couple evidently enact the roles of Michael Jackson and his on-screen girlfriend, performed by Ola Ray. The prison couple start their performance mirroring *Thriller*'s graveyard sequence, but in the place of filmic props, theatrical sets and scenery, they walk past an illusory burial ground, realized through a real-life walk through a prop-less prison yard. The distinct synthesized, rhythmic loop, directly lifted from 7.23 minutes into the original *Thriller* short-film soundtrack, segues into Vincent Price's infamous *Sprechgesang* as Price proclaims, 'The foulest stench is in the air … '. As he narrates, the camera pans outwards, revealing for the first time, at least twenty bodies in identical orange prison-suits. The men, with short orange sleeves against their brown skin, move in from the periphery, edging towards the couple with stuttered movements, some arms outstretched in the lingua franca zombie pose, some inching forward with limping legwork and bodies moving forward surreptitiously, a soulless army of the living dead. Meanwhile, the carefree leading couple skip past the orange crowd, seemingly oblivious, her right arm linked with his left; their respective empty arms swing to their upbeat gait.

A horde of at least fifty orange-suited bodies appear, approaching from a dark distance – some moving singularly, some in uneven clusters as Price melodiously warbles about 'grizzly ghouls'. The camera zooms in on individual bodies, faces forward. These masculine, dark-brown bodies are noticeably branded; bright, white 'CPDRC inmates' lettering decorates the front of their orange shirts, and a large, white 'P' for *preso* (prisoner) is emblazoned on their backs and legs. As the camera pans across further we momentarily see two green rooftops framing the periphery of what appears to be a yard, one with a white basketball net attached to it, and as it zooms outwards hundreds more orange-suited bodies are revealed. The camera pans right, returning to our leading couple who, no longer skipping gaily, are slowly surrounded by a plague of orange-suited zombie-humans. Just before *Thriller*'s soundtrack of ghoulish, guttural groans returns, over the repeated synthesized, syncopated bass groove Price recites the lyrics in a chilling tone, fluctuating between a sing-song and gravelly timbre. Steadily, Price slowly rolls the 'thr', dramatically accenting the final clause:

'The *evil* of the Thriller.'

CHAPTER ONE

Seeing sound

Locating music and YouTube's symbiosis

Music and/as mediation

Music has always been mediated. Take, for example, the voice in music's modern era. The voice does not sing alone. It is accompanied by, implanted in and mediated by technologies, while paradoxically just as it attains the status of a unique expressive carrier, so is it accompanied by a plethora of machinery that reveal the carrier to be radically hybridized (Prior 2013). Music is intrinsically based on an affiliation between subjects and objects, and these immaterial and material subjects and objects often 'collide and intermingle' (Born 2005: 7). At home or in transit, listening to *Thriller* through an mp3 player or via YouTube, one is never listening to Michael Jackson's voice alone, nor is one simply watching Jackson sing and dance across our screens. In these instances, sonic pleasure and audiovisual enjoyment can be triggered for a host of reasons. The technologized machine, and non-human artifice afforded by technology are often the cause of our pleasure as much as the grain of Jackson's non-verbalized vocalizations. Consequently, while one may derive much pleasure from music 'itself', one simultaneously enjoys the various technologies and practices associated with music's mediation.

Creating music through face-to-face interaction is filled with as many cultural inflections as mediated and digitally mediated musical communication. Yet we often fail to see the framed nature of such face-to-face relationships and social interactions precisely because these frames work so effectively, as Erving Goffman reminded us (1959). Historically the power to reproduce sound was once the reserve of the gods (Attali 1985: 87). Today, however, with billions of smartphones, microphones and speakers now in use, such power belongs to the majority of humanity (Sterne 2012: 1). Advancing technology affords billions of the world's population access to experience music. Yet new media practices are not necessarily new *mediations* 'compared to how we used to be' (Miller and Sinanan 2012: 2). So, what then *is* music mediation? And how has our understanding of mediation shifted with advancing digital, technological developments?

Mediation can be understood in several ways: as a communicative, connecting link between forms, and/or as an intervention, reconciliation or negotiation. Forms of mediation are commonly considered to be social structures that may incorporate online, mobile interactions between people in near and faraway places, using technological devices, machines, programmes and platforms. New forms of mediation are not antithetical to older forms, but rather sit together on a spectrum of communication. For Nancy Baym, new forms of mediation have been disruptive in consistent ways throughout history, evoking long-standing opposing tensions (2010: 154). Music similarly encompasses a variety of social structures, from producing its own varied social relations, to inflecting existing social relations, while still remaining bound up in wider institutional forces that effect music's production and reproduction (Born 2005: 7). Theories of mediation – for example the technological determinism of scholars like Marshall McLuhan – have thus been crucial in the development of music studies, from critical musicology to the cultural study of music. While I do not necessarily agree with McLuhan's well-known pronouncement that 'the medium is the message', it can be helpful to think of media usage along a continuum, and around the idea that technological characteristics transfer to those who use them. I consider both aspects of music mediation – how music acts as a connecting link between forms and as an intervention, reconciliation or negotiation – and complicates the historical narratives surrounding popular music's technological circulation and online mediation.

This chapter charts music's contemporary mediation, focusing on its increasing visualization and subsequent digital spreadibility (after Jenkins 2013), to contextualize the conditions surrounding the production of a YouTube work such as CPDRC's *Thriller*. We start with the rise of popular music through video, a format that became commercially available in the Western world from the late 1960s, which enabled novel forms of audiovisuality. Composers were not only able to visualize their music and artists to sound their images, but for the first time such audiovisual actions could be recorded and transfixed onto a technologized medium that could be circulated privately and publicly, far and wide (Rogers 2013). Technological developments from this point on have served to further imbue the audio and the visual to the point that today, YouTube has become the world's number one streaming service, of which music accounts for a significant proportion. Listening to music via YouTube, though, is not without complexities. As Interlude One described, hearing music and sounds through YouTube can often be a convoluted, frustrating and even unpleasant aural activity, as users must overcome pop-up, roll-out advertisements and jumpy navigation panels. Audiophiles find that YouTube's sound is habitually highly compressed, thereby affecting the pleasure and enjoyment of listening to music via YouTube's online platform.[1] This chapter seeks to understand the idiom 'YouTube videos' in all its polysemy, and calls for awareness of YouTube's frequent musical (and sonic) intermingling, which remains, for the most part, largely overlooked across academia.

YouTube, screen mediation and the interface

As a video-based platform, YouTube remains widely regarded by journalists as a visual genre – a hierarchy, no doubt, inherited from widespread television and cinematic practice. Academic literature on YouTube to date includes, but is not limited to, YouTube as media studies (Snickars and Vonderau 2009), educational methods and possibilities for teaching through YouTube (Waldron 2013), the experiences of YouTube users (Lange 2007), YouTube as database (Lovink and Niederer 2008), and YouTube video as/and participatory culture (Burgess and Green 2009). Sonicity's intertwined relationship with YouTube's visuals, and vice versa, cannot be underestimated, particularly when confronted by YouTube's overwhelming music-related statistics. YouTube's pervasiveness has led to it becoming the second most popular internet search engine, processing three billion searches a month in 2014, following only behind its parent company Google. YouTube users are not required to register before viewing YouTube video; registration is only necessary to upload content, and the amount of content one may share remains, at present, unlimited. Comscore's Dan Piech's 2013 statistical presentation based on data from the US, notes that online video is the most consumed content format on the internet, where the number of videos watched online increased by 800 per cent from 2007 to 2013.

Central to music's contemporary mediation is the increasing proliferation of screen media. After Dziga Vertov's groundbreaking film *Man with a Movie Camera* (1929), Lev Manovich argues that avant-garde film acts as a precursor to the language of new media, and the (computer) screen becomes a wider metaphor for the fundamental element of modern interface, where Manovich reads post-millennial screen culture as 'over-taking the printed word' (2001: 86). He explains:

> A hundred years after cinema's birth, cinematic ways of seeing the world, of structuring time, of narrating a story, of linking one experience to the next, have become the basic means by which computer users access and interact with all cultural data. In this respect, the computer fulfils the promise of cinema as a visual Esperanto – a goal that preoccupied many film artists and critics in the 1920s, from Griffith to Vertov. Indeed,

today millions of computer users communicate with each other through the same computer interface. And in contrast to cinema, where most 'users' are able to 'understand' cinematic language but not 'speak' it (i.e. make films), all computer users can 'speak' the language of the interface. They are active users of the interface, employing it to perform many tasks: send e-mail, organise files, run various applications, and so on. (Manovich 2001: xv)

The significance of the 'interface' lies in the fact that it is not simply a physical nor a digital technology. Rather it functions as a 'cultural interface', a carrier of cultural messages that users interact with across various media types (Manovich 2001: 64). Computers have evolved from 'work' machines to 'universal media machines' and as such bridge the gap between users and cultural data, yet these universal media machines continue to refer and relate to older media and cultural traditions – not least through skeuomorphic design.[2] Indeed while Manovich pays close attention to how concepts of the screen influence user experiences of viewing, telling us that a key proponent of new media lies in its existence in different and potentially infinite versions, he fails to address the important concept of scale within these infinite versions (2001: 36). Since screens have migrated from their once native residences in public cinemas and domestic living rooms, digital media has shifted the scale and categorization of screen culture, however futile, volatile and transient such classifications may seem (Simons 2011). In addition to traditional, domestic screen locations, Manovich's computer screens, and mobile, small screens on iPhones and personal games consoles, I also include the multitude of screen manifestations, including 'urban screens' such as billboards that adorn skylines and streets, 'skinned walls' or buildings with video walls in, wide-screen televisions and digital signage spread across public spaces and public transport (Simons 2011: 101–2). For Simons, all screens – regardless of their size or technology – present specific concerns, but most crucially display a hierarchy of content that is deemed worthy of attention and content that is not.

Music and the moving image: A fast-forward overview

The relationship between music and recorded moving image is historically intertwined, and has served as the basis for popular music and music video literature (see Frith et al. 1993; Vernallis 2004). From the turn of the twentieth century, George Thomas's combination of music and image on hand-coloured glass slides produced what is believed to be the first 'illustrated song' in 1894, while the first cinematic 'talkies' of the 1920s blended live music and film practice. The intersecting realms of visual music, visual poetry, direct animation, and abstract film from pioneering artists such as Oskar Fischinger, Norman McLaren, Harry Smith and Len Lye (among others) played an important role in experimenting with audiovisual relationships and aesthetics, establishing connections between the avant-garde and popular forms. Early proto-music video can trace its origins to the Busby Berkeley-style choreographed scenes from Hollywood film musicals such as *Top Hat* (dir. Mark Sandrich, 1935), Disney's *Fantasia* (1940) and *Gentlemen Prefer Blondes* (1953). Music video can also locate a historical connection to early twentieth-century film and video art, particularly the work of surrealist filmmaker Luis Buñuel.[3] With more than a subtle hint of irony, The Buggles' music video 'Video Killed the Radio Star' officially launched the world's first music video cable television channel in America on 1 August 1981. A major breakthrough in music broadcasting and distribution, MTV defined a generation by offering popular music videos twenty-four hours a day, seven days a week (Denisoff 1988: 1). MTV intended to appeal to a younger demographic with its bite-sized, fast-paced design.[4] Although the origins and concept of music video pre-dates MTV by several decades, the dramatic rise of MTV in the 1980s and early 1990s led to the combination of televised moving image and music becoming ubiquitous in popular music practice.[5] Alongside capitalists' interests, MTV was created out of a desire to use short promotional films that would allow TV audiences to see a pseudo-performance of a song in the absence of a live appearance. Widely recognized as the 'most pervasive and significant form of musical audiovisual text' (Shuker 2008: 107), by the 1980s music videos experienced a decisive shift in development thanks to increased budgets. David Bowie's music video for 'Ashes to Ashes' (dir. Bowie and David Mallet, 1980) cost over US$500,000 to produce, while the fourteen-minute video for Michael Jackson's *Thriller* (dir. John Landis 1983) became the first music video that cost US$1 million.[6] After Landis's triumphant success with Jackson, other Hollywood directors 'began to moonlight as videomakers, offering a touch of their sensibility to sympathetic artists', and as such 'the ranks of its directors expanded and fashion photographers, filmmakers and artists began to take up the video's reins' (Austerlitz 2007: 40–1). By the late 1980s music videos had flourished and became a reputable, and more crucially a profitable, enterprise and, before long, Hollywood's influence and impact led to a pattern of rapidly spiralling production costs as video makers sought to focus attention on their particular product in an increasingly congested market. A purely economics perspective on twentieth-century music video history then sets apart those made before *Thriller* with its million-dollar budget, from those videos that came after, like Duran Duran's 'Wild Boys' in 1986 which purportedly cost US$1.2 million, Michael Jackson's 'Bad' (dir. Martin Scorsese 1987) costing US$2.2 million and Madonna's 'Bedtime Story' (dir. Mark Romanek 1995) costing US$5 million to produce (Inglis and Hearsum 2013: 485). Following MTV's heady hey days, music – and, in particular, popular music – was presented as constantly imbued with the visual. By the end of the twentieth century, most record labels curtailed such flamboyant spending on music video, citing various reasons from declining viewership to declining budgets due to music piracy. With the scale and scope of major patrons removed from the equation for all but the minority of international pop stars, music video transformed and subsequently relocated to various other sites, particularly with the advent of digital platforms. While music video has experienced periods of fluctuating mainstream popularity over the past two decades – and notwithstanding MTV's recorded decline in audience figures since the early 2000s – the demand for music video never disappeared; rather it migrated online.

Web 2.0: Defining participatory culture

To adequately contextualize CPDRC's *Thriller* is to position it in light of its second-generation roots in the developments of the World Wide Web. Current understandings of Web 2.0 encompass a broad categorization representing a general shift towards user-generated content, participatory cultures and open-sourcing as it moves towards interactive, decentralized and multimedia frameworks. Arguing for a sociological approach to music studies, David Beer's research on Web 2.0 music culture and practice suggests four key interrelated categories of Web 2.0 applications: Wikis, Folksonomies, Mashups and Social Networking Sites (2008). Wikis, taken from the Hawaiian term 'wiki wiki' meaning quick, are applications that draw together open input to form communal projects. A key example would be Wikipedia, the online encyclopaedia comprised of the collaborative and collective efforts of many individuals that serves as an example of Web 2.0's version of 'collective intelligence'. I use the term collective intelligence after Pierre Lévy, who describes it as a form of universally distributed intelligence, constantly enhanced, coordinated in real time, that results in effective mobilization of skills, and is imperative for democratization (Lévy 1995: 13). Folksonomies are classified by Beer as vast archives that function through systems of metadata (primarily through 'tagging' the media content with descriptive keywords, on sites such as YouTube and Flikr). Web 2.0 mashups are appropriated from the popular music technique of combining two different materials to create something new, often associated with illegality since the majority of mash-up creators do not seek permission to use the mashup-up or sampled material (see Brøvig-Hanssen and Harkins 2012; Cook 2013). Social Networking Sites (SNS), meanwhile, are distinctive in their real-time interactive, transnational, mobile, networked, built-for-purpose for costless copying and sharing, with a clear commercial interest in maintaining the simulation of community, while simultaneously providing new opportunities for fashioning performances of the self.

Countering the drive for a sociology of Web 2.0, Christian Fuchs (2010) argues that what is primarily needed is not a phenomenological or empirical social research of Web 2.0 but a wider critical theoretical approach to the internet and society. Changing societal circumstances creates situations in which new concepts need to be clarified and social problems need to be solved. Three evolutionary stages in the development of the World Wide Web – Web 1.0, 2.0 and 3.0 – are each based on the idea of knowledge as a threefold dynamic process of cognition, communication and co-operation (Fuchs 2010: 767). These three levels of internet development each correspond with specific internet features. Web 1.0 can be remembered primarily as a tool for consumption. Our current Web 2.0 era offers a medium for unprecedented levels of human communication, while Web 3.0 is framed as a digital technologies network that will support human co-operation as we currently experience Web 2.0 services evolving into Web 3.0, with developments in smart home appliances embedded in wireless networks. In short, stemming from intertextual cultural practices of old, Web 2.0 offers an extension to existing mass media, popular and participatory cultures of screen media, literary print traditions – those inherited from Web 1.0 and of course, those that originate from long before.

Web 2.0 media phenomena also offer communications that are transformative in terms of speed and scale. As such they are widely celebrated as a location for the articulation of individual and collective social power, as they enhance the general public's participation in media production and cultural expression as well as positively impacting and empowering individual interpersonal interactions, both socially and politically. Such celebrations are not without noticeable detractors who lament Web 2.0 as extolling an apparent democratization of society. For some critics, democratization – despite its lofty idealization – serves in fact to undermine truth, sour civic discourse and belittle expertise, experience and talent (Keen 2007: 15). What Web 2.0 often offers, in practice, is quick and superficial remarks in the place of considered, gradual judgement. Thus, Keen argues, Web 2.0's democratization threatens the very future of our cultural institutions.

YouTube as archive?

Debates like Keen's are relevant to my conception of YouTube, and further point to the problems of thinking of YouTube as an archive, as many scholars describe it (Gehl 2009; Snickars and Vonderau 2009; Vernallis 2013). Among the sheer noise of YouTube's continually uploaded digital documents and incessant interactive conversations as users simultaneously fight for clicks, subscriptions, comments and likes, in the introduction to the first scholarly collection dedicated to YouTube, Pelle Snickars and Patrick Vonderau consider the many metaphors used when discussing YouTube's societal impact, as well as its social, economic and technological importance. YouTube offers an archival platform on the one hand, they write, but one with an apparent loss in quality and lack of preservational strategies. In any case, Snickars and Vonderau believe YouTube is not an either/or, and 'traditional media archives are facing the fact that sites like YouTube and Flickr have become default media-archive interfaces' (2009: 13–14). Interacting with YouTube is certainly reminiscent of using archives or libraries, Snickars and Vonderau remark, and metaphorically speaking YouTube appears to work not only like an archive or a medium, but also like a laboratory that registers user behaviour (2009: 15–6). Yet while YouTube certainly functions as a repository of songs, albums, music videos and whole reams of other audiovisual material, equating YouTube as a music or cultural archive remains deeply problematic. YouTube may host an extensive back catalogue of videos, music and other audiovisual material, but as a private, commercial business owned by Google it is not and cannot be considered an archive in the sense of being a complete or open public record: it simply represents the best and worst of participatory culture, with a heavy dose of everything in between.

The term 'participatory culture' here is understood as a culture in which private persons do not act as consumers only but also as contributors or producers of content. These 'produsers' are a key feature of Web 2.0's use of collective intelligence, who create and publish internet media content. I refer to Jenkins et al.'s definition of participatory culture as one with relatively low barriers to artistic expression and civic engagement, strong support for creating and sharing one's creations, and some type of informal mentorship whereby what is known by the most experienced is passed along to novices (Jenkins et al. 2006: 3). Still, as a Web 2.0 platform, YouTube – along with other Web 2.0 interfaces like Facebook, Vimeo and Instagram – should not be readily dismissed nor relegated because of the action of a few in the noisy crowd. Web 2.0 functions as a communication device, an ideology, a form of commodification and marketing strategy rather than a specific technological change and, on the whole, it represents collective changes in the way internet sites and web pages are made and used. Centred on participatory culture, collective intelligence and neoliberal ideologies, Web 2.0 sites offer new levels of social interaction, media consumption, online presentations of the self and opportunities for the production of new texts, new cultures and new communities, all of which reconfigure cultural production rather than eliminate previously held hierarchies (see boyd 2007; Jenkins 2006a, 2006b, 2013).

Web 2.0 and the digital divide

Scholars have argued that Web 2.0 can, in many ways, be considered television's successor. Jenkins, for instance, regards the territory as a space in which 'old and new media collide, where grassroots and corporate media intersect, where the power of the media producer and the power of the media consumer interact in unpredictable ways' (Jenkins 2006a: 2). The key features of Web 2.0's new 'convergence culture' include a more active participation based around participatory culture. In such discussions of participation, the widening inequalities inherent in these kinds of access must be addressed. Media scholars have recognized that participatory culture is not always progressive, nor does it necessarily represent a diverse culture (see Ivey and Tepper 2006; Burgess and Green 2009; Jenkins 2006a, 2006b). National and regional digital divides exist, in addition to a global digital divide that separates individuals from equitable access to technology, information and culture. Creativity and cultural expression go hand in hand with access, economy, education and technology and, despite some attempts to redress such inequities, opportunities for creativity and cultural expression often remain the preserve of those with the necessary resources. The digital divide *is* important because it affects citizens in a wide range of significant ways, as Ivey and Tepper describe:

> Increasingly, those who have the education, skills, financial resources, and time required to navigate the sea of cultural choice will gain access to new cultural opportunities. They will be the ones who can invest in their creative hobbies, writing songs, knitting, acting, singing in a choir, gardening. They will be the pro-ams [professional-amateurs] who network with other serious amateurs and find audiences for their work. They will discover new forms of cultural expression that engage their passions and help them forge their own identities, and will be the curators of their own expressive lives and the mavens who enrich the lives of others; they will be among [the] creative class. (2006: B6)

Although referring specifically to the United States in this case, Ivey and Tepper's observations have far wider implications that are profoundly relevant to this book's central case study. Not least because it reminds us that in discussions of digital media and its vast potentials, we cannot afford to neglect the other side of the sociocultural coin. Those citizens all around the world with fewer resources – those with less time, less money and less knowledge about how to navigate the cultural system – are relegated to rely on the cultural content offered to them by multinational media and entertainment businesses. Indeed, such citizens of the United States will have little choice but to engage with arts and culture through large portals like Walmart or Clear Channel radio. Their cultural choices are directed to limited options through the narrow gates defined by the synergistic marketing that is the hallmark of cross-owned media and entertainment. Finding it increasingly difficult to take advantage of Web 2.0's promise of democratization, such citizens are trapped on the *wrong side* of the cultural divide (2006: B6, italics added). Conceptualizing access to digital cultural interfaces, we must consider how a nation or region can prosper when – and indeed if – its citizens experience such varied and unequal culturally lived experiences (Ivey and Tepper 2006). Such observations on the increasingly polarized environment that faces digital media users only serves to demonstrate how Web 2.0 technologies, in tandem with economic change, are fusing to create a new cultural elite and a new cultural underclass.

In addition to increasingly polarized digital experience, the configurable practices of culture brought about through advancing Web 2.0 technology are gaining increasing levels of mainstream acceptance. Dynamic, interactive and collaborative characteristics are quickly becoming the normative Web 2.0 experience. Consequently, therein lies inherent dangers in terms of potential social factors that may affect accessibility, accuracy and consistency. Problematizing Web 2.0's neoliberal foundation on collective intelligence by questioning its internal qualitative, objective and consistent logic, Aram Sinnreich writes:

> If each of us has the ability to select and reject the nature of the information we encounter based on our individual tastes and preferences, the argument holds, then each of us will have a completely different sense of what is going on in the world around us. […] if each of us has the ability to alter and recirculate information as we see fit, there can be no confidence in the quality, veracity, or objectivity of the information we encounter. (2007: 142–3)

In the era of participatory culture's innate democratization, questions regarding authoritative, quantifiable facts among the sea of collective 'intelligence' – to follow Sinnreich's pessimistic view – democratic society is perhaps 'doomed in the era of the blog and the remix' (2007: 143). Yet while observing the ease in which new media tools enable the endless proliferation of material, others have argued that Web 2.0's neoliberal ideology is fundamental to understanding how it operates, as such rhetoric underlies each and every online activity (see Jarrett 2008; Fuchs 2010). Some, like Kylie Jarrett (2008), see interactivity in Web 2.0 as a technical reproduction of neoliberal or advanced liberal dominance, serving as disciplining technologies founded on the liberal ideal of subjectivity and centred on ideas of freedom, choice and activity. Noticing the speed at which normativity and standardization of expectation can form around such new media practices, Madianou and Miller highlight the flow in identity practice that online platforms offer. Paying caution to neologisms, they describe and define the proliferation of communication technologies over a wide range of platforms as a 'polymedia' environment, calling for the term to be used to encompass the recent, widespread possibilities of communications between separated persons (Madianou and Miller 2012). Identities across online platforms may be broadly similar or may shift in emphasis – from a professional identity to a social identity, and between media – such as text messaging versus face-to-face conversations via a webcam (Foresight Future Identities 2013: 25). In our polymedia environment, communication – between individuals and industries – is key. Publicly and efficiently navigating a communicative message through this murky, densely populated terrain, however, is fast becoming logistically troubled. In the networked era of memes and viral video, as the saying goes, 'if it doesn't spread, it's dead'.

Memes, media viruses, viral videos: Speed and biological metaphors in Web 2.0

Memes, viruses and viral media: contemporary advertising, marketing and media industry language is filled with such biological and genetic metaphors that loosely serve to illustrate how media content moves within cultures, and especially in Web 2.0 culture. With the arrival of Web 2.0's convergence culture, new media content sought to compete in an increasingly saturated market, yet the 'if it doesn't spread, it's dead' ethos continues (Jenkins et al. 2008). Speed and veracity are key to contemporary ubiquitous consumption of memes and viral media; those with the necessary resources have abolished the wait almost in its entirety. And in this speed-driven shift in forms of consumption, pleasure is now to be gained in the act of purchasing – no longer in the act of consuming the material (Bull 2013).

The etymology and evolution of these biological metaphors stems from biologist Richard Dawkins's coinage of the term 'meme' in his influential book on cultural evolution and memetics (1976). Dawkins applies the genetic metaphor to cultural practice, corresponding the key to successful memes with the key to successful genes in their propensity to replicate. The most successful memes are namely those that remain and spread, are subject to transmission *and* evolution. In Dawkins's words:

> Just as genes propagate themselves in the gene pool by leaping from body to body via sperms or eggs, so memes propagate themselves in the meme pool by leaping from brain to brain via a process which, in the broad sense, can be called imitation. (Dawkins 1989: 192)

Initially, Dawkins defined a meme as a noun that communicates the 'idea of a unit of cultural transmission, or a unit of imitation' (1989: 352). Cultural memes do not necessarily survive because people want them to, Dawkins points out, or because they suit any specific needs in human society. Successful memes survive simply because they do not die out, while unfit memes wither and are soon forgotten. Dawkins consistently conceptualizes memes across varying levels of organization, regardless of scale or society, as a single, discrete unit with no prescribed size. The fact that Dawkins understands memes as indivisible units has been problematized by subsequent authors working in memetics, and is not without its detractors. Douglas Rushkoff, building from Dawkins, described how media viruses are conceptually linked to biological ones and media viruses spread through the datasphere instead of the body or community (1994). However:

> instead of traveling along an organic circulatory system, a media virus travels through the networks of the mediaspace. The 'protein shell' of a media virus might be an event, invention, technology, system of thought, musical riff, visual image, scientific theory, sex scandal, clothing style or even a pop hero – as long as it can catch our attention. Any one of these media virus shells will search out the receptive nooks and crannies in popular culture and stick on anywhere it is noticed. Once attached, the virus injects its more hidden agendas into the datastream in the form of *ideological code* – not genes, but a conceptual equivalent we now call 'memes'. (Rushkoff 1994: 9–10)

Rushkoff's observation of the various ideological codes embedded within such media viruses is telling. The defining characteristic of memes and viral media, then, lies in the 'spreadability' of the media content, that which 'acts as a hub for further creative activity by a wide range of participants in this social network' (Burgess 2008: 102). Yet hidden agendas and ideological code can infiltrate our mediasphere through the spread of seemingly innocuous cultural memes. In the case of CPDRC's *Thriller*, the 'protein shell' may refer to a great many elements of the audiovisual content of the viral media – as we will later see in *Thriller*'s many YouTube remediations in Chapter 5.

Viral media has been a topic of much discourse from the biological to business and marketing, and social scientists and scholars have written about the defining features of viral media in Web 2.0 culture (Burgess 2008; Burgess and Green 2009; Jenkins 2006b, 2013). The term 'viral' – say in a viral video for example – places an emphasis on the replication of the original idea, seeking to explain the process of cultural transmission but does so in such a way that it strips aside the social and cultural contexts in which ideas circulate; this can often omit the human choices that determine which ideas get replicated (Jenkins et al. 2008: 2). Nonetheless, we have now reached a point where the widespread, vague use of the term 'viral' is unhelpful to the point of confusion (Jenkins et al. 2008). Because the term viral is used so frequently and freely in today's mediascape, it can refer to everything from word-of-mouth marketing efforts to remix videos to popular content in ways that don't help us understand the nature of these different activities and the potential relationships between them. Furthermore, vague uses of the term 'viral' fail to consider the everyday reality of human communication and relations, the actuality that 'ideas get transformed, repurposed, or distorted as they pass from hand to hand, a process which has been accelerated as we move into network culture' (Jenkins et al. 2008: 2). Viral phenomena, like CPDRC's *Thriller,* are neither straightforward nor wholly predictable, but rooted in the cultural politics of digital networks.

Mapping the rise and fall of YouTube's amateur ethos (or, what *is* a YouTube video?)

Before we examine CPDRC's *Thriller* in more detail, it seems wise to briefly situate this YouTube video in the context of what YouTube was, and what YouTube videos were up to at this point in time. Founded in February 2005 by three former PayPal employees looking for a way to upload, view and share video content, YouTube is today the world's leading – but not the first – video-sharing website. From the outset YouTube was designed and made its mark on the internet landscape as a site for sharing user-generated content. Initially launched with the tagline 'Broadcast Yourself'™, YouTube's early rise to fame hinged on the 'You' of YouTube – its inbuilt association with ordinary people sharing everyday experiences, a view promoted by one of YouTube's founders. In an interview with *The New Yorker* (2012), co-founder Chad Hurley emphasizes that YouTube's content was user-generated: 'Real personal clips that are taken by everyday people'. By extension YouTube's Broadcast Yourself motto became synonymous with constructing, communicating and ultimately mediating varying degrees of self-identity, capitalizing on ordinary individuals' desire for fifteen minutes of fame. As a result, those community members, known as YouTubers – those users who actively uploaded and interacted with much everyday user-generated content – commandeered YouTube's formative months and years. Alongside the banality of everyday content grew various niche communities, and users soon discovered videos that they found interesting and obscure. These so-called amateur, non-professional video-makers played a crucial role in the website's success in establishing it as the world's foremost video-sharing platform.

We now know that that YouTube started out as a site largely associated with amateur, DIY content. But how did a user-generated platform produce such large audiences so quickly? By offering audiences an alternative to television as a source for audiovisual entertainment and information, YouTube empowered the public with a degree of choice that exceeded that which most television schedules offered.[7] Since YouTube's official launch in 2005, YouTube's audience soared from 2.8 million unique users in 2005 to 72 million users the following year, overtaking every other online video platform, including Google Video (ComScore World Metrix 2006).

YouTube's swift acquisition by Google in October 2006 – the same month CPDRC uploaded their first prison music video to YouTube – served to reinforce the platform's increasing capitalist logic, which inherently values quick, quantitative feedback above qualitative.[8]

YouTube has since emerged both as a central archive for media content, including that produced by various communities of amateur and pro-am media makers as well as content appropriated from mass media sources, and as a distribution hub through which this content flows outward through a range of social networks (Jenkins et al. 2008: 40). As the site grew under Google's guidance, and all the while CPDRC were learning to navigate the world of YouTube with their homemade videos, the 'YouTube: Broadcast Yourself' logo that was in use from 2005 to 2012 was revised and the iconic 'Broadcast Yourself' tag line removed entirely from YouTube's trademark logo. Post-Google takeover, YouTube version 2.0 sought to monetize their website and share the profits with non-professional content partners as well as the already distinct 'professional content partners', initially done by introducing its 'Partner Program' in May 2007.[9] Still, despite mounting collaborations with YouTube studios and mainstream media corporations, YouTube continue to publicly promote themselves as a user-generated, community-driven organization. They describe themselves on their own website as an innovative, public service provider: 'a forum for people to connect, inform and inspire others across the globe and acts as a distribution platform for original content creators and advertisers large and small', that allows 'billions of people to discover, watch and share *originally-created* videos' (YouTube 2013, italics added).

YouTube certainly holds the potential to offer billions of people the opportunity to discover, watch and share video, but how much of this video content is like CPDRC's *Thriller* – originally created and user-generated – is debatable. A 2011 study of popular YouTube videos found that the majority of content on YouTube is not user-generated; rather 63 per cent of the most popular videos are in fact made up of user-copied content – video content made by professional users or duplicated from other YouTuber's original videos (Ding et al. 2011: 366). Even so, YouTube represents a platform where amateur curators assess the value of professional and commercial content and re-present it for an assortment of niche communities of consumers; thus participants or 'users' create value around uploaded video content in two key ways (Jenkins et al. 2008: 41):

1. They may focus greater attention on content which otherwise might have been lost, holding it in storage so that word of mouth can attract greater viewer interest;
2. They actively respond to the media content through the production of new media, often embedding it much deeper into public consciousness through this process of repetition and variation.

Value in uploaded YouTube video is multifaceted, constructed in a variety of ways, and inherently intertextual. YouTube's perceived value can vary from place to space, as we will see in CPDRC's *Thriller*. Through active repeated and varied remediation and circulation, both on and offline, YouTube videos can become deeply embedded in public consciousness as valuable social and cultural constructs that raise important questions regarding attention, participatory culture and everyday new media practice.

YouTube's overwhelming statistics, though not unproblematic, help illustrate YouTube's growth and situate the site within Web 2.0's context. By 2011, YouTube had localized in 25 countries across 43 languages, which saw 48 hours of video uploaded onto YouTube every minute, and three billion views each day. By 2014, more than one billion users visited the video-sharing platform each month, and over 100 hours of video were uploaded every *minute*. Firmly located in the top three most visited websites in the world at the time of writing, YouTube's amateur-video origins have since been somewhat countered by the site's increasing commercialization that started to escalate mid-2007.[10] Perhaps it is no coincidence that Google first introduced embedded, rollout advertisements on YouTube at the same time that Byron Garcia uploaded CPDRC's *Thriller* video – 17 July 2007. By August 2007, YouTube announced that they were now offering 'select partners the ability to incorporate YouTube InVideo ads into their content' – interactive, animated, hyperlinked overlays which appear over the bottom 20 per cent of a video (YouTube 2007b). Despite YouTube's steady media corporatization and increased professional commodification, it continues to be associated with user-generated, amateur content – even though such amateur aesthetic content is becoming harder and harder to find under YouTube's commercially driven algorithms.

This connection to DIY and amateur culture is noteworthy for several reasons. In some ways YouTube operates in a manner similar to musical and artistic ideologies, such as the Seventies punk movement, or Dadaism for instance, whereby new expressive practice was enabled by the very act of abandoning conventional requirements of artistry, expertise and technical ability. Inglis and Hearsum argue precisely that: in YouTube we have found a place where those 'without formal training, up-to-date equipment, and professional qualifications can actively engage in the audiovisual representation of popular music' (2013: 487). However, such an assessment of YouTube's accessibility, as with many Web 2.0 optimists, fails to account for the so-called second-level digital divide or production gap that separates those who consume internet content from those who produce internet content. Studies of Web 2.0 users have found that most users are nominal content creators who interact with the existing technology but rarely contribute (Nielsen 2006).[11] There are many reasons for this second-level digital divide, often related to material factors such as the type and frequency of internet connection, as well as those relating to the cultural markers of class and socio-economic status. YouTube undoubtedly offers access to those previously marginalized by the music industries' prior modes of practice. Even so, it remains nowhere near as egalitarian as certain reports claim of it for the varying levels of access, consumption and production must be accounted for.

To summarize, YouTube has quickly evolved to become the most viewed video internet site, and its cultural presence is recognizable, to varying degrees, in many – but by no means all – parts of the world. Quite often the videos that appear on YouTube – from the user-generated, DIY to the professional music videos, live recordings, advertisements, films, web series, television series, films, gameplay, vlogs, animations, pet/animal videos, tutorials, shout-out videos, unboxing videos, pornography, food preparation and everything else in between – are amalgamated under the umbrella term 'YouTube videos'. As a vast video-sharing, archival and social networking service with hundreds of millions of users and hundreds of thousands of professional and amateur video content being uploaded every day, defining YouTube videos as anything more specific than a catch-all for all videos that appear on YouTube becomes an arduous task, riddled with subjectivity. While we may struggle to define YouTube videos as a concept within a set of clearly defined parameters, very often we know it when we see it.[12] Thus, in many senses, using the contemporary category of 'YouTube videos' is indeed a redundancy, as YouTube videos encompass the widest possible range of themes and genre content. At the same time though, the term 'YouTube videos' is used and deemed useful, to some degree, within popular culture to denote a specific kind of online video, generally synonymous with the video-sharing platform's early amateur, user-generated content stage. This type of constructed definition of YouTube videos tends to be rooted in the common myths surrounding YouTube quality and content, as summarized succinctly by self-described YouTube guru and video marketing expert Greg Jarboe (Table 1.1).

Table 1.1 Three commonly held perceptions about YouTube (Jarboe 2011: 26)

Perception #1: YouTube is limited to short-form user-generated content.
(Reality #1: Thousands of full-length feature films, television episodes and albums can be found among YouTube's thousands of professional media partners, including Disney, Channel 4 and VEVO.)

Perception #2: YouTube videos are grainy and of poor quality.
(Reality #2: By 2011 YouTube had more HD [high-definition] videos than any other video site.)

Perception #3: Advertisers are afraid of YouTube.
(Reality #3: YouTube continues to monetize billions of videos per week, and the number of advertisers using display ads on YouTube increased tenfold between 2010 and 11.)

For critics like Andrew Keen, YouTube can be dismissed as an 'infinite gallery of amateur movies showing poor fools dancing, singing, eating, washing, shopping, driving, cleaning, sleeping, or just staring into their computers' (2007: 5). So while there is no single, universally held definition of 'YouTube videos', in many contexts, and due in part to the arrival of many other niche video-sharing platforms such as Vimeo, Vine and Netflix, in everyday parlance 'YouTube videos' remains connected to amateur-driven content alongside obscure and/or absurd user-generated videos of poor, pixelated quality (Burgess and Green 2009; Burgess 2008).

Music and/on YouTube

Music and YouTube's relationship is inextricably linked. For music aficionados, YouTube represents vast potentials – not least as an unlimited, open-access, digitized media collection filled with gems like unreleased back catalogue material, unofficial music videos and bootleg recordings. For many of my students and colleagues, YouTube's primary function is that of an online music jukebox: a free listening library where many songs and often many different versions – live, studio recorded, covers and so on – exist side by side. Not only are these accessible as live audio/visual streams or data that can be downloaded and played back on personal media devices, YouTube offers a quick and easy platform where music fans can 'try before they buy' or rather, in many cases, not buy at all. I include this anecdote simply to say that accessing music via free platforms like YouTube serves educational and music appreciation functions at the very least as a way to 'broaden people's taste' in music in many, many ways, as Arild Bergh, Tia DeNora and Maia Bergh noted – at least among certain age demographics – as their study pertained to teenagers and mobile musicking (2014: 322). Indeed, Burgess and Green's foundational study of YouTube established that music videos were prominent in the 'Most Favourited' category (2009: 50), while a 2012 study found that of the Top 1000 YouTube Channels, 25 per cent were categorized by the users as 'Music' channels – the largest category among YouTube's partner channels. Of course this categorization fails to take into account other video categories that feature music, albeit explicitly or implicitly. We see this illustrated in CPDRC's *Thriller,* which was originally uploaded with the tag 'People & Blogs', before it went on to become part of YouTube's general 'Lifestyle – Topic' category and associated video discovery channel. Thus music may often be the foundation, or a major feature of at least some of the other 75 per cent of YouTube channels not listed in the 'Music' category. YouTube statistics for the Top 10 Most Viewed YouTube Channels (2014) show that seven of these channels exclusively mediate (read: sell) music content, while the other categories – 'Games' and 'Entertainment' – often contain varying degrees of music and musical content as viewed in Table 1.2.[13] To date, music is *the* ubiquitous and unifying feature of YouTube's most viewed channels.

As we see from Table 1.2, music is also the unifying feature across YouTube's most popular videos. Using YouTube's API figures to compile an inventory detailing the thirty most viewed YouTube videos of all time in 2014, twenty-nine of these videos are music videos from artists including Psy and Katy Perry (with three music videos each), Eminem, Miley Cyrus and Justin Bieber (with two music videos each). Table 1.3 illustrates this in detail.

Tables 1.2 and 1.3 show us that as YouTube developed and became part of everyday media life, music and music videos feature prominently across the Most Favourited, Most Viewed Channels and Most Viewed Videos categories. There are many reasons why this might be the case. Music plays a central role for postmodern identity formation, a point Simon Frith makes; its significance and usefulness lie in its 'dual status as a marker of individualism and a signifier of group participation' (Frith 1996: 110–11, qtd in Burgess and Green 2009: 50–1). Others point to the role of the voice as holding particular significance as a site for identification in music, finding it 'the most intimate inscription of identity', as Stan Hawkins suggests (2009: 151). More recent research discusses how music is used to critique and interrogate identity as well as the negotiation and liberation of identity per se, beyond the individual/group nexus. Works by scholars in the fields of media and cultural studies, fan studies and celebrity studies are particularly notable (see Duffett 2014, Hawkins 2015, Perrott 2017, Devereux, Dillane and Power 2011). YouTube has thus evolved into a site where social identity can be negotiated

Table 1.2 Top 10 most viewed video channels on YouTube

	Username	Channel type/category	Video views	Subscribers
1.	Emimusic	Music	6,127,269,911	2,202,124
2.	PewDiePie	Games	5,354,293,949	29,119,450
3.	RihannaVEVO	Music	5,229,401,253	14,253,928
4.	Machinima	Entertainment	5,046,774,895	11,610,999
5.	JustinBieberVEVO	Music	4,983,090,279	9,824,489
6.	Officialpsy (PSY)	Music	3,920,350,960	7,337,074
7.	EminemVEVO	Music	3,805,735,243	12,916,118
8.	KatyPerryVEVO	Music	3,683,893,263	13,079,395
9.	shakiraVEVO	Music	3,605,634,040	5,099,129
10.	smosh	Entertainment	3,465,511,071	18,386,631

Compiled using data from Social Blade.com *(23 March 2014)*

Table 1.3 List of the 'most viewed' YouTube videos of all time (as of 30 June 2014)

Rank	Video name	Uploader/artist	Views	Upload date
1.	'Gangnam Style'	Psy	2,050,799,476	15 July 2012
2.	'Baby'	Justin Bieber featuring Ludacris	1,067,465,415	31 July 2014
3.	'On the Floor'	Jennifer Lopez featuring Pitbull	770,368,169	3 March 2011
4.	'Charlie Bit My Finger – Again!'	Harry and Charlie Davies-Carr	746,875,924	22 May 2007
5.	'Love the Way You Lie'	Eminem featuring Rihanna	721,533,588	5 August 2010
6.	'Party Rock Anthem'	LMFAO featuring Lauren Bennett & GoonRock	720,262,913	8 March 2011
7.	'Waka Waka (This Time for Africa)'	Shakira featuring Freshlyground	716,889,983	4 June 2010
8.	'Gentleman'	Psy	716,270,704	13 April 2013
9.	'Wrecking Ball'	Miley Cyrus	690,582,918	25 August 2013
10.	'Bad Romance'	Lady Gaga	597,172,829	23 November 2009
11.	'Roar'	Katy Perry	582,707,342	5 September 2013
12.	'Ai Se Eu Te Pego'	Michel Teló	581,100,306	25 July 2011
13.	'Danza Kuduro'	Don Omar featuring Lucenzo	580,458,515	25 August 2010
14.	'Call Me Maybe'	Carly Rae Jepsen	575,407,013	1 March 2012
15.	'Thrift Shop'	Macklemore & Ryan Lewis featuring Wanz	560,581,042	27 August 2012
16.	'What Makes You Beautiful'	One Direction	541,101,366	19 August 2011
17.	'Somebody That I Used to Know'	Gotye featuring Kimbra	531,515,680	5 July 2011
18.	'Not Afraid'	Eminem	529,387,448	4 June 2010
19.	'Rolling in the Deep'	Adele	524,647,561	30 November 2010

Rank	Video name	Uploader/artist	Views	Upload date
20.	'The Lazy Song'	Bruno Mars	521,692,105	15 April 2011
21.	'Rain Over Me'	Pitbull featuring Marc Anthony	499,830,618	22 July 2011
22.	'Oppa Is Just My Style'	Psy featuring Hyuna	498,518,954	14 August 2012
23.	'Dark Horse'	Katy Perry featuring Juicy J	495,583,058	20 February 2014
24.	'Firework'	Katy Perry	466,797,663	28 October 2010
25.	'Diamonds'	Rihanna	457,921,860	8 November 2012
26	'The Gummy Bear Song'	Gummibär	449,930,603	9 October 2007
27.	'The Fox (What Does the Fox Say?)'	Ylvis	435,718,748	3 September 2013
28.	'Never Say Never'	Justin Bieber featuring Jaden Smith	433,388,258	27 May 2010
29.	'We Can't Stop'	Miley Cyrus	430,005,360	19 June 2013
30.	'Just the Way You Are'	Bruno Mars	427,709,681	8 September 2010

Source: YouTube's public viewcount statistics as of 30 June 2014

and liberated, all the while such experiences flow into musical expression and appreciation. Experiencing music through YouTube – particularly for those who have taken up YouTube's early invitation to 'broadcast yourself' – can be a way to construct and communicate various modes of self-identity, however fraught, which may include diverse degrees of performance and performative mimicry. Despite palpable evidence to support music and YouTube's symbiotic relationship, relatively little has been written about their mutually advantageous reliance. Notable exceptions include Carol Vernallis's *Unruly Media* (2013), contributors to *The Oxford Handbook of New Audiovisual Aesthetics* (2013) and Mathias Bonde Korsgaard's *Music Video After MTV* (2017). Burgess and Green's pivotal text *YouTube* (2009) and Michael Strangelove's *Watching YouTube* (2010), while both important works in establishing YouTube as a serious platform worth studying, give little more than passing mention to music's unique place within YouTube's socio-culture.

At the turn of the twenty-first century, MTV was supplying music television to an estimated 342 million homes around the world and generating annual revenue of more than US$3 billion, while producers and consumers (real or imagined) were restricted by material and ideological codes that appeared resistant to change (Inglis and Hearsum 2013). Yet in a matter of a few years, the arrival of YouTube proved to be an instrument 'through which many of those apparently entrenched codes were actively confronted and challenged' (Inglis and Hearsum 2013: 487). Continuous and uninterrupted access to music videos in the post-YouTube world provided a significant change from their previous confinement to scheduled television time slots. As Jenkins posits:

> By providing a distribution channel for amateur and semi-professional media content, YouTube incites new expressive activities ... Having a shared site means that these productions get much greater visibility than they would if distributed by separate and isolated portals. It also means that they are exposed to each other's activities, learn quickly from new developments, and often find themselves collaborating across communities in unpredictable ways. (Jenkins 2006a: 274–5, qtd in Inglis and Hearsum 2013: 487)

Voicing the early optimism of possibilities that YouTube offered media scholars and practitioners alike, YouTube – much like other new media formats – offers in theory no new kinds of fan and media experience. Rather, in practice it offers collectors the opportunity to share their vintage materials to a wider audience, a chance for fans to create art through remixing contemporary, mediated content. As such, YouTube delivers a platform that enables everyone to 'freeze a moment out of the "flow" of mass media' and to focus greater attention onto the moments that matter most to that individual. (Jenkins 2006a: 275)

YouTube's sublime, promiscuous and open-accessibility ensured that video creativity was no longer the reserve of the industry, as Jenkins prophesized.[14] Consequently, music video was no longer the patron art of the recorded artist or label conglomerate. With the availability of cheap, more accessible, DIY technology, those with the necessary skills but, more importantly, free leisure time could create independent music videos that are not primarily tasked with selling the song, and therefore hold no responsibility to the record company. No longer seen as primarily the promotional tool it once was in the heady days of MTV, the digital era's music-like videos represent new revenue opportunities for artists and labels. Free from the traditional censorship means of MTV, CPDRC's *Thriller* is demonstrative of how YouTube music videos enable an approach and exploration of different identities that remain under-represented in mainstream televisual and cinematic media, such as the Filipino and the Filipino male body (and by extension, the Asian male body), the ostensibly queer and transgender figures. And although CPDRC's *Thriller* may be free of MTV's influence, it falls instead under newer, differing forms of YouTube censorship – one where its use of copyrighted musical material means that CPDRC's *Thriller* is not playable in Germany (or any other jurisdiction where Sony Music Entertainment have not lifted the ban) for just one relevant example.[15] I extend Vernallis's argument that it is precisely *because* of YouTube's short and often miniature music-like videos, that further investigation or 'extended dialogue' is often quelled (2013: 150). Cover songs, fan videos, bootleg recordings of performances, talent show auditions and so on, account for over half of all of YouTube uploads. Such new music-broadcasting opportunities have substantially reshaped traditional industrial, ideological and technological understandings of music video aesthetics. Music video was and is 'irreducibly strange', as Vernallis is quick to point out, therefore the concept of a singular 'music video aesthetic' has never been straightforward or unproblematic (2013). I agree with Vernallis's broad-but-necessary definition, adding that the global spread of capitalism means that we are selling music to international locations as never before, accompanied by the rise of new, neoliberal structures intended to protect prevailing media industry interests. With the onslaught of YouTube and other online participatory cultural spaces, the result can at times seem like another form of quasi-global homogenization, as news, arts, education and culture are swallowed up by YouTube's entertaining 'edutainment' philosophy. From patronage to prosumer, YouTube has provided a systematic space for music, new and old, as well as music-like video to flourish. And it is in the thick of the vast, brilliant and simultaneously murky material shared on YouTube that CPDRC's *Thriller* first captured the world's attention.

INTERLUDE TWO

'You're fighting for your life inside a killer, thriller'

A quarter of the way into CPDRC's *Thriller* performance, the camera zooms in on our leading characters' faces, and we notice their feigned, frightened facial expressions. Thanks to Garcia's personal and at times intimate proxemics, for the first time we also see that the role of the girlfriend, in her baby-pink halter top embellished with gold earrings and decorative bracelets, is sporting an obvious receding hairline, broad face, strong jawline. Although hard to discern among the highly compressed digital image, we picture the subtle trace of an Adam's apple, which leads many YouTube viewers to comment that *she* is a *he*. Simultaneously, the girlfriend's display of finely arched eyebrows and hair-accessories means she can, with relative ease, 'pass' as 'the girlfriend'. For Filipinos, the girlfriend bears the recognizable markers of an effeminate, cross-dressing male, a *bakla*, who occupies a unique – but often oppressed – place within Philippine socio-culture. Through performing the role of the girlfriend he mimics not only Ola Ray's feminine movements, but at the same time impersonates an imagined American pop culture. The gritty realities of years spent awaiting trial and conviction are instantaneously transformed by a drag queen's fantastical gestures.

The video's soundtrack, now featuring Elmer Bernstein's orchestral incidental 'scary music', builds to a dramatic climax as the girlfriend utilizes melodramatic body language and facial expressions associated with the damsel in distress. She raises her forearms so that her hands frame her furrowed face in an exaggerated act of feigned fear.

CPDRC's girlfriend's obvious overacting fulfils two distinct, intertextual functions. First and foremost, his performance – performed by inmate Wenjiel Resane – serves to directly connect audiences with Michael Jackson's girlfriend in the original *Thriller* short film. But Resane goes beyond mimicking Ray's subtle gestures. He imitates the character of the 'girlfriend' but, in doing so, exaggerates that which constitutes the 'girl'. To read Resane's overwrought impersonation of a source – in this case, Michael Jackson's *Thriller* girlfriend – as an act of drag, the subversive power of her act becomes clear. Resane's drag performance destabilizes and parodies the original *Thriller*, accentuating the radical features of this reinterpreted, remixed, reimagined prison *Thriller*. Second, the girlfriend's melodramatic mimicry highlights the video's fundamental, metaphorical contradictions: *Thriller*'s obvious narrative binary opposition between good (the girlfriend) and evil (the zombies), and Resane's dual inability to transform into an emancipated 'girlfriend'. The melodramatic impersonation of the girlfriend's 'feminine' markers (the damsel in distress movements, her distinctive clothing – the only one of the inmates in 'civilian' clothing among hundreds of men in orange jumpsuits – as well as her long hair, padded top and high heels), serve to amplify the visual markers of us (the civilians) and them (the incarcerated and/or zombies). Resane's performance troubles underlying social and gender binaries, and thus goes some way to fulfil what Judith Butler calls the 'critical promise of drag' (1993: 26). Resane's exaggerated performance as the girlfriend emphasizes a series of binary oppositions, and according to media reception and YouTube's comments, audiences readily construe. It is therefore in CPDRC's *Thriller*'s metaphorical contradictions that we can gain an understanding of the video's universal accessibility and activator of pleasure.

At just over a minute into the video, *Thriller*'s instrumental groove returns, replacing Bernstein's orchestral crescendo. The camera zooms in, closely profiling the male protagonist, as he stares forward, right arm outstretched, body shambling – body language that conveys that he has 'turned' from dancing human to dancing zombie. CPDRC's Michael Jackson, performed by Crisanto Niere, takes his place at the apex of the triangular formation, flanked by twenty-two men in identical suits who have additionally transformed into dancing zombies. Together the men move in near unison, closely following the movements of *their* Michael Jackson. Niere and his posse nod their heads to the right and pop their shoulders in time to the beat of *Thriller*'s pulsating rhythm, signalling the opening sequence of Michael Peter's hallmark *Thriller* choreography.

As the camera pans outwards we see all the surrounding inmates align the prison yard in neat, compressed lines, bordered by a two-story building with the first floor's metal bars glistening in the sunshine. Row after row of hundreds of inmates flank the core triangle, and the yard is awash with tiny orange and black pixellated dancers, concurrently moving their heads and shoulders in time to the beat, but with both arms remaining horizontally outstretched in classic zombie imagery as they perform a static reduction of *Thriller*'s choreography. The combination of low-resolution video recording with YouTube's high-compression results in a pixellation that although very much the norm in 2007, is rendered almost unwatchable a mere decade later, once high-definition video became the norm.[1] This pixellation, a kind of digital grain, only serves to add a further layer of intrigue as it becomes difficult to decipher precisely how many dancers twirl to *Thriller*. The pixellation, combined with an elevated, distant camera angle, makes it equally difficult to read individual dancers' facial expressions or to make out the moves of the dancers in the furthest distance, those half-hidden under the prison yard's dark porticos.

Halfway through, the camera quickly pans to the right and we grasp, for the first time, the magnitude of this performance. Row after row of hundreds of men in bright orange move their arms and twist their bodies to make the famous *Thriller* 'claw' movement in time to the chorus. On the beat of the chorus, Niere – CPDRC's 'Michael Jackson' – performs a solo pivot, and dramatically faces the camera while the remaining dancers follow suit a split-second later.

'You're fighting for your life inside a killer, thriller.'

Michael Jackson's voice rings clear over the prison amplifiers, as the core triangular ensemble drop to the floor leaving only Niere to perform a triple-spin, drop-kick solo with unmistakable flourish. The surrounding corps steadily rise to standing positions, arms stretched upwards with dramatic flair. These uncanny, fragmented zombie-inmates do not embody the living or the dead. Instead they roam the borders of this concrete purgatory, immortalized through and inside of YouTube, and trapped forever as the new mediated, eternally undead.

CHAPTER TWO

Performing postcolonialism Filipino history through four-part harmony

[C]onflict between cultures – brought about largely by colonialism – has had a ruinous impact on the musics of the world, causing many traditions to disappear altogether, especially in territories that were conquered by European nations and incorporated into colonial empires. Musical practices played important roles in this conflict, for in the early modern world there was arguably no music that was not constitutive of societies' ideological values and a signifier of deep cultural symbolism. Every act of musical performance was inextricably intertwined with religious or political cultural systems or imbued with expressions of social or ethnic identities. (Irving 2010: 2)

With a 350-year history steeped in violent colonial oppression, the Philippines – and Filipinos – are frequently half-jokingly dismissed as a 'people with no culture' (Rosaldo 1998). This colonial history is often reduced to the précis of 'three centuries in a Catholic convent and fifty years in Hollywood' (Karnow 1989: 9).[1] For Arjun Appadurai, Filipinos are a people homesick for a 'world they never lost', and as such, the Philippines presents a unique case of nostalgia without memory – a place where there are 'more Filipinos singing perfect renditions of American songs (often from the American past) than there are Americans doing so … [in spite of] the fact that the rest of their lives is not in complete synchrony with the referential world that first gave birth to these songs' (1996: 29). Alongside this 'ersatz nostalgia' (Appadurai 1996: 82), in news and media reports to global tourist literature, Filipinos are widely stereotyped and indeed promoted by their own government as an ever-smiling, and ever-singing nationality (see Subaihi 2013; Gonzales 2014). Take this excerpt from the *Lonely Planet: Philippines* guidebook[2] – arguably the world's leading international tourist literature brand – as one such example:

> [D]espite years of injustice at the hands of colonial and homegrown rulers, and despite being for the most part dirt poor, *Filipinos are the happiest people in Asia*. This incongruous *joie de vivre* is perhaps best symbolised by that quirkiest of national icons, the jeepney. Splashed with colour, laden with religious icons and festooned with sanguine scribblings, the jeepney openly flaunts the fact that, at heart, it's a dilapidated, smoke-belching pile of scrap metal. Like the jeepney, *poor Filipinos face their often dim prospects in life with a laugh, a wink and even a song*. (Bloom et al. 2012: 33, italics added)

Leaving aside, for now, the crude and deeply problematic association made between poor Filipinos and dilapidated scrap metal, this quotation entitled 'The National Psyche' blatantly connects poor (read: mass) Philippine spirit with laughter and song. This categorization that Filipinos are among the happiest *and* most musical nation of people in the world is widespread and such a stereotype, no matter how 'positive' it may be intended, can certainly be dangerous. Such constructed stereotypes play a crucial role in the establishment and pervasive acceptance of CPDRC's *Thriller* as a form of banal entertainment.

My purpose in this chapter is to trace a number of aspects of the CPDRC performances to show that the legacy of colonialism, and US neocolonialism in particular, lives on in contemporary Filipino experience. Building on the previous chapter on the role of music in YouTube video and redefining the music video after Vernallis, I now move to examine more closely our contemporary music video exemplar. I explore this distinctive case study's postcolonial themes in relation to new media and critical theory, and in the context of contemporary Philippine studies. Philippine studies – an interdisciplinary, multidisciplinary field of study – is understood here after Priscelina Patajo-Legasto, as incorporating enquiry about the Philippines and Filipinos, and it includes:

> all those discourses which, through a critique of Western hegemony and an affirmation of our own hitherto marginalised cultural practices, what directions we as a people, including those in the Filipino diaspora, should take to liberate ourselves from the legacies of Spanish and American colonist discourses and the continuing power of Western hegemony, that have metamorphosed into discourses of globalisation. (Patajo-Legasto 2008: xxii)

Not limited only to Filipino scholars, from the late 1980s to today Philippine studies scholarship has witnessed a wave of foreign academic attention, with particular focus on Philippine politics and society and anthropological ethnographic studies (see Cannell 1999; Go and Foster 2003; McKay 2007; Ness 1992; Pinches 2005). For Neferti Tadiar, the Philippines is a complex country dominated by misplaced dreams and ironic juxtapositions. It is, she says, 'a place of ironic contrasts and tragic contradictions, where politics is a star-studded spectacle set amid the gritty third world realities of hunger and squalor. A third world place in first world drag' (Tadiar 2004: 1–2). I connect the digital sharing of the Cebu prison pop performances – especially with reference to CPDRC's girlfriend character played by *bakla* Resane – as an example of Tadiar's third world space in 'first world drag', a complex extension of the colonial education experience as 1,500 inmates continue to shake their hips in time to the disco beats and sing along to hits in a former colonial language. By drilling American colonial values upon the Filipino people for half a century, CPDRC's performances demonstrate an aspiration to the American fantasy dream of life, liberty and the pursuit of happiness despite these prisoners never being promised such fantasies in the first place.

Throughout this discussion, I present how music plays a vital role in everyday Cebuano life – past and present – shaping how these Visayan Filipinos perform identity, and how it shapes lived experience. To examine the context surrounding the international viral video phenomenon that is CPDRC's *Thriller*, this chapter takes as its starting point the American colonial project in the Philippines from the beginning of the twentieth century, discussing how US education policies helped shape a century of US cultural influence over an archipelago located some thousands of miles away. I examine the fundamental essentialism that continually takes place because of this crucial link between Filipinos and popular music culture, tracing it to pre-Hispanic Philippines and following it all the way through to today. I address how and why this portrayal of the Philippines and Filipinos is continuously circulated among national and international academic, commercial and colloquial discourse, and connect this to how and why a video such as CPDRC's *Thriller* is so easily, and readily, perpetuated. But more significantly, the heart of this chapter asks the question from the perspective of the internationally popular CPDRC videos: whose interests are being served from portraying these inmates as inherently musical, innately happy Filipinos?

Philippine colonial history in four-part harmony

In this section, I first show that the inmates' dance routine indoctrinated a series of bodily practices and positions marked by highly asymmetric ideologies of domination and subjugation, which owe their force to historical legacies of US colonization – illustrated in examples such as the St. Louis World Fair.[3] With this background, I then present a nuanced reading of the CPDRC performances and attend to the longue durée of such colonizing activities, and their continuing influence on education policy in the Philippines.

To end the Spanish–American conflict of 1898, representatives of Spain and the United States signed into effect the Treaty of Paris on 10 December 1898, 'allowing' the US to purchase the Philippine Islands from Spain for US$20 million. The seizure of the Philippines by the US proved a logical extension of the nation's plan to participate directly in Asian markets, yet directly led to the Philippine–American War (1899–1902). Rich in natural resources including hemp, copper, gold, silver and iron, the Philippines' 7,100 islands provided the US with an attractive base in Southeast Asia. The US can be considered an 'empire in denial', Niall Ferguson (2003) claims, an imperial power that operated in a vastly different manner to previous European empires.[4] The US was an 'exceptionalist paradigm', widely considered an exercise in effective benevolence – a benign, civilizing mission rather than one of conquest aimed at 'transplanting the ideas and improvements of one civilisation on another' (Go and Foster 2003: 1–2). Scholars, activists and journalists have noted that today most Americans are unaware of the fact that the Philippines was part of the US empire until the end of World War II (see Campomanes 1995; Cooper 2013), for the US colonization of the Philippines remains largely omitted from most US history books.

Christi-Anne Castro believes that US colonial rule over the Philippines is often overlooked by Americans, despite the fact that it served as an early case study of US influence on nation-building abroad as well as a fundamental factor in the rise of US international power (Castro 2011: 6). Filipino-Americans are the second largest population of Asian-Americans in the twenty-first century, and according to the US Census, over 3.4 million people in the US trace their ancestry to the Philippines. Yet the Philippines, and Filipinos, remain an exotic Other for many Americans, unaware of the colonial heritage America left behind on the Far Eastern islands. Filipinos and Filipino-Americans remain near invisible in mainstream American culture today, 'alienated from whites (for being nonwhite), blacks and Latinos (for being Asian), and Asian Americans (for being insufficiently Asian)' (Pisares 2006: 191). Despite a history that is deeply intertwined with the US, and a significant diaspora population in many countries, from Singapore to Spain, UAE to the UK, Filipinos remain, by and large, invisible in global culture – mainstream or otherwise.[5]

'The miseducation of the Filipino': American occupation and the army of educators

Take up the White Man's burden,
Send forth the best ye breed
Go bind your sons to exile,

To serve your captives' need;
To wait in heavy harness,
On fluttered folks and wild –
Your new-caught, sullen peoples,
Half-devil and half-child
(Kipling, 'The White Man's Burden: The United States and the Philippine Islands' 1899)

The White Man's Burden has been sung. Who will sing the Brown Man's?
(Twain, 'The Stupendous Procession' 1901)

At the dawn of the twentieth century, the St. Louis World's Fair (also called the Louisiana Purchase Exhibition) constructed the Philippine Exhibit – the largest, most expensive and most popular of all the displays. This 'Philippine Exposition' incorporated forty-seven acres, 100 structures, and 1,200 indigenous Filipino representatives who were forcibly plucked from the recently acquired Philippine archipelago and shipped to the US to be viewed and to perform hourly 'exotic' rituals for the pleasure of the American masses (Figure 2.1).

Tasked with entertaining the Fair's crowds of daily visitors, the cover of the Philippine Exposition brochure promised visitors an experience that was 'second only to the world's fair itself', and 'better than a trip through the Philippine Islands'. The imported Philippine 'natives' were required to repeat rare, sacred tribal rituals in a monotonous daily routine, with the main attraction being the display of dog-eating undertaken by members of the Igorot tribe. Music performance played a vital role in these exhibitions. To further demonstrate the American civilizing prowess over Filipino subjects, the Filipino presentations concluded with musical performances, culminating in a stirring rendition of 'The Star Spangled Banner' (Delmendo 2005: 52). Music, and in particular the act of singing, is deeply rooted in the American colonial agenda.

As Kipling's poem tells us, US imperialism was presented as a rather thankless mission to civilize 'fluttered folk and wild'. The 1904 Fair displayed the displaced Filipinos in loincloths, promoting their 'new-caught, sullen ... half-devil and half-child' (Kipling 1929) acquisitions in a grandiose project showcasing new imperialist America.[6] The Fair sought to justify the US colonial and orientalist discourse, as indicated through the Fair's binary markers of difference between the 'Occident' and the 'Orient,' between the Western individual and the colonized 'Other' as substantially or ontologically different (Patajo-Legasto 2008: xvi). However US history pitches the acquisition of the Philippines as part of an 'informal empire', as mentioned earlier – one that was markedly different from the European imperial territories. For historian Paul

FIGURE 2.1 *'Better than a trip through the Philippine Islands'*: brochure front cover of the Philippine Exposition at the World's Fair St. Louis (1904) featuring an unnamed, so-called native Filipino. (Image reproduced with the kind permission of the Jonathan Best and John L. Silva Collection.)

Kramer, US colonial rule in the Philippines has disturbed accounts of US uniqueness since it was:

> ushered in with a war that looked much like Europe's colonial wars. It involved the United States in colonial state-building and international politics of a kind undertaken by European powers during the same period. (2006: 15)

Indeed the Second Assistant Chief of Constabulary, W. C. Taylor, confirmed the purpose of the US imperial project, revealing that 'America took these islands with the avowed intention of lifting them up out of ... savagery' (Bureau of Education 1902: 162). Thus, in view of the fact that military victory alone does not equate with victory, the most effective means of subjugation used by the US colonial rulers over the Filipino population was the establishment of a public education system that truly 'captured the minds' of the Filipinos (Constantino 1970: 21–5). The Education Act of 1901, part of the Taft Commission (or Second Philippine Commission) established by the US President William McKinley in 1900, provided free primary instruction to all Filipinos and sought to train them to be citizens of a new American colony (see Act No. 74 of the Educational Act, 1901). A pacification effort took place whereby US soldiers were enlisted as teachers, equating and trading the image of a figure of violence with that of paternity (Roma-Sianturi 2009: 7). The early education of the Philippines by US voluntary teachers is frequently considered as a commendable project. But as Dinah Roma-Sianturi reasons, education can be a deceptive gift.

In 1901 a group of American public school teachers landed in the Philippines aboard the USS *Thomas*, tasked to 'carry on the education that shall fit the Filipinos for their new citizenship' and close 'a chasm' between Americans and Filipinos, so that Americans and 'a people who neither know nor understand the underlying principles of our civilisation', still 'must be brought into accord with us' (Kramer 2006: 168–9). The Thomasites, a group of 1,000 American teachers in total, and their followers, were meant to restore the fabric of US nationalism among Filipinos still in recovery from Emilio Aguinaldo's First Philippine Republic defeat in the violent war of 1898–1901, which resulted in many deaths on both sides, displaced tens of thousands of Filipinos, and destroyed the economy (Kramer 2006: 169–70). Composed of men and women from primarily middle-class backgrounds, and lured by the promise of travel and adventure, the Thomasites were deployed across the archipelago to teach Filipinos the rudiments of egalitarian education (Roma-Sianturi 2009: 8; Racelis and Ick 2001). The harsh, physical violence of the Philippine–American War that killed at least 200,000 civilians was only to be replaced by a seemingly softer, American colonial ideology, the key to which was the introduction of a new foreign language and to quickly enforce it as the mandatory medium of instruction. The English language thus became a 'wedge that separated the Filipinos from their past and later was to separate educated Filipinos from the masses of their countrymen ... This was the beginning of their education. At the same time, it was the beginning of their miseducation, for they learned no longer as Filipinos but as colonials' (Constantino 1970: 25). Renato Constantino eloquently explains the enormous impact of the Thomasites on shaping Filipino identity and culture as he explains:

> The new generation learned of the lives of American heroes, *sang American songs*, and dreamt of snow and Santa Claus ... Thus, the Filipino past, which had already been quite obliterated by three centuries of Spanish tyranny, did not enjoy a revival under American colonialism. On the contrary, the history of our ancestors was taken up as if they were strange and foreign peoples who settled in these shores ... We read about them *as if we were tourists in a foreign land*. (1970: 25, italics added)

The results of US colonization was that Filipinos, their history and their culture, were left to feel as strangers in their own home, and much of the advances in media technologies at the turn of the century only served to accelerate the colonial project. Leisure activities including listening to gramophone recordings, radio broadcasting, playing songs from printed sheet music, and going to the cinema were deployed to voraciously spread the medium of American songs and other audio and visual media. Together, such activities repeatedly ensured English became the language of modern-day entertainment. The tempo at which the introduction of the English language abruptly disconnected the Philippines from Spanish influence was indeed remarkable. Education united both the highland and lowland in embracing the US colonial presence, comprehensively ensuring the oppressor's ideology was benignly conveyed through entire systems. The power of education and language in colonial operations is vast, as Ngũgĩ wa Thiong'o asserts:

> the maintenance, management, manipulation, and mobilisation of the entire system of education, language and language use, literature, religion, the media, have always ensured for the oppressor nation power over the transmission of a certain ideology, set of values, outlook, attitudes, feelings, etc., and hence power over the whole area of consciousness. (Thiong'o: 51, qtd in Roma-Sianturi 2009: 6)

Such insidious manipulation through mandatory primary education and language, as Thiong'o observes, is precisely how American ideologies effectively took root across the archipelago in such a relatively short period of time. Such was the effect of, and adherence to American colonialism that most Filipinos remained loyal to the United States during the post-Pearl Harbour Japanese occupation of the Commonwealth of the Philippines (1942–5). Through the work of the Thomasites and 'those who came in their wake, Filipinos were led to think of themselves as if they were Americans, that is, as other than who they were supposed to be' (Rafael 1997: 271). The Thomasites operated as an army 'of education', as Thomasite teacher Adeline Knapp wrote in her memoirs (Gov.ph 2003). As mentioned in the introduction, every army in the world has music, and the Thomasites were no different. They built upon the previous contributions from the US army soldiers who began teaching English to Filipino students, sang American songs, danced American dances and transformed the Philippines into the third largest English-speaking nation in the world.

Today, current practice remains not wholly dissimilar to American colonial practice. From third grade through college, English is the medium of instruction in a significant number of Philippine education courses (see Fullmer 2012). In line with other globalized nations, there is an increasing wealth of employment opportunities in the Philippines afforded to those with proficiency in English, from the international call centres of Manila, Cebu and Baguio, to a host of international employment destinations. Although the Philippine economy is the 39th largest in the world, the rapidly increasing Filipino population and successive Philippine labour migration policies mean that the Philippines continues to depend on sending over 10 per cent of its 101 million population to work abroad. It is hardly surprising, then, that today's Philippine education hinges on catering to the demands of an overseas employment market, with English language skills placed at its core. Since the US-supported Marcos regime (1969–86), the comparative advantage of the current Philippine economy is founded on the exportation of Filipino bodies throughout the world as cheap labour. The culture of Filipino *balikbayan* (periodically returning émigré visitors; literal meaning *balik*-return, *bayan*-country) is intertwined with a steady tradition of sending Overseas Filipino Workers (OFW) to far off lands in search of higher-paid work. OFWs, of which some three million reside in the US alone, are widely praised in local and national media as being among 'the best workers in the world' – modern day Filipino heroes whose special power is sending money back home (Ong 2009: 164).[7] Such is the reliance on OFWs that former President Gloria Macapagal-Arroyo coined the term Overseas Filipino Investor (OFI) for Filipino expatriates whose annual remittances create business, purchase property and repay interest from the World Bank debt. Therefore proficiency in English remains highly valued as many of the colonized are still being processed for 'integration into First World developmentalism through transnationalization and the global division of labour' (Tolentino 2008: 673). The price of transnationalization is paid for dearly by Third World people, Rolando Tolentino contends, most especially women, feeding into the logic of colonialism that is, in fact, neocolonialism (2008: 673–4). The lure of better-paid employment abroad combined with a historical culture of Filipino workers sent around the world as domestic workers, seafarers and mail-order brides means that OFW are as prevalent today as ever.

Centuries of dealing with a range of colonizers, missionaries and traders have left their mark on the political, cultural and economic life of Filipinos. The periods of Spanish colonialism (1521–1898), American imperialism (1898–1946), the postcolonial state (1946–66) as well as the Marcos dictatorship (1966–86) immersed Filipinos in complex sociocultural situations that left deep imprints of the West as superior and advantageous, with some scholars arguing that education too was used to train Filipinos to be good colonial subjects and to conform to American ideals (Kelly 2000: 29). Vincente Rafael reads the act of the *balikbayan* as mirroring the real tragedy that is shared by the majority of the Filipino population still caught up in the delusions of colonial hegemony. The real failures of Philippine nationalism, for Rafael, lie in its inability to 'retain and control the excess known as overseas Filipino' (1997: 272). By now, the effects of US imperialism within the Philippines are embedded to the point that Filipino/American Studies scholars have gone so far as to claim that the identity of 'Filipino American' is not just an apparent oxymoron, but an inherent redundancy. Oscar Campomanes reminds us that '[t]o be Filipino is already, whether you move to the United States or remain where you are, to be American' (Campomanes in Tiongson et al. 2006: 42). Conrado de Quiros makes similar assertions, stating that the physical fact of Filipinos migrating abroad is just the tip of the iceberg, because '[m]ost of us are expatriates right here in our own land. America is our heartland whether we get to go there or not' (de Quiros 1990: 140, qtd in Rafael 1997: 272).

Since Philippine independence from the US in 1946, the Philippine government has also played an important role in seeking to construct a Filipino identity that is attuned to the needs of the globalized economy. The Philippine state's legitimacy in entering the global economic arena, both in terms of socio-economic environment and domestic political economy, is described as both 'premature' and 'weak' by some scholars. Rommel Banlaoi argues that the characteristics of the Philippine state were in opposition to those characteristics required of a mature and strong state when entering the global market (2004: 203–4). Such mature and strong characteristics include:

i. The ends and purposes of government have become settled and founded on a significant ideological consensus;
ii. Most social groups (ethnic, religious, linguistic and the like) have been successfully assimilated, or have achieved protection, equality or self-determination through autonomy, federalism or other special devices;
iii. Secessionism no longer constitutes a major goal of minorities. Territorial frontiers have become legitimized and sanctified through legal instruments;

iv. Leaders are selected on the basis of a regular procedure like elections. No group, family, clan or sector can hold power permanently;

v. Military and policy organizations remain under effective civilian control;

vi. The mores of governance preclude personal enrichment through various political activities.

Since the Philippines entered the global competitive market through the World Trade Organization (WTO) in 1995, it is widely recognized as a nation determined to face the challenges of globalization (Banlaoi 2004: 203). Yet the rather orientalist and essentialist notion of the 'highly trainable' disposition of the Philippine workforce continues to be singled out, as the US Embassy Bureau of International Labor Affairs report found (2003: 7). From this pervasive notion of Filipino discipline and trainability, it becomes rather easy to see how myths of Filipino musical dispositions can swiftly creep into national and international discourse.

Confronting the 'innately musical Filipino' trope

The Philippines is regularly cited by politicians, poets, journalists and academics as a nation filled with innately or inherently musical people. Filipino historian and playwright Horacio de la Costa romantically eulogized that music is regarded as one of the 'jewels' of the Filipino, providing a bond that binds across a nation of over one hundred languages and dialects (de la Costa 2005: 143–4). The Filipino-American Symphony Orchestra assert that Filipinos are 'naturally gifted in music', and according to the Orchestra's website, their goal is to showcase this 'innate Filipino artistic talent'. Meanwhile contemporary travel literature and guidebooks single out Filipinos 'innate musical talent' (Bloom et al. 2012: 46). This propensity to homogenize Filipinos as an intrinsically musical people is, however, by no means unique to the Philippines.[8] Yet history points to two potential reasons for this prevalent attitude. First, pre-Hispanic Philippine music and dance traditions are maintained in some remote areas of northern Luzon, the central Visayas, southern Mindanao and the Sulu archipelago (Rodell 2002: 174–7), and has long been a cultural meeting place for Chinese, Malay and Muslim people. By the sixteenth century, Spanish-governed Manila was, according to musicologist David Irving, an intercultural nexus, 'the world's first global city', and as such, it was effectively 'a microcosm of the world' (2010: 19). In such an ethnically diverse society as the Philippines, Manila represented a crucial conduit for the regional diffusion of multiple styles and genres of Western music, from the sacred to the profane (Rodell 2002; Irving 2010). Early accounts by Spanish colonizers describe the native Filipinos as competent, good musicians, who quickly and enthusiastically picked up Spanish church music instructions. Early Spanish colonization brought with it Filipinos' expertise in complex polychoral European music due to the Filipino 'innate musicality', as Franciscan friar Juan de Jesús attested in 1703. He claimed that even 'without teachers the Filipinos are decent enough musicians', who 'make musical instruments and play them with skill' (Jesús qtd in Irving 2010: 118). Navigator John Meares's eighteenth-century account of his voyage from China to America would appear to reinforce Jesús's utterances. His description of hearing Filipino musicians performing in Mindanao in February 1788 confirms that the Philippines served as a meeting point of people and cultures from East and West, illustrated by a happenstance upon a local musical performance (with a predictable dose of eighteenth-century colonial mentality):

> We were equally surprised at hearing a very tolerable band of music, which was composed of natives of the country. It consisted of four violins, two bassoons, with several flutes and mandolins. This unexpected orchestra [was] acquainted with some of the select pieces of Handel; they knew many of our English country dances, and several of our popular and favourite tunes; but in performing the Fandango, they had attained a degree of excellence that the nicest ears of Spain would have heard with pleasure. The Malayans [sic: Filipinos] possess, in common with other savage nations, a sensibility to the charms of music, and are even capable no inconsiderable degree of perfection in that delightful science. (Meares 1788, qtd in Irving 2010: 69)

Leaving the colonial primitivism of Meares's report to one side, the above descriptions presents an account of pre-Hispanic and Spanish colonial Philippines as a musical place and people, who display multi-genre talent, knowledge of and expertise in European repertoire.

Second, in more recent history Filipinos have been supplying musicians to the world throughout the twentieth century. As part of the US empire, the Philippines became purveyors of their own style of Western popular music, especially vaudeville, dancehall, jazz and, later, rock'n'roll. During the 1920s and 1930s, the harbour cities of Manila and Cebu in particular, became cultural crossroads where citizens took part in the dual roles of consumers and performers of all facets of popular culture and the American jazz era, from music, art and literature, to fashion (dress and hairstyles), theatre and cinema. Many Filipinos took paid gigs as musicians on passenger ships, travelling to the US and beyond. In later decades and up until the present day, Filipino musicians have played in service industry sites all over Asia.

The international success of Filipino choral groups (both children and adult) that tour the world only serves to bolster this view about the skills of Filipinos as accomplished musicians, especially singers. And more recently, the significant number of Filipinos featured in international television music and talent competitions, such as Mikey Bustos on *Canadian Idol* 2003, 4th Power/The Cercado Sisters on *Superstar K* (South Korea, 2014) and the *X Factor* (UK, 2015), and *X Factor Israel* 2014 winner Rose Fostanes, an openly gay, middle-aged Filipina caregiver living in Tel Aviv.[9] Such is the widespread popularity of Filipino singers succeeding in international talent shows, American satirical news site *The Adobo Chronicles* featured an article titled 'Filipinos Barred from "X Factor," (and) Other Reality TV Singing Competitions', which more than a few readers appeared to interpret as fact. Like many other nations and nationalities, Filipinos may believe they are a musical people based on their own experience of music at home, but in addition there is ample validation from the wider world that Filipinos are valued as musicians and singers.[10] All of this is not to say that the 'innately musical Filipino' myth is true. Rather I share some of the possible explanations as to why the myth continues to be globally ubiquitous. After all, the prevalence of Filipino musicians internationally directly relates to the general phenomenon of OFW – English-speaking, trained, migrant labour – the Philippines' largest, and most profitable export.

Tracing the history of this inherent musicality myth brings to the fore the explicit role of colonization in music training, from Spanish friars teaching Filipino natives Catholic hymns in four-part harmony, to American enculturation during World War II through the medium of radio and popular song. The central dimension of this musical stereotype that extends to a nation or peoples, is that there remains a degree of prevalent cognitive investment in this association. Such an association, however minute, may or may not rise to the level of belief, but it becomes more than mere recognition that such an association is widespread. Positive stereotypes – though often treated as flattering, harmless and therefore seemingly innocuous – are especially potent because they may insidiously influence people's general beliefs about the nature of social group differences, and ironically, can go on to trigger negative and harmful stereotypical beliefs (see Kay et al. 2013).

Locating music and dance in Cebuano cultural history

So what do we know about music and dance in Cebuano cultural history that might help explain the origins of the exceptional CPDRC *Thriller* video? While I have just acknowledged the potential peril of stereotypes, one must also address the prevailing – if not lighthearted – cultural, regional reputes among Filipino social identity. In Filipino culture, *Ilocanos* – native Filipinos who live along the Ilocos coast, mountainous ranges and agricultural valleys of northern Luzon – have a reputation for being very hard-working, and extremely frugal (*kuripot*), undoubtedly due to notoriously harsh farming conditions (Rodell 2002: 6). Meanwhile Visayans – including Cebuanos – are considered the archetypal opposite. For Filipinos, the abundant marine resources and rich volcanic soils of the Visayas, along with the prevalence of Visayan guitar-making industries, have led to a culture that values music, art and, above all, fun (Rodell 2002: 7). The marriage of former president Ferdinand Marcos, an Ilocano, and his Visayan wife Imelda Romualdez, provides a well-known summary of the Filipino study of contrasts: Marcos, an Ilocano of simple tastes and alleged conservative spending, proved a contrast to Imelda's flamboyant lifestyle, whose shopping sprees and impromptu singing at prolific parties spoke of her Visayan origins (Rodell 2002: 7). Thus, by fate and/or design, the Visayan Islands, and Cebu in particular, provide a particularly colourful – yet not unproblematic – history of music traditions that extends beyond pre-Spanish acquisition.

Situated in the central Visayan region of the Philippines, 365 miles south of Manila, Cebu's place in history is famed for being the birthplace of Christianity in the Philippines (and by extension, Asia) in 1521. Cebu, or *Lalawigan sa Sugbo* in Cebuano, is an island at the centre of trade and commerce in the southern part of the Republic of the Philippines, which over 3.85 million people home. Cebu is the oldest city in the country, the entry point for the first Spanish settlement in the Philippines and the location of Portuguese explorer Ferdinand Magellan's death in the Battle of Mactan (1521). The capital of the province, Cebu City, is centrally located and well-connected nationally and internationally by land and sea.[11] The island is rich in historical sites, shrines and stories, while facing similar extreme and contrasting socio-economic conditions, and the constant threat of natural hazards as other Philippine cities. Historical accounts support this painted picture of the Visayans as noticeably, and even exceptionally, musical. Visayans, legend tells us, 'were said to be always singing except when they were sick or asleep' (Scott 1994: 107). With the exception of funerals, historian William H. Scott explains that:

> all Visayan feasts ... were accompanied by dancing and gong playing – weddings, birth of children, planting and harvesting of crops, preparations for war, and victory celebrations afterwards. (1994: 111)

Another historical account of antiphonal song in the Philippines demonstrates that such songs were introduced to the Philippines as early as the first migratory wave of Malays (Proto-Malays) who arrived in the Philippines between 12,000 and 8,000 BC. As Gutierrez notes,

> Just to what definite part of the Philippines these alternating songs first took ground one can only guess, for their chronology is so widespread that studies made by different ethnologists reveal that practically all primitive and pagan mountain tribes have one kind of song or another sung alternatingly. Among the Christian Filipinos these alternating songs are especially popular in the Visayas, more so in places where the Cebuano language is spoken. (1961: 25)

This type of antiphonal song, known by the ancient Visayan term *ayayi* and acquiring the term *balitao* in present Cebuano vocabulary, is said to have been in existence 'since time immemorial' (Gutierrez 1961: 25). In Gutierrez's account, wherever early Cebuanos gathered, whether it was during communal work or:

> merrymaking, the *balitao* was ever at hand in the hearts and throats of the men and women. These early people especially the women were very proficient in the art of rhyming and verse making. (1961: 26)

One of the most significant Spanish influences on Philippine culture is reflected in the history of the *balitao* song and dance.[12] Through the actions of Spanish friars and their followers, the *balitao* was transformed into a vehicle for the new faith of Catholicism, incorporating narratives of the Nativity, Passion and Crucifixion of Christ. These changes mirrored the ubiquitous Christianization faced by Cebuanos and the general Filipino population in the sixteenth and seventeenth centuries (see Gutierrez 1961: 26–7). All of this is to say that the Visayans, if we are to believe such historical accounts, were an exceptionally musical people, to the extent that the Spanish settlers used this perceived musicality as a velvet glove to occupy the land and colonize the population.

The omnipresence of music in historical Cebuano socio-culture has continued in contemporary Cebuano life. The Philippines and Filipinos, as indeed in many other cultures, continue to celebrate historical occasions and rituals through the nexus of music, movement and dance. The belief that Visayans are the most musical of all Filipino regions is partly due to their bustling calendar of fiestas. In Cebu, the tradition of fiestas celebrated through music and dance is particularly ubiquitous. Since all cities and municipalities in Cebu province have their own respective annual fiestas, the Cebuano calendar boasts no less than fifty-three annual festivals, all of which feature varying levels of dance, music and colourful costumes. Table 2.1 depicts a selection of these festivals that heavily feature dance and music in their programme.

Table 2.1 28 of the 53 Cebuano festivals held annually that prominently feature dance and music

Date	Title	Location & notes
3rd Sunday of January	Sinulog Festival	Cebu City's most popular and grandest fiesta; Co-opted and celebrated in other Filipino cities including various barangays in Manila.
19 January	Tagbo Festival	Poro, Camotes Island
20 January	Silmugi Festival	Held in Borbon, in honour of its patron saint.
10 February	Bodbod Festival	Catmon; Noted for its street-dancing competition participated in by the different *barangays* (districts/neighbourhoods).
February (movable)	Kabayo Festival	Mandaue City; Organized by the Cebu Equine Owners, Breeders and Sportsmen.
14 February	Sarok Festival	Consolacion; Mardi-gras parade and street dancing.
18 March	Soli-Soli Festival	San Francisco, Camotes Island; Freestyle dance competition uses the soli-soli plant as its dominant material.
3rd Sunday of April	Tostado Festival	Santander; Named after the town's famous delicacy, the 'tostado'. Street dancing is the highlight of the festivity, and dancers use the different movements of making a tostado in their choreography.
Easter Sunday	Kabanhawan Festival	Minglanilla; Games and entertainment featuring street-dancing celebrations.
22–27 April	Kadaugan sa Mactan	Lapu-Lapu City; Features musical productions commemorating the historical battle of Mactan between Magellan and Chief Lapu-Lapu.
7th May	Mantawi Festival	Mandaue City; Showcase for the city involving street dancing, dioramas and floats.
2nd Week of June	Camotes Cassava	Tudela; Includes cultural nights and competitions.

Date	Title	Location & notes
12 June	Tartanilla Festival	Cebu City; Coinciding with the Philippine's Independence Day, this Cebuano fiesta preserves the tartanilla (horse-drawn carriage) heritage.
June (Movable)	Kinsan Festival	Aloguinsan; Named after the town's famous fish that visits the coastal area every June; Features parades and dancing.
June (Movable)	Kuyayang Mardi Gras	Bogo City; Kuyayang refers to the dance movements conveying courtship and love characterized by the Bogohanon's cariñoso character.
Last Week of June	Palawod Festival	Bantayan; Palawod is the fishermen's daily toil, their means of livelihood, life and pride. The street dancing captures and preserves the Bantayanons' unique traditional fishing rituals inherent to the island through music and dance.
25/26 July	Kaumahan Festival	Barili; A festival of revelry showcasing the town's agricultural products through dancing on the streets to the pounding beats of the drum, chanting and singing thanking God for a bountiful harvest.
25 July	Caballo Festival	Compestella; Highlights include the Caballo dance ritual championship, which features several competition categories including Best Solo Performance and Best in Street Dancing.
2nd Week of August	Dinagat Bakasi	Cordova; Celebrating an exotic eel locally known as 'bakasi', the dance replicates the gliding movement of the Bakasi.
9 August	Bonga Festival	Sibonga; Thanksgiving fiesta for the abundant fruits found in their town The festival includes street dancing competitions.
30 August	Haladaya Mardi Gras	Daabantayan; Dance, parade and thanksgiving of Datu Daya, the leader of the first Malayan settlers.
3rd Sunday of September	Kabuhian Festival	Ronda; Features dance movements based on the various livelihood programmes of the town.

Date	Title	Location & notes
3rd Sunday of September	Karansa Festival	Danao City; The Karansa dance, expressing one's joy and happiness, is performed in four steps that jibes with the official Karansa beat.
4 October	Sinanggiyaw	Dumanjug; Through dance and field presentations, performers focus on three aspects: planting, harvesting and thanksgiving.
14–15 October	Inasal (Halad/Lechon) Festival	Talisay City; Showcasing history and heritage through street dancing and food festival featuring the famous 'Inasal' or 'lechon' – the Philippine's beloved roasted pork.
4th Week of November	Kabkaban Festival	Carcar; Cultural catalogue of the town's past with a parade and street dancing.
8 December	Sadsad Festival	Oslob; Thanksgiving fiesta to the Immaculate Conception through dance displays.
8–9 December	Tag-Anitohan	Tudela, Camotes; Street dancing and ritual contest participated in by the community.

Compiled using data from: Your Guide to Cebu, Philippines. *PDP Digital, Inc. 2005 [Third Edition, 2007]: 60–4*

Pride of place on the Cebuano calendar is the *Sinulog* fiesta. As is the case with many religious feasts, the *Sinulog* can be traced to the pre-Spanish, indigenous, pagan era of wooden idols and *anitos*. Welcoming growing numbers of tourists to Cebu each year, today the *Sinulog* has become an annual festival commemorating the Filipino conversion to Roman Catholicism, celebrated throughout Cebu and in more recent years, initiated by Cebuanos and/or religious orders in other parts of the Philippines and among the international Filipino diaspora too, from Auckland and Dubai to Los Angeles. The fiesta's main feature is the collective performance of the *Sinulog* dance and street parade, to the sounds of the *Sinulog* dance-prayer expressing devotion to the Infant Child Jesus. To dance the *Sinulog* dance is to worship the Santo Niño, providing liminal spaces of celebration and bonding (Ness 1992). From early childhood, Cebuanos perform the *Sinulog* steps to the clear beat of gongs and trumpets, which was formally solidified into the *Sinulog* Street Dance parade in 1980. Music, dance – particularly collective and collaborative dance in unison – is a regular feature in the lives of many Cebuanos through the multitude of annual fiestas, especially the *Sinulog*. These embodied, musical movements profoundly symbolize how music and dance in Cebu is entrenched in the collective memory, national identity and power relationships between past and present.

Popular music, dance and postcolonialism in the Philippines

> I hope that in due time the enchantment of Western civilisation shall gradually wear off and in its place a truly integrated Filipino consciousness will develop even more richly as the spirit of a proud and sovereign people that it must be. (Felipe Padilla de Leon, 1973: 274)

Relocating Philippine cultural identity post-Philippine independence was not without challenges. Nationalist critics denounce the continuous American cultural imperialism over the Philippines, noting the domination of all forms of popular culture including American films, music, comics and literature over Filipino popular culture for decades (Constantino 1970; Fernandez 1981). Such 'an active, ongoing, multimedia, multi-sensory bombardment' renders Filipinos powerless and complacent, according to Fernandez, and 'before most Filipinos become aware of Filipino literature, song, dance, history [...], education, language ... the media have already made them alert to American life and culture and its desirability' (Fernandez 1981, qtd in Lockard 1998: 128–9). Certainly, Filipino scholars have been divided on the values and meanings of popular culture in today's society, an argument that reflects the Frankfurt and Birmingham School divide where critics view popular culture products as 'purely escapist slop concocted by the hegemonic order and which the undereducated and the underprivileged lap up to the max' (Lockard 1998: 129). Eleanor T. Elequin characterized the post-American-colonial Philippine popular music of the 1950s, 1960s and 1970s as largely derivative of American melody and rhythm. For Elequin a 'seeming confusion or absence of direction in thought can be inferred' in the philosophies of Filipino popular songs, where it appears that 'not knowing how to relate to what was reality, we ran away from it' (1986: 81–99). Post- and neocolonial identities were furthermore transferred not only through popular music compositions, but also through the embodied movements of dance.

While the Philippines operated as an American colony, schools were used as a site for the preservation of Filipino dance, including Spanish and American colonial dances. Basilio Esteban S. Villaruz, Professor of Dance at the University of the Philippines, theorizes contemporary Philippine 'dances of the people' into six classifications, summarized as follows (Villaruz 2006: 29):

i. Those that propitiate the spirits – *diwatas* (spirits) and *anitos* (ancestors) – by the power of the *babaylan* (shamans);

ii. Those that are imitative of animal life or activities (i.e. hunting, fishing, planting or mock-war dances);

iii. Those meant for socializing and celebrating, whether for courtship, communal harmony, ceremonies or political hierarchy;

iv. Those inherited from Spanish and American colonialism, most of which are for social purposes and are meant to preserve social amenities and protocols;
v. Those mentioned above, religious and secular, which have been appropriated by tourism programmes for cultural and/or economic ends;
vi. Theatrical dance, which was a product of evolving societal forces, including ballet, modern dance, jazz and tap, and has now become a staple in Philippine theatrical consumption.

As Villaruz's classifications demonstrate, while the Spanish colonial era introduced Filipinos to a variety of European musical influences, the increased technological mediation of the twentieth century brought with the American colonial period live dance bands, recorded dance music and various dance crazes while popular songs inundated the Philippine market. In tandem with music, dance – those dances inherited from pre-Hispanic ancestors and *anitos*, as well as those imparted from Spanish and American imperialism – continues to play an important role in everyday contemporary Filipino culture. Dance shapes religious and secular celebrations, as well as providing novel economic prospects and tourism opportunities – including in unlikely locations such as prisons, as we shall see in later discussions of CPDRC's development of penal tourism.

We see that Garcia built his music and dance rehabilitation programme based on an existing and prevalent musical-Philippine and musical-Cebuano stereotype, or to use J. Lorenzo Perillo's term, the Filipino musical-mimicry stereotype. The musical-mimicry stereotype normalizes the dancing inmates as essentially Filipino, as Perillo fluently argues, while simultaneously creating an 'elated sense of collective identity for a multicultural archipelago that has survived centuries of psychologically fragmenting and violent colonialism' (Perillo 2011: 615). However, to go one step further than Perillo, the reason that the CPDRC performances successfully connect with local, national and international Filipino audiences is precisely because they conflate the Filipino musical stereotype with regional Philippine stereotypes of the Cebuano. Such stereotypes, in combination with their presentation on YouTube, discourage critical engagement with *Thriller* and are in direct contrast to traditional conventions of dance/movement therapy, revealing instead underlying ideologies of punitive punishment, discipline and control.

Performances of US popular music and dance continue to play a dual role in contemporary Philippine culture that is increasingly often projected online and traverse across various terrains and mediascapes. Dance shapes religious and secular celebrations in the Philippines and especially in Cebu, as well as providing economic prospects and cultural tourism opportunities through the manufacture of the *Sinulog* Street Dance Parade and its associated high-profile activities. Indeed dance remains an important facet of public school education in the Philippines today; however, with more of a focus on mass exercise over individual expression, calisthenics over creativity. This is echoed in the CPDRC dance ethos as the inmates 'demonstrate physical ability rather than develop an artistic concept' (Perillo 2011: 614). Watching the neat and orderly rows of hundreds of inmates copying the choreographer's every manoeuvre within the confines of an invisible square-foot box, hardly ever coming into physical contact with their fellow dancers, by all appearances bears more resemblance to imperial drills than to a prospective dance/movement therapy initiative. Considered in this light then, music serves an almost supplementary, albeit convenient, function; the addition of pop music soundtracks is precisely what prevents the exercise being deemed a purely militaristic – and therefore explicitly disciplining – endeavour. Though CPDRC's *Thriller* aims at displaying rehabilitation in action and reducing violence among inmates, it does so by effectively extending racial and colonial inequalities and so it becomes crucial to understand the deep-seated colonial contexts of music and dance history in the Philippines in order to situate *Thriller* accordingly (Perillo 2011: 608–13). The explicit audiovisual objectification of the inmates in CPDRC's *Thriller,* in conjunction with prevailing stereotypes of Cebuanos and Filipinos that function as ambivalent and/or benevolent racism, make possible insidiously dangerous mediations.

Ideological progress and zombie performances

> If concrete people envision historical agency to exist only outside of themselves, that is, if they imagine that real power exists in icons, they transfer their own power to these figures. (Beller 2006: 215)

When examining history from present vantage points, it becomes easy to reflect upon CPDRC's *Thriller* in light of the 1904 Philippine Exposition performances at St. Louis. Although a century apart, both historical events become part of an ever-expanding digital archive, history and the digital functions to level out, compress and decontextualize. Both the St. Louis and Cebu performances stress innate ideologies of 'progress made visible', but crucially, it is a 'progress' according to Western standards. The Philippine Exhibit at St. Louis explicitly and implicitly functioned as an exercise in governmental propaganda to justify the United States' recent acquisition, purposely depicting the native tribes and villages in such a way as to reinforce the US as paternalistic missionaries, dutifully 'taming' the wayward Philippine peoples. For example, the desire to display the Igorot tribes, clad only in loincloths, as 'barbaric human beings' was such that even as the Fair entered into the winter months, the organizers refused to provide the native Filipinos with warm clothing or even trousers in the belief that visitors to the Fair would not pay to see Igorots in Western dress.[13]

Whatever became of the many Filipinos after the St. Louis Fair ended? Some returned to the Philippines. Some, unaccustomed – and, tragically, ill-equipped – to deal with the colder midwestern climate, caught pneumonia and died. Others, primarily Igorots, found themselves in Chicago, enslaved once again as live exhibits in other human zoos (Delmendo 2005). Themes of progress, civilizing, and Westernized advancement are similarly palpable in CPDRC's performances. The publicly released videos and live performances can be read as an exercise in governmental public relations; a twenty-first century exhibition showcasing the success of the Garcia clan in securing the previously unsecure, and stabilizing the previously unstable and volatile prison population. In their live and mediated performances, unconvicted CPDRC inmates produce a similar vein of spectacular audiovisual entertainment for the masses. These performers and their appearances must be strictly controlled. Despite wearing a mixture of civilian clothing and prison uniforms during their everyday imprisonment, during the monthly prison conversions into a public tourist site, all inmates must appear in their full orange prison uniform down to the matching shoes on their feet. And levels of visual control extended to the initial casting of the lead characters for CPDRC's *Thriller* in the first place. In a documentary funded by USAID and The Asia Foundation, both lead dancers explain that Warden Garcia forced them to perform the roles primarily because of their appearances (Diokno 2008). Crisanto Niere, who played the role of Michael Jackson, explains how he became *Thriller*'s lead dancer in an interview with filmmaker Pepe Diokno (Figures 2.2 and 2.3):

> Sir Byron got me and made me dance. 'My face looks like it's for "Thriller,"' he said. The zombie – the one from Michael Jackson. That's how they see me. (Niere qtd in Diokno 2008)

Missing a number of his front teeth, Niere pauses as he explains the reasons why he was singled out for the lead role in *Thriller*: because 'I look like a zombie'.

Bakla Wenjiel Resane, who performs the role of Jackson's girlfriend, also describes how Garcia forced him to dance; despite Resane's (initial) objections, he felt powerless to refuse.

> I don't know with Sir Byron, what he saw in me. He had me called, and told me I'd carry the dance. I didn't want to, but I couldn't do anything. The planning [is all] by Sir Byron. He's the one *who programs us* here. (Resane qtd in Diokno 2008, italics added)

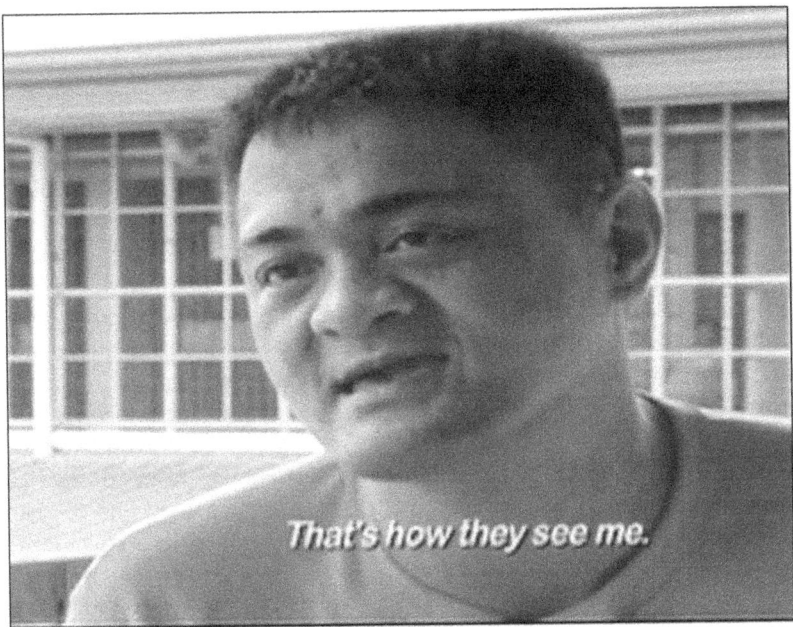

FIGURES 2.2 AND 2.3 *Crisanto Niere, dancing 'preso', describes why he was chosen as the lead dancer in* Thriller. *Interview in* Dancing for Discipline *(dir. Diokno 2008)*. © *Pepe Diokno.*

As Resane articulates, and Figures 2.4 and 2.5 illustrate, programmatic control is striking and overwhelming in the CPDRC performances, but also too in the St. Louis Philippine Exhibit. Both performances highlight the close Philippine–US relationship that remains equally intertwined and nonetheless complex today as it was 100 years ago. By conflating two performances of the subaltern Filipino – the displaced slave forced into exhibition, and the hybrid, postcolonial dancing inmate also forced to dance – both performances can be seen as splitting subjectivity, existing in Homi Bhabha's 'third space' (2006).[14] Bhabha's conceptual model of the third space refers to a liminal space between two or more colliding cultures, which offers new possibilities for rearticulating negotiation and resignifying cultural meaning. This subversive place is exemplified through the mimicry of hybridized cultures and identities whose agency can be read against the authority of the state – in this case, the US. The St. Louis World's Fair's enforced exhibition of indigenous Filipinos reflected the imperial, Orientalist values of the Fair's organizers and the US government at the turn of the century, and the Fair's inherent racism has subsequently been widely critiqued by many both in and outside the academe. Yet we find ourselves, a century later, seduced and (however temporarily) excited by portrayals of incarcerated Filipino men (and women), dancing to a pre-programmed Western soundtrack from Michael Jackson and the Village People, Justin Bieber and Bruno Mars. Audiences assume, because of the implied and thus assumed rehabilitative nature of the programme, the universal supposition that music could but only equate to pleasure. Because of their original appearance on the initially user-generated, participatory website YouTube, audiences largely take for granted that dancing inmates *must* be an irrevocable force for good. The dancing inmates continue to dance for their lives, reinforcing essentialism with every step, day in day out, while simultaneously attempting to assert agency through the very moves that bind them. In celebrating such spectacles uncritically we divert attention from the fact that imperialisms may just as easily be perpetuated from within. Thus an inherent paradox is faced by new, mediated subjects in the neocolonial world. On the one hand, digital media platforms have given a voice to postcolonial and subaltern subjects, while on the other hand it simultaneously problematizes the Filipino performers, presenting them as uniform, 'highly trainable', Orientalist stereotypes. CPDRC's *Thriller* music video – with hundreds upon hundreds of clearly marked Filipino prisoners at its core – offers a hybrid, in-between space that both disrupts and reinforces the possibility for resistance. And as such, it becomes a metaphor for twenty-first century postcolonial Philippine attempts to assert its independence from the United States.

FIGURES 2.4 AND 2.5 *Programmatic control in practice. Photographs from the daily CPDRC dance rehearsals, featuring an inmate wearing a vest bearing the slogan 'I'm Easy To Use And Operate'. January 2013.* © Photo: Author.

INTERLUDE THREE

Fade to black

By CPDRC's *Thriller*'s third minute, the recognizable synthesized groove returns, this time with additional, accentuated ghoulish groans as the central corps morph into a looser triangular formation enacting the hallmark zombie movements: arms outstretched and unsteadily dragging their feet.[1] The girlfriend reappears in the frame for the first time since the chorus started. Once again she enacts the damsel in distress tropes – arms daintily stretched to the side, hands framing her furrowed face as she bounds across the concrete. The camera closes in on her, monitoring her movement among the crowded yard as the syncopated *Thriller* groove fades into Bernstein's shrill orchestral soundtrack. The instrumental 'scary music' takes over, punctuated with the once diegetic sounds of monster growls, glass and wood smashing and Ola Ray's high-pitched screaming.

Timing her actions to those on the soundtrack, CPDRC's girlfriend character – Wenjiel Resane – pirouettes her way into the centre of the dance corps as the bedraggled zombies slowly encircle her. At 3.52 minutes she falls to the ground, knocking over one zombie-inmate in her midst and the central corps descend upon her as Bernstein's soundtrack is punctuated by Ray's piercing cry. The horde of inmate-zombies surround the girlfriend, captured by a range of long and full shots by Garcia's digital camera – both public and social proxemics. She tries to crawl away but several outstretched zombie arms find her and grab at her hair, while one or two zombies tug at her baby-pink top. The fuzzy video quality, frenzied soundtrack and increasing number of violators turn this into a disturbing audiovisual scene, with more than subtle connotations of ultra-violence.

Without Landis's Hollywood monster masks and tongue-in-cheek horror movie set, the unmasked prisoners act the scripted parts of soulless corpses; yet in their prison garb they appear exactly as themselves. The inmate's literal 'show of face' enacts new and decidedly more complex meanings to their *Thriller* performance, which obfuscates the boundaries between good and evil, between fact and fiction and between truth and fantasy. CPDRC's *Thriller* ending is markedly different to the original *Thriller* ending.[2] In Landis's short film, just as the zombies were about to close in on the girlfriend she suddenly wakes up, believing it was all a nightmare as she is comforted by her once again human boyfriend, Michael Jackson. As they exit the room arm in arm, Michael Jackson breaks the fourth wall and Vincent Price's laugh sounds as Jackson turns to face the camera (and the audience), revealing a pearly white wide grin against yellow, were-cat eyes (Figure 3.1). The camera moves in for a close-up of Jackson's face, becoming an intimate proxemic of Jackson's knowing smile and big yellow eyes.

Price's evil laughter – mediated through prison speakers to the inmates' ears and remediated across the communicative distance via YouTube – interrupts the sustained orchestral cadence. But instead of revealing a visual

FIGURE 3.1 *Michael Jackson's knowing smile (12.01 minutes) in Michael Jackson's* Thriller, *directed by John Landis.* © *Epic Records/Vestron Music Video, 1983.*

metafictional break in narrative complete with knowing nod to the audience as the original *Thriller* finale so aptly does, Price's laugh in CPDRC's *Thriller* soundtracks what is primarily read as the beginnings of a theatrical gang rape – or an act of zombie cannibalism upon the girlfriend – that unfolds under the camera's steady, distant surveillance. However, just as the horde of menacing inmates are about to completely descend upon the girlfriend, the screen suddenly cuts into a white, orange and black constellation that ultimately dissolves to a lingering blackness (Figure 3.2). There is no knowing nod in CPDRC's version; the inmates never break the fourth wall; instead the YouTube video ends shrouded in mystery regarding the protagonist's fate.

In visual culture and televisual semiotics, the dissonant finale wherein the image dissipates into a lingering blackness can have an effect on audience comprehension of the ending. In CPDRC's *Thriller*, the video ends with the image of the orange-clad zombie horde about to descend upon the girlfriend that is suddenly edited, and the scene fades and pixellates into black. This surreptitious ending has shaped audience perception and understanding of how they see the performance ending, as the YouTube comments reveal (see Chapter 6). The visual semiotics and production choices behind this

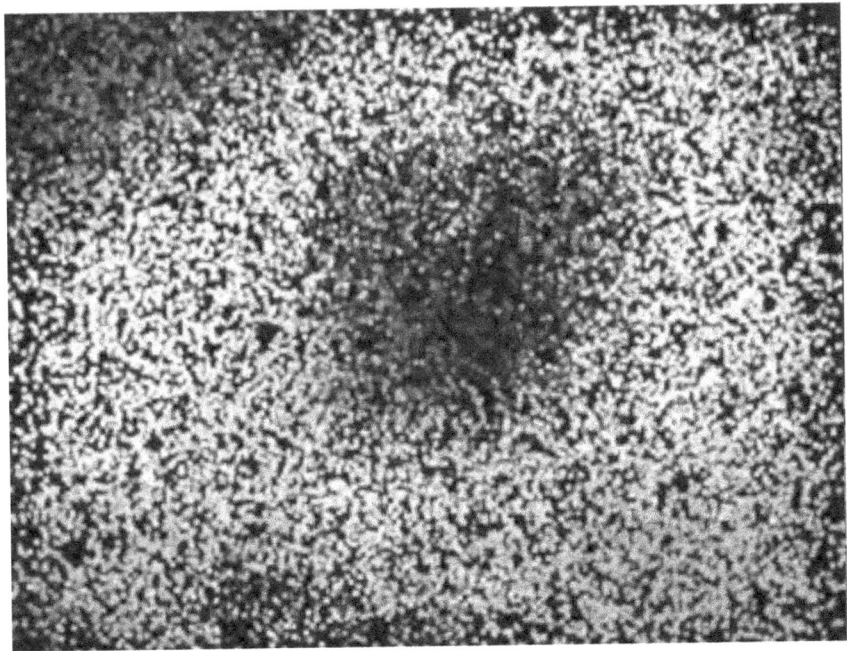

FIGURE 3.2 *The final image breaks down into a constellation of black, white and orange at 4.13 minutes into CPDRC's* Thriller. © *Epic Records/Vestron Music Video, 1983.*

text are revealing, signifying at least two possible endings. The decision to film from that particular camera angle – perched high above the inmates and zooming in on specific dancers at particular moments within the choreography, coupled with the decision to cut and edit the final scene in such a way is remarkable.[3] In popular television and film, the fade to black clearly marks the end of a scene, but additionally the fade to black can hold extra meaning – utilized to signify declining to describe a sex scene in screen media, or to allude to the death of the leading protagonist – usually on screen at that moment (as in the famous final scene of *The Sopranos* that ends with a lingering blackness). With an air of narrative ambiguity, but deliberate filming choices and distinct use of digital editorial software to manipulate the final scene, CPDRC's *Thriller* video fades to black and abruptly ends. Along with it we can negate Garcia's claims at uploading the video exclusively as an educational exemplar for other prison guards to learn from. This video was perfectly choreographed, consciously staged, conscientiously filmed, knowingly edited, digitally disseminated and globally broadcast by Garcia as a prison spectacle. CPDRC's *Thriller*'s subsequent circulation as a form of mass entertainment has shown just how precarious, and indeed dangerous, such mediations can be.

CHAPTER THREE

Penal tourists 2.0

The birth of CPDRC's pop programme

'Political scions': Introducing the Garcia family of Cebu

On 27 December 2004, CPDRC inmates staged protests and hunger strikes at the old, dilapidated and severely overcrowded *Cárcel de Cebú* facility that was located in the centre of Cebu City. Refusing to transfer to the new, purpose-built facility in the outskirts of Cebu because of alleged misinformation, and while demanding better treatment, over 1,000 inmates were forcibly removed from the old facility by the Regional Mobile Group of the Philippine National Police. Shackled by the ankles and wrists, the inmates were transferred to the hills of Cebu to the new CPDRC building under the orders of the new Cebu Provincial Governor, Gwendolyn Garcia.

Gwendolyn Garcia (Figure 3.3) was elected as governor of Cebu earlier that year – a position she succeeded from her father, Pablo P. Garcia. Representative Pablo Garcia will forever be remembered for his role in reintroducing the death penalty into the Philippine constitution in 1993. Despite being the first country in Asia to abolish capital punishment for all crimes in 1987, and against the wishes of civil libertarian and human rights activists who maintained the death penalty functions as an 'added nail' to the coffin of the poor, Garcia – as Cebu Representative and Chair of the House of Representatives Committee on Justice – served as principal author of the bill, authorizing the death penalty for forty-six separate offences including non-violent crimes such as treason, car theft and bribery (see UCA News 1993).

FIGURE 3.3 *Gwendolyn Garcia's portrait and profile, featuring choice photographs highlighting the key aspects of her tenure: Garcia playing/posing with a Cebu-made bandurria (or laud), a choreographed musical fiesta performance, and the new* Museo Sugbo *at the Governors of Cebu exhibit in the Cebu Provincial Capitol Building, May 2017. © Photo: Author.*

In a press release statement on 1 December 1993, Pablo Garcia explained that the death penalty bill, Republic Act 7659, would be 'signed into law by Christmas as a "Christmas gift" to the Filipino people' (UCA News 1993). Executions resumed, and by 2002 there were fifty-two offences carrying the death penalty, primarily affecting the poorest defendants who could not afford lawyers to defend themselves. Also disproportionately affected were those who were tortured in custody, or sometimes unable to understand the language in which court proceedings were conducted (ICDP 2013: 20). Ongoing campaigns by NGOs, the Philippine Commission on Human Rights, and the Catholic Church led to President Gloria Macapagal-Arroyo's policy to commute death sentences to life imprisonment, announced at Easter 2006. The Philippine Congress voted overwhelmingly in favour of abolishing capital punishment, and on 24 June 2006 the new bill prohibiting the imposition of the death penalty in the Philippines (RA 9346) came into lawful effect.

Once the bane of the Cebu government with severe overcrowding, gang violence and housed in a dilapidated building that dated back to the Spanish colonial era, the Cebu Provincial Detention and Rehabilitation Centre's fortune changed when Gwendolyn Garcia was elected Governor of Cebu. The eldest daughter of the Congressman and his wife Judge Esperanza (Inday) Fiel Garcia, Gwendolyn Garcia's foray into politics surprised few since the Garcia family are among Cebu's (and by extension, the Philippines') most renowned political dynasties. Upon entering office in 2004, Gwen Garcia's tenure prioritized the promotion of Cebuano culture and heritage. Under her watch, the century old *Cárcel de Cebú* was transformed into the Cebu Provincial Museum, *Museo Sugbo*, and the Cebu Provincial Tourism and Heritage Council was founded, promoting Cebu city and countryside to a new, international generation of tourists.[1] Determined to eradicate the widespread gang violence and corruption among inmates (and prison wardens) at the old *Cárcel de Cebú*, Governor Garcia took an unconventional approach to cleaning up the old CPDRC; the first order of business was to appoint her younger brother Byron F. Garcia – a business management graduate and complete novice to penology – to oversee CPDRC's reinvention as chief security officer and prison warden.

Moving prisons

By January 2005 the facility officially moved from the old *Cárcel* to the brand-new, modern, purpose-built facility in the hills of Barangay Lahug on the outskirts of Cebu city, and Warden Byron Garcia began his mandate of turning CPDRC into a leading centre for detention and rehabilitation. To this end, he fired dozens of corrupt prison officers, separated gangs, eradicated drug use and, importantly, implemented a strict routine of labour and exercise. Carrying on the Garcia family dynasty, Congressman Garcia's son – the new Warden Garcia – publicly declared that although he could have easily chosen a comfortable corporate career, he instead chose the road less travelled. Taking to his personal website, Garcia announced that he chose to use his distinguished lineage as son of a 'political scion transcended from his political and landlord roots to do "the very least for my brethren" – turn dregs into human beings' (byronfgarcia.com 2007). Equating his role as warden with that of a 'mission', and highlighting the personal and familial difficulties his job brought with it, Garcia goes on to explain how he 'chose to be with the thugs of society, he chose to be with the dangerous men of society and he chose to be in a thankless and demeaning job where his relatives thought it was such a crazy thing to do' (byronfgarcia.com 2007). Garcia's passionate, emotive prose paints him as a kind of martyr, suffering but still bringing salvation to the thugs and dangerous men of society.

In keeping with the spirit of his unorthodox approach to penology, Garcia claimed in several media interviews that he was inspired to introduce music to the inmate's exercise regime after seeing the 1994 classic film *The Shawshank Redemption* (McCarthy 2008). One of *Shawshank*'s central scenes – that where the lead protagonist Andy Dufresne defies the prison warden by broadcasting an LP of Wolfgang Amadeus Mozart's 'Canzonetta sull'aria' (A little song on the breeze) duet from *Le nozze di Figaro* over the prison's public address system – was, for Garcia, the precise moment of inspiration. In this scene the camera pans from above the prison yard and we witness hundreds of prisoners stand and stare at the prison loudspeakers, trance-like, as the soprano voices soar through the prison yard (Figure 3.4). At the same time the film's narrator, Ellis Boyd 'Red' Redding, recounts:

> I have no idea to this day what those two Italian ladies were singing about. Truth is, I don't want to know. Some things are better left unsaid. I'd like to think they were singing about something so beautiful, it can't be expressed in words, and it makes your heart ache because of it. I tell you, those voices soared higher and farther than anybody in a grey place dares to dream. It was as if some beautiful bird had flapped into our drab little cage and made these walls dissolve away, and for the briefest of moments, every last man in Shawshank felt free.

Red's narration ends with the prison wardens furiously demanding that Dufresne turn off the record. He moves towards the record player as if to comply, before responding defiantly by turning up the volume instead – unable and unwilling to move the needle before the song has come to an end. This scene is Hollywood through and through, rich with allegory and metaphor. On the one hand, it is a cinematic portrayal of the powerful, romanticized associations between music and freedom in a place where the most fundamental freedom is so clearly restricted. On the other, it serves a cautionary tale of what can happen when the seeming pleasures of musical experience are seen to be misused, or used without permission, by those

THE BIRTH OF CPDRC'S POP PROGRAMME

FIGURE 3.4 *Still from* The Shawshank Redemption *(dir. Darabont 1994) showing the prisoners stopping en masse to listen to Mozart's aria through the prison address speakers.* © Frank Darabont / Castle Rock Entertainment.

in power. Even at the fictitious Shawshank prison, for a prisoner to play a Mozart aria is dangerous – the result of which is violence and further punishment for the film's protagonist. Waving batons, and breaking down the door, the prison guards react to the prison musical interlude by sending Dufresne to the 'hole' for two weeks of solitary confinement. Even – and perhaps especially – in Hollywood, music is a powerful and dangerous weapon when placed in the wrong hands.

Back in CPDRC, Warden Garcia explains that he was motivated by *Shawshank*'s big-screen portrayal of music as a transformative force for uniting unruly prison populations. In numerous media interviews, he publicly testifies to the communicative power of music, especially in communicating with prisoners. But rather than use a soundtrack of classical music as featured in the film, he deemed pop music to be a more suitable communicative medium for choreographing routines to the Cebu inmates. However, Garcia soon emerges as a man of many paradoxes. In earlier accounts with journalists, Garcia presented an alternative account of the programme's origin. In an interview with *National Public Radio* (NPR), he describes the visual–ocular, accidental yet aesthetic impetus behind the programme's evolution from general inmate leisure time to choreographed routines. Garcia explains:

> I wanted a program where everyone would exercise an hour a day. One day, I saw these waves of orange people [in the exercise yard]. I thought it looked very nice. (Garcia qtd in NPR 2007)

In a similar report from Australian news agency *SBS*, Garcia elucidates how one day he saw inmates marching in the central quadrangle, which triggered the thought '"Why don't I convert that march into a dance number?" I thought of dancing after that' (Lazaredes 2007). In contrast to the *Shawshank* narrative which came later, these two earlier accounts point towards the gaze of the prison warden as the point of origin. From this position, it seems Garcia based the Dancing Inmates programme on visual, surface appearance, cloaked in pop music with more than an underlying hint of objectification.

Grand designs: The birth of the penal tourist

Accepting a job at a newly opened, state-of-the-art jail in 2005, little did Vince Rosales know that he was about to change the course of history at the Cebu Provincial Detention and Rehabilitation Centre. Rosales sees the world in art, grand designs, formations and dance. Rosales may appear as an unlikely candidate to enter into the business of prisoner rehabilitation through music and dance. The grandson of the famous Cebuano dancer, Tita Inday – one of the founding members of the first Sinulog street dance in 1980 – Rosales graduated with a Bachelor of Science degree in Architecture some years before, though limited opportunities to put this degree into practice in his native Cebu meant seeking out other employment prospects. And so he found himself working as prison officer at the new CPDRC facility, alongside another recent hire, Warden Byron Garcia. Growing up dancing with his *Lola*, the steps for the Sinulog – as well as many other dances – were ingrained in his memory. Thus when the opportunity arose in his new job to assist Warden Garcia's latest unorthodox idea, Rosales was quick to volunteer to informally choreograph this new Dancing Inmates initiative, while Garcia selected the playlist and filmed the routines on his personal camera. And so Rosales, rather unceremoniously, became CPDRC's first choreographer.

In October 2006 Garcia posted his first YouTube video of the inmates performing 'The Algorithm March' – a Japanese song and dance-craze that penetrated popular culture across Asia that year – citing a desire to show other prison managers his innovative, disciplinary music-dance technique in action. Using his personal YouTube channel and username 'byronfgarcia', he uploaded the record-setting performance of 967 inmates dancing to the song, and once the inmates had mastered the marches, Garcia formally employed internal prison guard Rosales (CPDRC) and external choreographer Grace Laydor to help teach the prisoners, and work alongside Garcia's creative designs. What began as a gentle one-hour workout soon developed into a rigorous programme that ordered all able-bodied inmates to dance outdoors for around four hours daily. Auditions were held for inmates who wanted to be part of the core ensemble or troupe of lead dancers. All remaining inmates – the chorus, if you will – then performed a reduction of the principal troupe's more complex choreography.

On top of his everyday duties as prison officer, and with no experience in choreographing large ensembles, but instead a college education spent designing skyscrapers and making miniature models of buildings and landscapes, Rosales spent many long hours formulating the best methods to get 1,500 inmates to follow his dance instructions. Garcia's first YouTube upload of 'The Algorithm March' was virtually ignored by the internet community with relatively few views. It was not until Garcia's seventh YouTube posting of the inmates rehearsing to Michael Jackson's *Thriller* some nine months later that the world took notice. As the YouTube views quickly spiked, Rosales acted as liaison to the multitude of journalists, photographers and other international press who turned up at the prison following the CPDRC's viral success. In the weeks and months that followed CPDRC's *Thriller* YouTube debut, Garcia and Rosales facilitated visits from curious foreign tourists and distinguished guests, including local reality TV personalities from *Pinoy Big Brother: Celebrity Edition*, boxing champion and politician Manny Pacquiao, the American-Filipino family of Bruno Mars, Japanese singer Ai Haruna and the Korean Sun Dance Troupe, who all arrived at CPDRC to watch the monthly shows he designed. The potential for CPDRC to become a leading tourist attraction was not only clear, but already in action.

Warden Garcia revived the facility to the extent that Governor Garcia's profile of achievements included a statement that under her term the CPDRC prisoners, once considered the 'dregs' of society, now 'gained respect and worldwide fame' (Governor's Profile 2012). Here, she mirrors her brother's emotive language that plays into populist stereotypes of prisoners as akin to inhuman, social waste. Still, the virtual YouTube views continued to transform into real, tangible visitors, spending real, genuine pesos. As a result Governor Garcia – together with her brother – legitimized the programme as a successful venture, as local, national and international media interest grew from month to month. Equating the inmates' worldwide fame with universal respect, both Governor Garcia and Warden Garcia continued to publicize and celebrate their respective roles in the formation of the CPDRC Dancing Inmates. Consciously choosing to capitalize on the international attention from YouTube audiences and media conglomerates, by the end of 2007 Warden Garcia – most likely in discussion with his sister and her Cebu Provincial Tourism and Heritage Council – opened up CPDRC to host live, monthly performances open to any member of the public to attend (see Figure 3.5).

The immense popularity of these shows soon transformed CPDRC into a bustling tourist attraction, sought after among national and international visitors. A 2012 edition of the popular *Lonely Planet Philippines* guidebook lists CPDRC in its recommended tourist 'Sights' of Cebu, alongside butterfly sanctuaries and museums, tempting international backpackers and business travellers alike with the following enticing description of CPDRC's free spectacle:

FIGURE 3.5 *Poster produced by Cebu Provincial Capitol advertising the CPDRC Dancing Inmates 'LIVE' performance on 29 May 2010. © Cebu Provincial Government, Cebu Provincial Capitol Archives.*

> This is where you can catch the inmate dance performances that became an internet sensation on YouTube several years back ... The performance was the brainchild of chief warden Byron Garcia, whose love of '80s pop inspired him to groove up the regular prison exercise drill. There are free performances on the last Saturday of each month; first register your name with the Capitol building. (Bloom et al. 2012: 207)

Advertised through local newspaper features, government-issued posters, international press and word of mouth, the CPDRC became a hybridized destination of leisure and rehabilitation – ticking the boxes for today's drive towards experiential tourist destinations, especially set against the context of an otherwise out-of-the-way, economically deprived area of the Philippines and Southeast Asia.

Mediating penal spectacles 2.0

CPDRC functions as a so-called maximum-security detention centre while simultaneously transforming into a tourist site once a month. New repertoire was regularly added to the performance portfolio, with requests coming from the YouTube community via public YouTube comments, as well as requests from Cebu government officials. Older songs were remixed so that one five-minute routine could accommodate a mash-up of two or more requested pop hits. Take their 2007 performances of 'Do the Hustle' by KC and the Sunshine Band remixed with 'In the Navy' by the Village People, or their 2009 Michael Jackson tribute medley that weaved together 'Ben', 'I'll Be There' and 'We Are the World'. New material was also composed especially for the Dancing Inmates. The 'CPDRC Song' is just one example of Garcia's multidisciplinary role within CPDRC, as he straddles the line between official security consultant, video producer, press officer and, then, songwriter.

> We're the dancing inmates of CPDRC/We dance and entertain the world and make you all happy/A new approach to rehabilitation/Representing Cebu province and the rest of our nation/We're the dancing inmates of CPDRC, fun and laughter, smiles in every corner/Got the world's attention, 'cause we've got moves/And now all millions of you say you've watched us on YouTube/CPDRC, CPDRC, CPDRC Inmates, CPDRC Inmates. (Garcia, 'CPDRC Song' 2008a)

Uploaded to YouTube in October 2008, the rap, hip hop track is primarily in Cebuano with the final chorus sung in English. It uses a simple four to the floor beat played on a drum-machine backing-track, over which a group of unnamed MCs and singers – presumably the inmates themselves – recite lyrics extolling the virtues of the Dancing Inmate programme, and success under Byron F. Garcia's leadership. Garcia's self-penned stanzas spell out his 'new approach to rehabilitation', explicitly connecting the Dancing Inmates of CPDRC with the cheery Filipino stereotypes: fun, laughter and smiles. Through the 'CPDRC Song', the inmates indeed evoke Bloom et al.'s depiction of 'poor Filipinos' from the *Lonely Planet* guidebook's depiction of the Filipino psyche in Chapter 2, who 'face their often dim prospects in life with a laugh, a wink and even a song' (2012: 33). These lyrics – when sung by the inmates in combination with the accompanying music video, featuring photographs of smiling, dancing inmates and a wealth of visiting tourists posing after the shows in the prison yard – become yet another mouthpiece for Garcia to spread his music and dance as rehabilitation philosophy.

The special 'live' shows for members of the public developed into a monthly performance ritual, that in turn became an integral part of the lived prison experience at CPDRC. At the most fundamental level, the live shows offer a chance for those living behind bars to have direct, human contact with the outside world. The shows, in theory, offered a chance for inmates' family and friends to visit. However, in reality a significant portion of the live audiences comprised not of local Cebuanos but rather of Filipinos from further afield, as well as foreign tourists. A tribute to Governor Garcia's success in raising Cebu's international tourism profile, South Korean and German groups were – remarkably enough – among the most common visitors to the facility.[2]

What many CPDRC local and international visitors had in common was their use of social media to document their visit to the shows. Regardless of nationality, the use of cameras and recording equipment was welcomed, and even encouraged by the CPDRC staff, as visitors and tourists shared photographs and videos of the CPDRC inmates on their social media accounts, actively documenting their time in prison to share with the world outside. Each performance ends with an invitation for audience members to enter the prison yard, dance with the inmates, and if so desired, have photographs taken with the inmates before exiting through the gift shop.[3] Brown describes the recent shift towards tourism in working prisons, the practices of interpretation and presentation, and the issues these raise. 'The entrance to prison tours sets the stage for how to treat the event', she writes, 'emphasising the tour as both museum and theme park – an experience to be carefully documented through the accumulation of a visual record (photos/postcards) and the purchase of souvenirs' (Brown 2009: 100). And tourists to CPDRC certainly purchase souvenirs, from the problematic replica orange 'CPDRC Inmate' T-shirts, as image one of Figures 3.6–3.9 illustrates, to specially printed mugs and postcards featuring the Dancing Inmates mid-performance.

The 'tourist gaze', John Urry and Jonas Larsen (2011) suggest, demonstrates that the act of photographing is both active and discursive. As the Instagram examples reproduced in Figure 3.6 attest, photographs and videos taken of and with the inmates are certainly active and discursive, and go on to enjoy a life beyond the ephemeral three-hour live *palabas* (spectacle) or *hataw sayaw* (dance show). Brown's observations on penal spectacles are fitting here, where we see 'the politics of the gaze intersect with the production of punishment in ways that proliferate with little acknowledgement or consideration of what punishment may mean, but with an additional sense of veracity and moral authority, of "having been there"' (2009: 16). Photographs have become digital, audiovisual objects, archived, tagged, disseminated and magnified by YouTube and other social media sites indefinitely. Such ritualistic, public spectacles of inmates clad in identical orange uniforms, serve as a constant reminder of their status as incarcerated people. As the live audiences take their seats behind the steel fencing in the panoptic towers high above the prison yard, the moralizing framework is further construed. The allure of mediated prison culture is only too evident today, across various media (and genre) platforms. The popularity of television and web series like *Oz* (1997–2003), *Prison Break* (2005–9) and *Orange is the New Black* (2013–present) are just

30 likes
ami19__ The news. Oh, I thought I was going to miss the movie, and I thought I was looking for a t-shirt in the back, and I was looking for a t-shirt. 😅 lol the news so I'm so glad 🍺 lol. #CPDRC #仰天ニュース #仰天ニュース #prison #jail #jail #jail #セブ

22 likes
ellyaileen Kind of wierd to be so happy next to criminals, but it was a fun experience watching them dance and it was fun to dance with them 😊 #dancinginmates #cpdrc #cebu #onlyinthephilippines

51 likes
maimaipunipuni セブの刑務所。
囚人のダンスvery interesting 💃🎵
#CPDRC #Cebu #jail
SEE TRANSLATION

4 likes
keemkai Selfie with the inmates! :)
#dancinginmates #CPDRC #cebu

FIGURES 3.6–3.9 *Example of four photographs taken by different international tourists and visitors at CPDRC and publicly shared on Instagram. 3.6. Screenshot taken of a South Korean news feature on the CPDRC that depicted Instagrammer ami19_ shopping for official CPDRC T-shirts in the prison gift shop. 3.7. Danish Instagrammer ellyaileen writes: 'It's kind of weird to be so happy next to criminals.' 3.8. Instagrammer maimaipunipuni writes in Japanese: 'A prison in Cebu. Prisoner Dance is very interesting.' 3.9. Filipina Instagrammer keemkai captions her two photos: 'Selfie with the inmates!:)' All four public posts use the hashtags #CPDRC, among others.*

some of the more recent examples of the internationally popular media set behind bars, all of which boasted notable accompanying soundtracks.[4] Soon after CPDRC's *Thriller* achieved viral success, Garcia capitalized on the requests for live performances that the dancing inmates received. In Diokno's 2008 documentary on the CPDRC inmates, financed by USAID and the Asia Foundation, Garcia reveals the extent of the international response to *Thriller*. One unnamed Philippine company, Garcia says, made a 'donation' of PHP ₱160,000 (over GBP £2,000) to let their employees visit the facility and view the 'dancing prisoners' (Diokno 2008). Later in the same documentary, Garcia announces the news of the forthcoming live performance to the inmates, proclaiming that:

> many companies want to come here and watch you. This is going to become a tourist destination! Beware if you stop dancing … If you stop dancing, we won't get any money. (Garcia qtd in Diokno 2008)

Garcia shares with the inmates their national popularity, transfers to them a sense of pride in commanding the interests of a prosperous company, and shoulders them with a shared responsibility in raising funds to keep the prison afloat. What happened to that PHP ₱160,000 – whether it went on improving prison amenities, was divided among the inmates, or pocketed by the prison staff – remains a mystery yet to be solved.

CPDRC's growing reputation as a tourist attraction for the island of Cebu follows several other prisons that have opened their doors to allow the public access to this 'Other' world. Sites of 'dark tourism' or thanatourism include historic prisons such as Alcatraz, and even former sites of torture such as Auschwitz-Birkenau, Robben Island and Tuol Sleng, which receive millions of visitors each year. 'Dark tourism' or 'thanatourism' is theorized by Philip Stone (2006) as 'the act of travel and visitation to sites, attractions and exhibitions which have real or recreated death, suffering or the seemingly macabre as a main theme'. As a form of dark tourism, thanatourism and/or kitsch pop entertainment, CPDRC functions as an addition to the multiple contemporary mediations of prison culture, and in doing so, embodies popular cultures' growing fascination with prison life. Even the most cursory glance at mainstream media reveals not only the extent to which the number of films, television series and documentaries that celebrate themes of punishment and retribution are increasing in frequency, but so too are a host of videogames, toys, websites, fashion and tourist destinations (Novek 2009: 376–84). Prison rodeo shows, for example, involving select inmates competing against each other and some 2000-pound bulls for a nominal cash prize, have a rich legacy in various (southern) states in the United States. The Angola Prison Rodeo at Louisiana's State Penitentiary was established fifty years ago as a 'fun' event by a handful of rodeo-loving inmates and employees, and has now become a highly lucrative business. Year-on-year increases in public curiosity led to an expansion of their specially built arena in 2000, to now accommodate 10,000 spectators.[5] Former prisons too now operate as accommodation for business and pleasure from the luxuriously refurbished Charles Street Jail in Boston, Massachusetts to the 'unfriendly, unheated, uncomfortable' former KGB prison in Latvia.[6] Yet however puerile paying to stay in jail may seem, the decision to visit a fully functioning jail like CPDRC, with real, living, convicted and non-convicted inmates inside, marks a completely different undertaking than any of the other historical prison tourism experiences.[7] These practices tend to create and maintain a significant conceptual and emotional distance between tourists and inmates, as Brown (2009) describes, which can in turn trivialize inmates' suffering, and/or even harden public attitudes in the form of 'penal populism' (Wilson 2008: 177–81). For tourists visiting working prisons like CPDRC, the experience becomes akin to a 'living museum'. In light of these observations it seems fair to ask who are the real beneficiaries of a commodified, prison tourism industry. Watching over live, criminal bodies – real and fictional – is indeed a lucrative business.

*

In a place where visitors are searched with military precision for any kind of contraband, it is notable that music, especially popular music, has the unique ability to permeate the maximum-security walls of the prison. The CPDRC performances underline the porous nature of music, in particular the ability for songs and dances to transcend physical borders and offer a sense of expression, a carefully framed celebration of liminal liberation otherwise unknown to those incarcerated. Popular music and dance have strong associations with feelings of liberty and hope, especially when utilized in a penal institution where prisoners' autonomy is limited to the bare minimum. There are several cases of music and dance being utilized in prisons, most commonly as an explicit form of optional therapy offered to inmates, often alongside further education opportunities and art programmes (for example Pat Graney's 'Keeping the Faith' prison dance and performance project in the US, Pimlico Opera's musical collaborations with the inmates of Wandsworth Prison, and 'Jail Guitar Doors' – Billy Bragg's campaign to give UK prisoners access to guitars). Of course such concepts of hope are questionable: is this hope real or illusory? Or is it a hope that popular music and dance can bring about a composite of reality and illusion? At CPDRC, the combination of popular music and dance performance brings about a hope that simultaneously exists as real, illusory and perhaps somewhere in between.

Through this new dance-as-rehabilitation ideology delivered in choreographed moves and nostalgic pop songs, inmates have encompassed, with implicit or explicit coercion, a distinctive way of passing time, a way that some, if not many, inmates enjoy on some level. Garcia has found a way of getting inmates involved in a daily exercise plan, a feat that medical officials around the world have attempted to implement in prisoner health plans.

In his essay 'Cultural Diversity and Cultural Differences', Bhabha (2006) argues that in order to examine cultural problems of difference and diversity, we must look at the boundaries between cultures. It is precisely at this boundary, at the point at which two (or more) cultures meet, where cultural differences can be seen. At CPDRC the boundaries between a Philippine prison spectacle, popular music, tourism, mass entertainment and internet cultures are undoubtedly blurred. Since its foundation in 2005, YouTube has demonstrated how video sharing impacts greatly on internet culture operations and communications. As Chapter 1 outlined, in this Web 2.0 era, sites like YouTube operate as important locations for citizen journalists who take advantage of a world where many cameras are ubiquitous, embedded in a great many cellphones. CPDRC's performances represent the boundaries between and within participatory cultures, shining a light on both the participation gap (access to cultural experiences and the skills acquired through participation in online social networks) as well as the digital divide (access to technology).

CPDRC's *Thriller* and other musical repertoire are symptomatic of YouTube's power to express a form of cultural community collaboration. Yet the inmates' active participation in one of the most popular online communities highlights the parasitic relationship that can exist between those captured on video and those profiting from their labour, particularly in light of YouTube's partnership with Google which monetized the site at an unprecedented rate – through the use of roll-out advertisements and increasing pressure on YouTubers to sign in using their full name. For the inmates, there is no reciprocal relationship in terms of internet revenue. They remain the subject of the viewer's gaze, their individual bodies vanishing into a collective vision of orange and black. They have limited power to return the gaze to the audience present in Cebu, and they, the seen, are powerless to participate in the YouTube comments or social networking undertaken about them by millions of viewers who tune in on smartphones and tablets across the world. To many viewers, the inmates remain an entertaining image, a powerless commodity that appears to present the inmates as themselves but ultimately functions as a fantasy production that glosses over years spent awaiting justice.

Uploading, sharing and publicly inviting free-for-all commentary on the pop performances of unconvicted men and women awaiting trial at CPDRC – many of whom are easily identified, and/or named in the accompanying media reports and in the video themselves – demonstrates the extent to which we must reconsider music, dance and other creative practices in relation to online social networking and digital technological advances. As increasing aspects of our lives are lived out online, the ramifications of making the fruits of the CPDRC labour available online without restriction may have real life consequences for the dancing inmates.[8] CPDRC's *Thriller* highlights several potentialities. One, it might be that YouTube has arrived as a new form of cyber rehabilitation, where transgressors of the law undergo publicly mediated forms of restoration, recovery and eventual return to society. Two, it points to the return of historic, and well-documented forms of oppression and public humiliation, albeit digitalized en masse to a degree and on an international scale that we have never before experienced. Three, it highlights the slippery foundations of morality as we struggle to find our footing in YouTube's digital era: is it ethical to publish audiovisual media of individuals who may not be in a position to give consent? Four, perhaps a bigger question is whether it is morally-sound to look, to listen to such published works displaying the realities of imprisonment that are only on the increase in a post-Web 2.0 era?

INTERLUDE FOUR

'Music is the language of the soul'

Sitting in the curiously chilly library of Ateneo de Manila University one sunny afternoon in December 2012, I stumbled upon a most peculiar video through one of my regular YouTube trawls. After catching up on the most recent CPDRC routines (and after indulging in a few obligatory cat-playing-the piano videos), I happened upon an old black and white film called *Manila – Castilian Memoirs 1930s*, digitized and uploaded as an eight-minute-and-fifteen-second YouTube video (Dickason 1934; Travel Film Archive 2008). The unnamed narrator, an added voiceover to what was evidently originally a silent film, describes a 1930s tour of Manila, which was at that time firmly established as a 'proud' American colony. The video displays both US and Spanish colonial histories, with clear traces of a recent Spanish past as we observe stylish Manileños going about their business in camisa blouses and shopping for the latest fashionable hats. The narrator furnishes each visual image with additional details as they unfold, providing an overview of a cosmopolitan Manila life, from city sidewalks and cigar factories to *caramatas* (horse drawn carriages) and caribou pulling carts. It was the film's depiction of Bilibid prison at six minutes in, however, that particularly caught my attention.[1] The narrator describes Bilibid prison as embracing seventeen acres and harbouring some 3,500 transgressors of the law, making it the largest penal institution in the world.

> Retreating every afternoon at four-thirty o'clock, is an impressive half-hour ceremony, when visitors are admitted to a central tower, from which the ward buildings radiate like the spokes of a wheel, thereby enabling spectators to view the entire scene with ease. (Dickason 1934)

At this point the film shows the marching band performing in the prison yard, brass instruments shining in the sunlight. Following this musical performance, the entire prison company perform a display of short callisthenic exercises – a feature our narrator is quick to point out notably distinguishes Bilibid from other penitentiaries (Figures 4.1, 4.2, 4.3).

The narrator continues, stating that during the calisthenics performance the men are treated not unlike soldiers as they are subjected to a system that 'grants privilege and metes out punishment according to conduct and industrial skill'. He continues:

> Uniforms of different colours indicate whether they are trustees, prisoners of the first, second or third class or apprentices. A drill by the crack Bilibid Scouts, bearing wooden arms and comprising chiefly life and good behaviour prisoners conclude the afternoon display. (Dickason 1934)

The Bilibid performances were remarkable, as the narrator noted, and set this facility apart from others both intra-nationally and internationally. According to our unnamed reporter, the motivation behind this musical revue and performance programme is drawn from an imperial rhetoric that remains all too familiar today. The goal of this 'model' programme is to prepare inmates for eventual good citizenship through regular work, recreation and rest. Such is the popularity of this programme, 'so beneficent is the regime that most of the guards are stationed outside to restrain immigration rather than inside as is customary to thwart emigration' (Dickason 1934).[2] This familiar language of inmate transformation connects at once with Foucault's reconditioning of a soldier, while simultaneously reminding us of Garcia's declarations of 'Responsive Rehabilitation' in his 2006 article for *Cebu Sun Star* newspaper. In this Garcia states that the CPDRC approach to rehabilitation is:

> discipline, physical fitness, dismantling of the culture of corruption and preemptive decongestion. It is a concept that views behavioral change and culture in the microcosm of a sick society, which is, the jail. ... While the goal is to keep the body fit in order to keep the mind fit, such may not actually happen if it is not done in a manner deemed *pleasurable*. Music, being the language of the soul, is added to that regimen. (Garcia qtd in Campbell 2007)

The addition of music to the exercise routines gives a task that might ordinarily be seen as objectionable, a pleasurable appearance in comparison.

FIGURES 4.1, 4.2, 4.3 *Scenes of Bilibid prison marching band, followed by a demonstration of Bilibid inmates performing a display of calisthenics to music in the prison yard, to an audience of assembled guests, in 1930s Manila. (Stills from* Manila – Castilian Memoirs 1930s, *dir. Dickason 1934. © Imperial Pictures Inc.)*

Garcia's approach at a holistic, and seemingly quintessentially Filipino, approach to discipline can be traced at least to the US colonial rehabilitation practices evidenced at Bilibid prison. Garcia too aims to prepare his inmates for eventual good citizenship through a combination of keeping the body fit in order to keep the mind fit, which crucially – as previously mentioned, may not happen if it is not done in a matter deemed pleasurable. 'True rehabilitation may need revolutionary change in policies and approaches', Garcia claims, and 'at the CPDRC, the experience in responsive rehabilitation has proven that revolutionary change can be done from within' (2006). Consciously or subconsciously, Garcia taps into a prison practice that on the one hand harks back to the American colonial project. On the other, he connects his argument for music as the language of the soul to a historical idea of music as the language of the soul. This discourse can be traced to the classical world, but came into its own in nineteenth century German philosophy. As Arthur Schopenhauer eloquently expressed in *The World as Will and Idea,* music holds a special status among the arts.

> [music] is such a great and eminently splendid art, it creates such a powerful reaction in man's inmost depths, it is so thoroughly and profoundly understood by him as a uniquely universal language, even exceeding in clarity that of the phenomenal world itself. (Schopenhauer 1819)

For Schopenhauer, the wardens at Bilibid prison in the 1930s, and countless others since, music *is* powerful. We can see how Garcia is replicating an argument with tradition, a historicized belief in music's magnificence and an ability to be truly universal. And it is in this quest for universality that music's use becomes 'dangerous', for when exercising all forms of power comes an inherent responsibility. Moreover, this statement indicates at least two possible interpretations. One, it suggests a holistic approach, a cost-effective method of keeping the inmates in good health throughout their incarceration. Two, it may also refer to keeping the inmates mentally fit in order to absorb the prison's – and by extension the state's – disciplinary ideology. The meaning inferred and interpretations yielded from Garcia's statements are not wholly self-evident. The performances are justified, and feed into the discourse that surrounds them. Conversely such discourse is constantly vindicated by the frequent public performances, creating a digital feedback loop with real-life, human consequences.

CHAPTER FOUR

Beats behind bars

Docile bodies and the digital panopticon

'Disco has gone to war': Mediating music in detention

The camera enters a makeshift interrogation dungeon, where a hooded detainee is left isolated in the middle of the darkened room, alone with the diegetic soundtrack of a hardcore anthem blasted from a PA system perched in the corner. The song is repeated over and despite the intensely loud volume, the lyrics are – as with many metal and punk lyrics – rather difficult to decipher. On closer enquiry, the track in question is 'Pavlov's Dogs' by New Jersey hardcore band Rorschach, released in 1990. The coarsely recited lyrics obliquely reference Ivan Pavlov's experiments on respondent conditioning, as the soundtrack screeches: 'Everything evil/Becomes serene/ Drilled in my head.'[1]

This bleak snapshot of a scene from the war thriller *Zero Dark Thirty* (dir. Bigelow 2012) depicts the level of understanding and perhaps even widespread acceptance across mainstream media of music's connection with imprisonment and detention, either as an EIT (enhanced interrogation technique) or as a form of torture, particularly in US government-run operations post-11 September 2001. Media reports increased after 14 September 2003, when US military commander in Iraq – Lt. Gen. Ricardo Sanchez, authorized the loud and sustained use of music on detainees, specifically to 'create fear, disorient ... and prolong capture shock' (Associated Press 2008). Sergeant Mark Hadsell, of US Psychological

Operations Company (Psy Ops) highlighted the US belief in the sociocultural and violent power music has. In *Newsweek* magazine, Hadsell states *his* understanding of the process, rooted on an ideology of fear and alienation through being forced to listen to unfamiliar music:

> These people haven't heard heavy metal. They can't take it. If you play it for 24 hours, your brain and body functions start to slide, your train of thought slows down and your will is broken. That's when we come in and talk to them. (*BBC News* 2003)

Hadsell articulates a very particular belief in using music (in this case heavy metal) as an instrument to imprison the mind and body. In another example Moustafa Bayoumi, writing in 2005, explains that the reported instances of 'Western music' being used as a weapon among US military were on the increase. In his essay 'Disco Inferno', he describes the experiences Afghani and Iraqi men faced at the hands of American forces:

> Near Fallujah, three Iraqi journalists working for Reuters were seized by the 82nd Airborne. They charged that 'deafening music' was played directly into their ears while soldiers *ordered them to dance*. And back in Mosul, Haitham al-Mallah described being hooded, handcuffed and delivered to a location where soldiers boomed 'extremely loud (and dirty) music' at him. Mallah said the site was 'an unknown place which they call 'the disco'. (Bayoumi 2005, italics added)

In contemporary conflict and practices of detention, music – the popular music of Metallica and Britney Spears in Bayoumi's account – is used as a tool of cruelty and transgression. By blasting songs at extremely high volumes, in addition to the humiliation tactics of forced dance and other stress positions such as being hooded and handcuffed, soldiers exploit music to degrade their prisoners. 'Disco isn't dead', as Bayoumi remarks. Rather, it's 'gone to war' (2005).

The Oscar-award-winning film *Zero Dark Thirty* conveys the unintentionally deft choice and use of music in detention by the Hollywood writers' interpretation of EIT, and although the scene is dramatized, it plays on tropes that have become commonly understood as practised forms of 'no touch torture'.[2] Rorschach's lyrics to 'Pavlov's Dogs', while somewhat unintelligible due to the sheer volume combined with stylistic expression, nonetheless neatly echo the assumed sentiments of the captive inmate. The sounds of lead singer Charles Maggio screaming 'Everything evil/Becomes serene/Drilled in my head' only serves to magnify the on-screen, visualized violence. This may appear as an exceptionally graphic, fictional depiction of 'white-collar' or 'no touch torture', yet it represents an all-too-conventional interrogation practice. The implication of such white-collar torture is one based on a notion of progress: that by not physically touching the prisoner, torture has been somehow civilized, professionalized, stripped of its teeth (Kagen 2013). This film scene – along with similar scenes from US TV show *Homeland* (2011) – depicts narratives of sonic warfare that play on the now-accepted understanding that constant exposure to excessive and intense sound will lead to 'diminished intellectual capacity, accelerated respiration and heartbeat, hypertension, slowed digestion, neurosis, [and] altered diction' (Attali 1985: 27). Such effects fall in line with even the most conservative understandings of the term torture.

Though not without notable detractors, such uses of music in detention are largely accepted as the US push the boundaries of interrogation, in practice and by definition, to enable such methods to circumvent legal definitions of torture.[3] At the turn of the twenty-first century, the ensuing rise of online social media networks enabled the play and replay of leaked photographs of the cruel and inhuman punishments served to detainees at US-run Guantánamo Bay and Abu Ghraib. Under the Freedom of Information Act, the American Civil Liberties Union released copies of the FBI internal memos concerning the alleged abuse and torture at Guantánamo, in Afghanistan and Iraq. One particular memo dated 22 May 2004 described in detail specific methods of 'interrogation' sanctioned by US military personnel and, by extension, mandated by the President of the United States, which included playing loud music, hooding detainees, the use of dogs and forcing inmates to strip off clothing and remain naked. The International Committee of the Red Cross reported that the abuse of Iraqi detainees was widespread, not limited to Abu Ghraib prison but other facilities as well, including al-Baghdadi air base, Hubbania camp, Tikrit holding area and the ministry of defence, and ultimately, some cases were 'tantamount to torture' (Cloud et al. 2004). A multitude of images of inmates, cuffed and hooded, being physically and sexually abused by US military quickly circulated among international print and digital media. In addition, the proliferation of hundreds upon thousands of news reports on music's increased use as a weapon served to further cement in global consciousness the fact that music has and continues to be used on detainees as a form of (or as part of) 'harsh interrogation' within the so-called US war on terror (BBC News 2003; Cusick 2006; Johnson and Cloonan 2009).

Sounding punishment: Prison, spectacles and the 'ideal spectator'

Theories on the public spectacle of punishment through history provide a framework by which to consider how CPDRC's *Thriller* represents a return to dramatic, spectacular forms of punishment that focus on the prisoners' bodies (Foucault 1977; Brown 2009; Roth 2010). But before we consider how music came to be used as a form of punishment and in places of detention like CPDRC, let us briefly pause to consider: what is punishment?

Why do most nations use prisons instead of other types of punishment? Punishment, from the Old French *punissement* and derived from the verb *punir*, is universally understood as a painful or unpleasant experience that is inflicted upon an individual in response to an offence, carried out by persons who have the authority to do so. Since punishment through its very definition involves inflicting pain upon a person, and fundamentally such an action is reprehensible, philosophies of punishment are divided on the issue. Two differing philosophies to punishment arise – the retributive: those who believe that inflicting pain as punishment is fundamentally different to inflicting pain on innocents and therefore is not inherently wrong, and the utilitarian approach: those who justify punishment only if it results in a 'greater good' through the secondary rationales of deterrence, incapacitation or rehabilitation. In theory and in practice, retribution should be limited, impersonal and balanced, since revenge is considered personal and very often disproportionate.

For Émile Durkheim, certain acts of punishment under certain conditions operate as social rituals, bringing together communities and providing a forum for reaffirming and intensifying their commitment to such shared values (Miethe and Lu 2005: 6). Whereas Immanuel Kant (1996: 105) – an advocate for retributive rationale – believed that punishment by a court can be inflicted upon a transgressor, but never solely as a means to promote some other good for the criminal himself or for civil society. Rather it must always be inflicted on him only because he has committed a crime, and he must previously have been found punishable before any thought can be given to drawing from his punishment something of use for himself or his fellow citizens, for the law of punishment is a categorical imperative. For Kant, to inflict evil upon others is to ultimately inflict it upon yourself.

Hearkening back to the gladiator combats of Ancient Rome to the scaffolds of medieval Europe, punishment was a public act that doubled as a sociocultural forum, tasked with uniting communities, and providing social rituals whereby community members could reflect on social and moral values. Music played a vital role in such social gatherings. Gladiator spectacles opened with processions led by musicians playing trumpets, cymbals and the remarkable hydraulis (water organ), sonically marking the start of the event and continuing to provide music during and in between the fights (Wisdom 2001: 42–61). Medieval punishment practices were similarly grounded on community ritual, with music playing a seemingly innocuous yet fundamental role.

From the medieval period through to the nineteenth century, the stocks and the pillory were two of the most widely used forms of physical punishment that occurred across Europe and the United States as forms of public spectacle primarily to punish the petty crimes of ordinary men and women. Humiliation, public ridicule and physical pain were the key features of these devices, as both the stocks and pillory consisted of specially crafted wooden or metal boards containing holes for head and hands, and usually located outdoors in such public places as crossroads, marketplaces and elevated platforms in town squares. Crowds of common people would flock to these spectacles and were openly invited to jeer and shout insults, spit and pelt victims with dead animals, offal, rotten food and excrement. Such acts of violence were undertaken through the agents of the state, and grounded in religious rhetoric surrounding the concept of hell; carrying out such publicly painful acts was justified in the belief that by doing so, one was in essence saved from the burning fires of eternal hell (Bending 2000). Physical punishment and retribution were permitted to be inflicted upon offenders as they merely mirror the relationship between God and mankind, and pain and suffering formed a crucial part of medieval Christian teaching, further serving as a way to purge oneself of evil sins in order to enter the next life.[4]

Herzfeld-Schild's study on musical instruments for punishment in the Middle Ages draws from historical legal, iconographic sources to describe one painting in particular detail – the Flemish artist Pieter Bruegel the Elder's *Netherlandish Proverbs* (1559). This large-scale oil-on-panel painting depicts over 100 different visualizations of folk metaphors, idioms and proverbs commonly in use during the sixteenth century. Among these various illustrations is a man imprisoned on a pillory, playing an instrument that bears resemblance to a violin, alluding to the Medieval proverb 'he plays on the pillory' (Herzfeld-Schild 2013: 14). This old adage relates to a specific kind of punishment used in the Middle Ages and Early Modern Era where felons had to wear symbolic musical instruments, usually wooden or iron 'neck violins' or 'neck flutes', while being pilloried through the streets in order to be humiliated in public. Such historical documents suggest that 'these punishment practices originally date back to a more ancient use of real instruments in a penal system that was applied and understood as a "healing punishment" (*poena medicinalis*) to banish the ill and re-establish the good in the delinquent, the community and the world as a whole due to musical sounds' (Herzfeld-Schild 2013: 14). Tellingly, this research points towards a historical ideology where specific punishments were meted out for specific crimes using music as a form of mockery on perpetrators, and where societal order is restored through a kind of symbolic re-enactment performance, and where sounds, symbolic or real, emanated not from the punisher but from the punished themselves (Herzfeld-Schild 2013: 14–22). Cultural and historical ideas of music – by means of real or symbolic instruments – and the performance of the *punished* rather than the punisher, have been apparent for quite some time. Such practices operate to solidify music's crucial role in the spectacle of punishment: as a form of humiliation, and as power itself.

Foucault's *Discipline and Punish: The Birth of the Prison* (1977) provides a foundation to help understand how the dancing inmates of

CPDRC operate in terms of penal control, displays of discipline and public punishment. For Foucault, the public spectacle of punishment served several intended and unintended purposes for society, which can be summarized as follows:

Intended purposes:
i. Reflecting the violence of the original crime onto the convict's body for all to see.
ii. Enacting the revenge upon the convict's body, which the sovereign seeks for having been injured by the crime.

Unintended consequences:
i. Providing a forum for the convict's body to become a locus of sympathy and admiration.
ii. Creating a site of conflict between the masses and the sovereign at the convict's body.

The ritualized nature of public punishments, from the tortuous to the executions, often exceeded the sovereign's intended purpose by inciting empathy and respect from spectators – an aspect we see in the YouTube reception to CPDRC's *Thriller* (see Chapter 7 for details on CPDRC's YouTube comments). Other times sites of public punishment led to riots in support of the convict. Conquergood's writing on performance and punishment in penal institutions argues that through the theatricality and spectacle of the scaffolds, audiences were encouraged to identify deeply with the convicts as fellow human beings and sinners, as described in the expected reactions of spectators at the scaffold:

> They [the audience] did not shrink in moral revulsion from even the most despised and heinous criminals. The typical response was 'there but for the grace of God, go I.' ... This way of seeing encouraged a deeply sympathetic, theatrical identification in which the spectators could imaginatively exchange places with the condemned, instead of holding themselves aloof in distanced judgment. The ideal spectator at executions became a deeply engaged, co-performative witness. (2002: 351)

The format and formality of public execution rituals served to create a kind of '*ideal spectator*', a way of seeing that encouraged audiences to be deeply sympathetic and identify as the criminals themselves. As sovereigns across Europe began to lose their power to more impersonal forms of government, power was 'exercised in the name of society as a whole and was legitimised as being in defence of society' (Burkitt 2008: 89). By the nineteenth century, such acts of public violence decreased as the state's next form of punishment was born – the prison.

CPDRC's 'docile bodies'

Penal systems, as we know them today, followed a long tradition of violence and public torture towards convicts. Foucault's 'docile bodies' are a key feature in CPDRC performances. Foucault's detailed account of the contrasts between modern and premodern approaches to punishment starts with the politically ritualistic, ceremonious nature of public torture and executions, where the body was the locus of punishment, to the shift to an apparently 'gentler' and more 'civilised' form of punishment via imprisonment. By the nineteenth century, public hangings, pillories and stocks were no longer necessary in many jurisdictions as prison systems slowly became an omnipresent force for policing the population. The beating and whipping of offenders moved indoors so that on the surface, punishment appeared to 'progress', through the guise of gentleness. Yet such a shift was not for humanitarian reasons. Reformists were unhappy with the unpredictable, unevenly distributed nature of the violence that the sovereign would focus on the body of the convict, Foucault argues. Because the sovereign's right to punish was so disproportionate, it was ultimately ineffective and uncontrolled. Thus, such changes in penal history served 'not to punish less, but to punish better' (Foucault 1977: 80). Punishments were no longer expected to be acts of revenge against the criminal's body, but instead now measured against the weight of the crime. The theatre of public torture gave way to public chain gangs, and out of this movement towards widespread punishment, a thousand 'mini-theatres' of punishment were created wherein the convicts' bodies were put on display in a more ubiquitous, controlled and effective spectacle (Foucault 1977: 29–31).

Changes in penal history included the declared purpose of punishment moving from retribution – either as a deterrence to others or for the sake of an ideal justice – to the reformation and rehabilitation of the criminal. Furthermore, the transformation from judges to 'experts' (who include psychiatrists, social workers and parole boards) to hand down sentences, in conjunction with the new, self-declared purpose of punishment as an act of self-amelioration, marked a drastic change in the history of discipline and punishment. As a result, prisoners were forced to do work that reflected their crime, thereby balancing the books by repaying society for their infractions. This allowed the public to witness the convicts' bodies enacting their punishment, enabling both convict and audience to reflect upon the crime. For Foucault, 'the body becomes a useful force only if it is both a productive body and a subjected body' (1977: 26), and as such the 'useful force' of the body is wholly dependent on the productivity of said body. The capitalist economy turned bodies into objects that can be easily ruled by those in power, from princes to prison guards.

Questions regarding the scale of microscopic discipline over the active body became imperative as the state gave birth to a new 'mechanics of power'. 'The body was entering a machinery of power', wrote Foucault, describing power's subjection of the body as a machine that explores it, breaks it down and rearranges it. This 'political anatomy' established

> how one may have a hold over others' bodies, not only so that they may do what one wishes, but also that they may operate as one wishes, with the techniques, the speed and the efficiency that one determines. Thus, discipline produces subjected and practiced bodies, 'docile' bodies. (1977: 138)

The shift from brutal physical punishment to less painful, more intrusive psychological power over inmates signalled the beginning of the modern age for prisons, where control of the soul is the ultimate goal.

Extraordinary levels of control are involved in creating a YouTube video like CPDRC's *Thriller* – and prisons are first and foremost spaces of control. Many early CPDRC videos uploaded onto YouTube feature extended introductions preceding the dance routines, wherein Warden Garcia seizes the opportunity to introduce his captive audience, live and imagined, to the most prominent inmates – usually singling out those charged with the most severe crimes such as multiple murder, or the lead dancers performing the roles of Michael Jackson and his *Thriller* girlfriend (see Garcia 2009b). Using a microphone amplified by the prison speakers, inmates must say their name and the offence that they have been charged with. In news reports and interviews as well as during live and mediated performances themselves, Garcia introduces prominent inmates to the audience by their name, and also by their offence and duration of the sentence to be served at CPDRC. Prisoners are presented as people, but are permanently associated with their (alleged) crime. It makes no difference that in CPDRC *all* of the dancing inmates are awaiting trial and technically innocent until proven guilty of a criminal act. Their (possible and/or presumed) crimes are inscribed and affixed to their names, and especially, their faces. Thus it is perhaps no surprise that Garcia imparts an ideology that reflects aspects of Foucault's theories on modern penology, such as the desire to impart to the viewer a visual lesson in morality.

Murderers on the Dancefloor, a 2008 twenty-three-minute British documentary based on the CPDRC, reveals the extent of the surveillance and control enacted in CPDRC. The film's title both plays on the noughties disco-pop song by British singer Sophie Ellis-Bexter, while equally reinforcing the inmates' presumed status as murderers. It opens by connecting CPDRC inmates with the most violent crimes, as the voiceover – by director Sarah McCarthy – announces, 'Cebu Detention Centre is a maximum security prison, meaning 70 per cent of the inmates are here on murder or rape charges' (McCarthy 2008). Garcia, interviewed by McCarthy, steadily articulates his achievements: 'What I did is something that you only see in the movies,' he affirms in all seriousness. 'I have put a true meaning, in the real sense of the word, of jailhouse rock' (McCarthy 2008). Subsequent press interviews with the inmates highlight their lack of consent in Garcia's YouTube broadcasts, most pointedly displayed in an interview with lead dancer Wenjiel Resane, who states that 'We didn't know that Mr. Byron put it on the internet and that it became so popular' until reporters began arriving at the facility requesting interviews with the star dancers (Journeyman Pictures 2007).

Explaining his reasons for choosing the song 'Thriller' for the inmates to perform, Garcia knowingly or unknowingly draws from a history of retributive rhetoric, fused with contemporary prison culture. He asserts his intended purposes as follows:

> I saw in the lyrics and video of Thriller much of what jail culture is like … The Dancing Inmates come as themselves. People perceived to be evil … What I wanted inmates to do in dancing to the Thriller was for them to be convicted to sin. When I uploaded this on the YouTube, what I wanted viewers to see is how evil dances in our lives without knowing its deathly consequences. (Garcia 2007a)

Garcia ascribes the alleged violence of their crimes onto their bodies, conflating unconvicted men as men perceived to be 'evil' and therefore 'convicted to sin', acting as judge, jury and executioner within the most ubiquitous and public platform available in the twenty-first century – YouTube. Inmates perform *Thriller* perhaps as rehabilitation, as Garcia attests, but in dancing the *Thriller* as a metaphor for their perceived wrongdoings, thus repaying the state for their purported transgressions.

Viewing the prisoners as public spectacles on a global scale becomes impossible to ignore. Flouting the detainees alleged crimes and inscribing them 'in sin' in such a public manner certainly invites what Foucault designates 'unintended consequences'. YouTube's open access enables international audiences to leave comments of admiration and concern, as the inmate's body becomes a locus of transferred emotion (discussed in more detail in Chapter 7). And still, presented as it is on YouTube, alongside VEVO's official music videos of Michael Jackson's back catalogue, alongside millions of user-generated cat videos, CPDRC's performance of *Thriller* is often perceived as a quick click fix – an entertaining few minutes' respite from an otherwise banal day in the office.[5] CPDRC's *Thriller*'s pop-music-video appearance means it is not generally viewed as a site of conflict between the masses and the state. Rather, as the comments that appear with the video illustrate, it is experienced as a form of mass entertainment – a conflation of pop music, leisure and imprisonment.

Despite CPDRC's *Thriller* pop exterior, a contemporary version of the medieval *poena medicinals* (healing punishment) or 'play on the pillory' penalty, Garcia has constructed a twenty-first century mini-theatre of punishment wherein the inmates' bodies are put on public display in the most controlled and effective spectacle. This contemporary, mini-theatre of punishment is then projected online, through YouTube. As such the CPDRC 'replaces bodily pain with performance rehearsals', and as Perillo affirms, functions to 'redistribute public responsibility online to discursively reinscribe and bring criminals to justice' (2011: 610). In the CPDRC performances, dance performance is pitched in opposition to punishing the inmates' physical body, and discipline is physically displayed through controlling corporeality.

The type of discipline we witness in CPDRC's *Thriller* was born at the precise moment when the inmates' bodies became obedient in responding to the choreographer's instructions in the prison yard. The dance routines, but more importantly their mediation, represent a shift from disciplinary societies, as Gilles Deleuze contends, but the result is a 'move towards control societies that no longer operate by confining people but through continuous control and instant communication' (1992: 3–7). This is crucial in relation to CPDRC, as the benefits of exposing prisoners to pop music and dance, as well as widespread fame and (mis-)fortune through their commercial spectacle, must be considered as part of a wider inclination towards new, open forms of punishment that are being introduced 'without a critical understanding (of) what is happening' (Murphy, Peters and Margison 2010: 355). As a result, the inmates become useful to the prison warden's requirements and thus enact the quintessential modernist approach to discipline, producing what Foucault designates 'docile bodies': bodies that not only do what we want but do it precisely in the way that we want (1977: 138). The individual bodily behaviour of each inmate, their posture, demeanour, clothing, footwear – every movement they make – is governed by Garcia's (and by extension, the Philippine state's) rules and regulations. Accordingly, through their embodied performance, the inmates have become 'subjected and practiced bodies' (138), that embody the very essence of docility. The act of surveillance over inmates creates a power-relation, with the 'gaoler made the watcher, the holder of knowledge, and the prisoner induced to enact the corresponding role of the watched' (Counsell and Wolf 2001: 127). This power-relation impacts directly on the behaviour of the inmate, 'for in "disciplining" their activity in accordance with knowledge's conception of them, individuals inscribe power on their own bodies, in effect performing hegemonic models of the human subject' (Counsell and Wolf 2001: 127). There is no power relation, Foucault contends, without the 'correlative constitution of a field of knowledge, nor any knowledge that does not presuppose and constitute at the same time power relations' (1977: 27). The body, power, knowledge and performance are always inextricably linked.

Born digital: Digital panopticism and the act of detail

Surveillance, and the screen, it seems, are key to CPDRC's *Thriller*. At CPDRC, Garcia aligns his success in restoring order to the facility first and foremost through increased surveillance over the inmates. Surveillance cameras were installed in every area of the new CPDRC facility, and these cameras were connected to the internet. As a result, the camera's footage was accessible through screens in Garcia's office, home computer monitors or wherever he chooses to log in and to inspect the inmates in any section of the prison. The dance programme's origins, in yet another reported version of Garcia's account, came about through closely watching the inmates on these very surveillance screens (Journeyman Pictures 2007). In this narration, Garcia claims to have seen the inmates marching in the prison yard through checking the surveillance camera's computer screen. Watching the inmates this way, they appeared on screen neat and organized, and so he decided the inmates should add dance to their exercise regime. In this version of events at least, the screen plays a most crucial role from the programme's inception. Also in this version the entire dance programme was conceived online, 'born digital' as it were.[6] By viewing the inmates through the frame of the computer monitor, it was not only possible but plausible for Garcia to smoothly transition into filming and uploading video footage of their dancing, for they were born *on screen*. Demonstrating the CPDRC's surveillance cameras to visiting journalist Nick Lazaredes in 2007, Garcia points to a computer screen that shows small groups of five or six inmates rehearsing their dance moves – in between the daily sessions in the prison yard – in corridors and stairwells around the prison. From the beginning, the inmates were viewed by Garcia as bodies on a mediated screen – bodies that could be transformed, ordered and controlled through distinctively hierarchical means.

The Foucauldian notion of 'docile bodies' once again becomes useful. As discussed earlier, docile bodies are those that are produced through uniquely modern methods, including hierarchical observation, which is based on controlling subjects merely through surveillance. This mode was magnified through Jeremy Bentham's mid-eighteenth century panoptic prison design that enabled maximum control of inmates by a minimum of staff (Figure 4.4). Panopticon prisons were not put into practice until the twentieth-century but since then its concept has permeated contemporary society in a variety of sites; from military barracks, lecture halls and hospital rooms, to shopping malls and factory floors. This enables the objects of control to be highly visible with the highest level of visibility reserved for criminals and asylum inmates, while those who exercise power remain somewhat obscured.

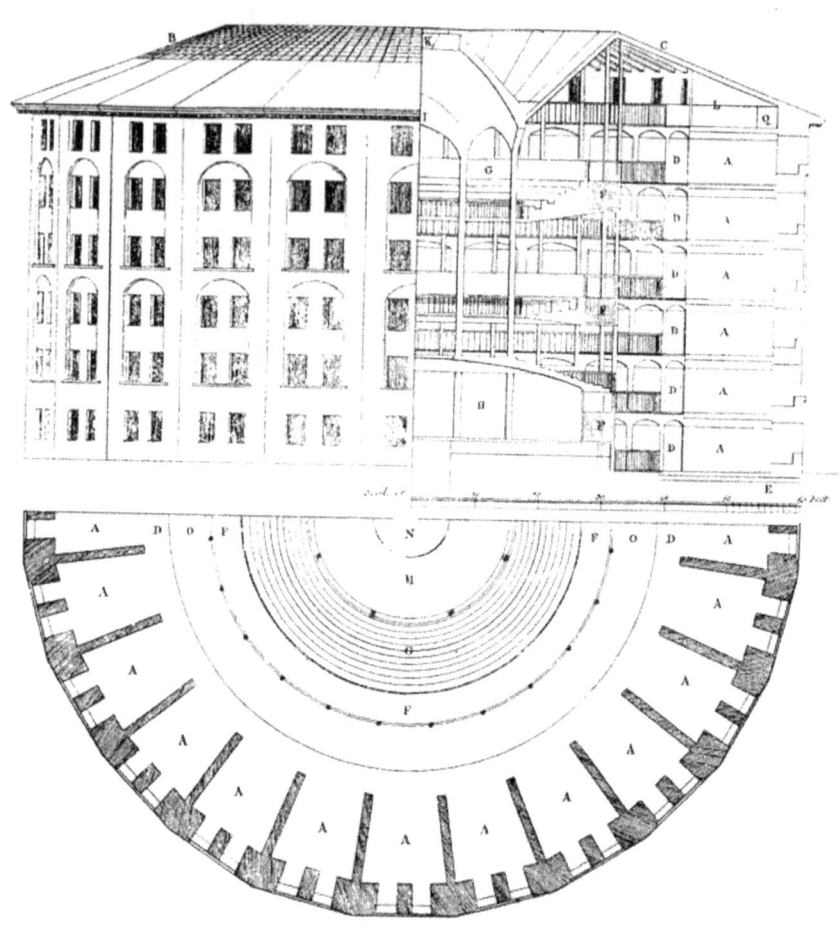

FIGURE 4.4 *Plan of panopticon by Jeremy Bentham from* The works of Jeremy Bentham, *vol. IV (1843, originally published 1791), 172–3. (Source: Public Domain)*

Panopticonism is based not on the fact of observation but on the constant possibility. Inmates do not know precisely when the monitor will direct their attention at them, but rather they are consciously aware of their permanent visibility, and as such, this constant possibility of being viewed 'assures the automatic functioning of power' (Foucault 1977: 201). The principal of panopticonism gradually spread throughout the world, 'by the gradual adaptation and diversified application of this single principle, you should see a new scene of things spread itself over the face of civilised society' (201). Prisons evolved into sites of reform for the body, and more crucially, the soul. Thus while surveillance as a disciplinary technique was not newly invented, instead it became ubiquitous through the small and subtle mechanisms that 'obeyed economies too shameful to be acknowledged [...] – it was nevertheless they that brought about the mutation of the punitive system, at the threshold of the contemporary period' (1977: 139). The effects of surveillance transitioned into society at large, resulting in a move towards societies that 'no longer operate by confining people but through continuous control and instant communication' (Deleuze 1992: 3–7). Discipline is without question, as Foucault meditates, a political act of detail.

What is apparent from conceptualizing this prison as a panopticon is the inherent hierarchy given to a gaze that assumes visibility over audibility. Understood in this way, the panopticon provides a useful point of departure for studies of surveillance, something to move beyond rather than a model of how surveillance actually works in practice. The very concept of a panoptic gaze overlooks (or undermines) the auditory aspects of the subjects of the gaze. By cloaking their noise and hiding their individual sounds under *Thriller*'s high volume, no such knowledge can be realized. The uni-directionality of the panoptic gaze is further construed when we consider its aural properties; the infectiously popular music soundtrack masks the inmates' individual utterances, and silences their voice.

In Bentham's original design for the panopticon, sound, listening and vocal economy have clear functions in the practice of surveillance. This fact is somewhat overlooked by Foucault, who gives only a footnote reference to Bentham's auditory surveillance, stating that:

> In his first version of the Panopticon, Bentham had also imagined an acoustic surveillance, operated by means of pipes leading from the cells to the central tower. In the Postscript he abandons the idea, perhaps because he could not introduce into it the principle of dissymmetry and prevent the prisoners from hearing the inspector as well as the inspector hearing them. (Foucault 1977: 317)

The very act of surveillance through the panopticon, then, originally included sounds from the outset, although sound was later abandoned. The uni-directionality of the panoptic gaze is further construed when we consider its aural properties; how the musical soundtrack, crucially, masks their utterances and silences their voice, and the sound-transmission system experienced by YouTube audiences forms an additional layer of observation. If the exercise was performed without the musical soundtrack, would we – could we – hear the inmates? When publicly circulated via YouTube, the recorded performances of CPDRC's *Thriller* serve as an exercise in surveillance, discipline and control over the Filipino prisoners. But rather than focusing exclusively on the ocular, the operations of power presented here are equally, if not more firmly, grounded in the sonic. It is precisely the soundtrack of this YouTube video that makes it so insidious. If we recall Dawkins's and Rushkoff's virus theories from Chapter 1, the song forms Rushkoff's 'protein shell' (1994: 9) of CPDRC's *Thriller* as a media virus, and its repetitive bass riff attaches itself to all the nooks and crannies of contemporary popular culture.

In CPDRC, inmates are not only observed in their cells, mealtimes, labour and family visits, but particularly during their exercise or 'leisure' time in the prison yard – the four-to-six-hour daily dance routines. Within the dance rehearsals, a further four-tier security surveillance structure is in place. First, the prison choreographer strictly surveys the dance rehearsals and tutors the inmates from the front of the prison yard, teaching the inmates to count each step while they grow accustomed to the music – music that is very often new to some inmates.[7] After multiple rehearsals when the routines are more polished, and in the run-up to the live performances, the choreographer sits high above the inmates in the panoptic balcony. Second, each section of dancers has an appointed 'leader' selected by Garcia – usually a more senior (or bigger) inmate, such as former police officer Leo Suico – who oversees his section and ensures each dancer is in time and in line.[8] Third, an array of prison guards who align the perimeter of the yard on the ground. And fourth, prison warden Garcia and his team watch and supervise each step they take from high up on the prison watchtowers, occasionally shouting down instructions to the choreographer or inmates over a microphone connected to the speaker system. In early CPDRC rehearsal videos Garcia can be seen calling out for choreographic changes, stopping rehearsals to suggest certain prisoners move to the front of the corps, and appearing smiling while singing along to whichever of his favourite songs is blasting from the prison loudspeakers. It becomes increasingly apparent that it is not the prisoners' experience that is captured on camera and then globally disseminated, rather we, the YouTube audience, are privy to Garcia's panoptic production – Garcia has chosen the soundtrack to their toil; Garcia watches from above; Garcia records and shares *his* viewpoint with the world through YouTube – a unique and elaborate performance of punishment, discipline and control.

CPDRC inmates do not know precisely when dance rehearsals will be called, or what songs they will have to perform to, but as soon as the opening strains of *Thriller* are heard, physical positions must be assumed (for the monitor – and the audiovisual recording device – will direct their attention at them). Through their close entrainment to specific musical cues, they are consciously aware of their permanent, on-and offline visibility, which 'assures the automatic functioning of power'. The soundtrack is what renders this otherwise questionable exercise thoroughly palatable – both for the inmates in the prison yard, and for the audiences watching at home. With noise is born disorder, and its opposite, the world, according to Jacques Attali; and with music, comes both power and subversion (1985: 6).

> [A]ny theory of power today must include a theory of the localisation of noise and its endowment with form ... Equivalent to the articulation of a space, it indicates the limits of a territory and the way to make oneself heard within it, how to survive by drawing one's sustenance from it. And since noise is the source of power, power has always listened to it with fascination. Eavesdropping, censorship, recording and surveillance are weapons of power. (Attali 1985: 7–8)

Attali's account demonstrates a duality: power may be exercised through hearing, but also through the production of noise and sound – in light of CPDRC, the production of music can be understood via the playing and sharing of mobile music videos. The configuration of power in this prison setting then points to an enlarged conceptualization of surveillance as multi-sensory, interactive and inclusive of noise, sound and hearing. I follow Marie Thompson's (2012) line of thinking about noise here. Rather than a negativity or failure, as noise is often conceptualized (see Hegarty 2008), if we consider noise as an affective force, it provides a framework that allows for noise's capacity to diminish and destroy, but also to enhance and create (Thompson 2012: 13–14). In CPDRC, noise is a vital source of power, and we see how the noise of music soundtracks piped through the prison yard are used to cloak, muffle or even silence certain populations and people. Yet despite the constant threat of panopticon surveillance, through noise lies the potential to produce new experiences and meanings for inmates – to laugh, cry, sing or shout as though no-one is listening.

Dance and docility at CPDRC

> If you ask a military man what is their sign of courtesy, their sign of courtesy is a salute, right? So now, we made it such a point that this physical fitness program will be the sign of their discipline – through dance. (Garcia qtd in Diokno 2008)

As discussed, Warden Garcia's initially mandatory calisthenics regime was *only* met with success when music was added – initially a compilation of his favourite 1980s and 1990s pop songs. Played over six loudspeakers across the prison yard, the sounds of Queen, the Village People, Soulja Boy and Flo Rida enticed inmates to singalong, clap and move together in time to the beat. Delighted with the results, Garcia recorded the rehearsing waves of orange dancers with a view to share his experiments and his idea with other prison officials. Several homemade videos followed, including routines to songs from the musical film *Sister Act* and Pink Floyd, so that by the time 'Thriller' was uploaded, Garcia had a firm understanding of the communicative potential that this new media platform, YouTube, held.

More than the exercise or the physical movement of dance, Garcia attributes the power of music as the platform to reach the inmates' 'inner-psyches'. Using his YouTube channel as a platform to explain his philosophy, Garcia describes his belief that 'therapeutic music and dance is meant to help prisoners cope with their depression and anxiety, improve their well-being as they go through a transition phase and reintegrate to society'. His manifesto continues:

> Music is a protocol to heal them of emotional and psychological disorders and trauma as a result of the offense or incarceration. Because penology practices make living hell in jails, the tendency is we breed next generation demons when they are discharged. If prisoners are healed while in prison, then we make them better persons when they are released and stay away from crime. (Garcia 2006)

Here Garcia affirms his beliefs that first and foremost, all inmates are convicted in sin, and secondly, that his programme 'heals' inmates and absolves them of their sins through the familiar trope of the therapeutic power of pop music – a statement he reaffirms in countless media interviews. Yet, as mentioned, to date no official reports confirm exactly how the programme has healed inmates, nor how and if it actually reduces recidivism rates. Instead, through the calculated dance routines Garcia attempts to rid the inmates of their criminal ways through disciplinary training and instil in them the air of an enlightened member of society instead. He moulds the inmates, training them in acts of discipline and control, of following strict and detailed orders, so they can be released back to society as noticeably changed, 'better persons', that somehow through disciplined dancing they have become 'reformed', 'honest beings'. Garcia is clear in his connection between using music and dance to shape the prisoners, physically and mentally, into upright citizens who will uphold Philippine law. Such description of the inmates echoes the eighteenth-century militaristic creation of a soldier. According to the Ordinance of 20 March 1764, a soldier was seen as something that can be made:

> out of a formless clay, an inept body, the machine required can be constructed; posture is gradually corrected; a calculated constraint runs slowly through each part of the body, mastering it, making it pliable, ready at all times, turning silently into the automatism of habit; in short, one has 'got rid of the peasant' and given him 'the air of a soldier'. (Ordinance of 20 March 1764, qtd in Foucault 1977: 135)

Through compelling dance performances to familiar, popular songs, inmates are believed to be reconstructed individuals. Through the action of repeated, daily dance, bodies undergo tangible, corporeal changes. Accordingly, at

CPDRC physical posture has been corrected, and as a result a calculated constraint runs through each part of their bodies, making it pliable and ready at all times to obey the choreographer's command. In short, through dance one has got rid of their criminal, peasant, social waste status and replaced it with the air of authority akin to a soldier. At CPDRC, dance is clearly utilized to separate inmates from their allegedly criminal pasts and thus recondition them into absolute, functioning citizens.

The relationship between exercise and positive behaviour in penal institutions is well noted among academics (Kielyl and Hodgson 1990; Mannocci et al. 2015). International medical and therapeutic publications provide much evidence that exercise can improve physiological and psychological health, particularly in older people or those currently inactive (Callaghan 2004: 476–83; Jackson and Shapiro-Phim 2008). One such study – on the relationship between physical exercise, acute and chronic illnesses and mental well-being in a New South Wales penal institution – revealed that there is a great need to include exercise as a factor in inmate health plans, due to the unquestionable benefits of exercise (Cashin, Potter and Butler 2008: 66–71). There appears to be an explicit correlation between emotion and mass. The mood improvement of certain inmates who participate in exercise is clearly stated, and when that mood in more than one person is changed, it can have more drastic effects. As Schechner notes, when moods are practiced in large groups or mass spectacles, the physical enactments of emotion or what he designates 'mood displays' (anger, enthusiasm, joy, etc.) are transformative when the mood changes in more than one individual. For Schechner (1988: 249), these mood displays change character when they are ritualized into mass actions such as spectator sports, political rallies or militarized parades; then individual expression rigidifies, is channelled into exaggerated, rhythmically coordinated, repetitive actions, while emphasis shifts from the free expression of feeling to an evocation and channelling of aggression for the benefit of the sponsor: the team, corporation, politician, religion, party or state.

At its most fundamental level, dance is an expressive form of exercise that releases endorphins, activating the body's opiate receptors to act as an analgesic, which can cause a sense of euphoria in participants. Through this new dance-as-rehabilitation ideology delivered in choreographed moves and nostalgic pop songs, inmates have encompassed, with implicit or explicit coercion, a distinctive way of passing time, a way that some, if not many, inmates enjoy on some level. Garcia has found a way of getting inmates involved in a daily exercise plan, a feat that medical officials around the world have attempted to implement in prisoner health plans.

The addition of music to forms of exercise, is also proven to greatly enhance the positive attributes felt by exercise alone, and as expected, embodied movement without music is not sufficient to restore 'inept' bodies. Music is added to the physical movements of CPDRC's inmates, and serves to 'penetrate their psyche' (Garcia qtd in Ortigas 2007). Music further assuages inmates as a tool of distraction, taking their minds off their impending trials, as Garcia confirms: 'Inmates say to me: "You have put my mind off revenge, foolishness, or thinking how to escape"' (BBC News 2007). Garcia credits music as part of a wider holistic, therapeutic process, as a form of music therapy to help the inmates reintegrate into society after the trauma of their detention and/or their criminal activities. These features are not necessarily mutually exclusive, of course, as the act of dance is widely understood as a pleasurable pastime that increases fitness levels and general well-being. The benefits of moving together in time with others, what war historian William McNeill designates 'muscular bonding' (1995: 2), is also proven to produce euphoric feelings of belonging, including among prison populations (Cashin, Potter and Butler 2008: 66–71). Describing the positive, euphoric effects that marching in unison can have on a soldier during times of trial, McNeill draws from his personal experience of service after being drafted into the army of the United States in 1941. In his book *Keeping Together in Time: Dance and Drill in Human History*, McNeill argues that the act of physically moving in time with others was an intrinsic source for good in the life of a soldier. He explains:

> Words are inadequate to describe the emotion aroused by the prolonged movement in unison that drilling involved. A sense of pervasive well-being is what I recall; more specifically, a strange sense of personal enlargement; a sort of swelling out, becoming bigger than life, thanks to participation in collective ritual. [...] Moving briskly and keeping in time was enough to make us feel good about ourselves, satisfied to be moving together and vaguely pleased with the world at large. (1995: 2)

McNeill continues, recounting how the rhythmic input from muscles and voice after 'gradually suffusing through the entire nervous system, may provoke echoes of the fetal condition when a major and perhaps principal external stimulus to the developing brain was the mother's heartbeat' (1995: 7). Thus McNeill imagines that the action of dancing in time to music, both a rhythmic beat of a drum and/or the sound of the human voice, might arouse in adults something like the 'state of consciousness they left behind in infancy, when psychologists seem to agree that no distinction is made between self and surroundings' (1995: 7).

The connection between marching together in time and embodied discipline in action remains foregrounded, and does not escape the attention of CPDRC audiences. Initial feedback from audiences of the CPDRC dance performances equated their choreographed dance with intrinsic discipline, as YouTube viewers remarked on the performances as acts of discipline. One viewer in particular observed that the dances were 'a marvellous show of discipline'. Philippine Roman Catholic Cardinal Archbishop Ricardo Vidal continues, 'If only they had practiced that (discipline) in their lives, they wouldn't be here' (Awit 2007). The Archbishop, along with a significant number of CPDRC's YouTube audiences, clearly associate choreographed movements to pop songs with an essential, positive character reformation.

The transfer from an individual expression of emotion to the channelling of an idea for the benefit of an institutional ideology is explicitly evident in the CPDRC performances. For Louis Althusser, ideology is reproduced in familiar, apparently benign institutions that are part of everyday social life. He argues that the primary purpose behind ideology is the formation of individuals as 'social subjects'. Althusser outlines the different institutions that form what he designates 'Ideological State Apparatuses' (ISAs), which are in contrast with the repressive state apparatuses that include the government, the police, the courts and noticeably, the prisons. These state apparatuses are repressive, Althusser suggests, because they function 'by violence' in both physical or non-physical forms, and therefore they are different to the Ideological State Apparatuses, which *'function "by ideology"'* (Counsell and Wolf 2001: 36). I agree. The ordered dance performances and shows of discipline at CPDRC inherently support the ethos of the detention centre, and by extension, the ethos of a correctional facility. Despite the inmates' status of presumed innocence, CPDRC creates 'social subjects' out of the incarcerated individuals, and these social subjects voice the shared values of Garcia and his administration. These values include decided political statements and public relations opportunities such as the 'innocent', CPDRC finale Sinulog performance of 'Mabuhi ang Sugbuanon' (*Cebuano*, 'Long Live Cebu') that featured a cameo appearance from Cebu Governor Gwen Garcia dancing the leading role (Garcia 2008b). Governor Garcia's performance singing and dancing alongside the inmates is described by her brother as 'thrilling', as he recounts: 'For a governor to be seen in the company of prisoners, dancing and enjoying herself is no movie. It is no thriller, it is not a dream, but for those who witnessed that event, including me, would say – it is thrilling to watch' (Garcia 2008b).[9] Their performance of Bonnie Tyler's 1980s hit 'I Need a Hero' was equally politicized via Garcia's spoken preface dedicated to all (his?) 'peace heroes'.[10] Furthermore, the dancing inmates have been used as vehicles for explicit religious proclamations, as in their 2007 performance of 'Gregorian Chant' that includes a Roman Catholic mass conducted by Cardinal Vidal and the inmates' bodies composed to form a large, crucifix formation in the middle of the prison yard. Together this array of recorded performances illustrates the extent to which the dancing inmates have been subjected to serve Garcia's ideological operations. Since Garcia took control of CPDRC as Chief Security Official in 2006, the prison underwent a transformation from an overtly (repressive) state apparatus, that is, one based on corrupt guards, violent, drug addicted inmates, to something more akin to Althusser's Ideological State Apparatuses, one where Garcia's carefully constructed new rehabilitation programme functions by means of a benign, almost invisible authoritarian outlook. CPDRC remains a detention centre, and therefore according to Althusser continues to be a repressive state apparatus. But the dance programme, which is regarded as positive and rehabilitative in much Filipino and international media, retains an underlying ideological element that is often overlooked or simply disregarded (see BBC News 2007; Campbell 2007; Ferran 2007; Israel 2010a; Israel 2010b; Awit 2010; Alesevich 2013; Lazaredes 2007; Ortigas 2007; Riminton 2007; Seno 2008). Still, it is perhaps this shift that marks the real revolutionary change that CPDRC audiences notice. The inmates' physical movements embody their remoulding as social subjects; what is normally invisible in the outside world – this shaping of human subjects – is made visible within CPDRC and beyond through YouTube videos.

CPDRC's *Thriller* viral video – precisely through its inbuilt shareable, sticky features – becomes a technology of power, of social control over real individuals who reside at the other side of the world. Significantly, CPDRC's *Thriller* has established the ideal conditions for panoptical power to manifest itself through both ocular *and* aural surveillance. The ubiquitous presence of video cameras must produce a knowledge among inmates that they are potentially under surveillance at any given time, thus their behaviour is likely to be altered by that knowledge of a potential global gaze upon them. After 'The Algorithm March' evolved into intricately choreographed, mandatory routines, Garcia reported to any and every visiting media representative that prison violence subsided, the inmates' health improved and recidivism rates dramatically decreased (Seno 2008). Yet neither the CPDRC nor the Cebu government have validated such statements with any evidence, quantifiable or other, to verify these claims. Press interviews with Byron Garcia, (former) Governor Gwendolyn Garcia and one or two sanctioned, lead-dancing inmates defend to the media Garcia's belief that mandatory dance is a favourable form of incarceration.[11] Indeed, Garcia consistently denies any claims of abuse towards the inmates in forcing them all to participate in the routines. 'Nobody forces them [the inmates]', Garcia states in a 2007 interview; 'They dance because they *want* to dance' (Garcia qtd in Campbell 2007, italics added). In this statement, like many others he made, Garcia reinforces the happy and innately musical Filipino trope by implying that dancing to pop anthems is accepted as a willing, even natural form of expression for incarcerated men and women in the Philippines.

As an early internet viral video, CPDRC's *Thriller*'s novelty is easy to decipher. The audiovisual incongruity of watching scores of allegedly hardened criminals dancing to pop and disco soundtracks yields potentially comic results. Yet some critics argue that the novelty of the programme simply misses the point. In one media report, criminal justice professor Edward Latessa attests that more appropriate programmes including 'substance abuse or family reunification programmes should be implemented with such coordination and vigor' (Ferran 2007) as the dance programme has been initiated.[12] One of the critical issues surrounding CPDRC's *Thriller* and subsequent programme lies in the act of providing leisure opportunities in the guise of rehabilitation that ultimately may do more harm than good. To read CPDRC's *Thriller* in this light, while dance helps pass the time and can bring ensuing internet fame, perhaps it does little to train or educate the majority of inmates in the transferable skills needed to help them restart their lives after release. Thus, a boundary between the glorification and humiliation of (suspected) criminals is in danger of being crossed through the CPDRC dance and tourism programme. The commercialization and internet mediation of the Dancing Inmates, as well as the live monthly performances in Cebu, becomes dangerous as they run the risk of alienating local Cebuano residents who see alleged perpetrators of crime being celebrated internationally. Families who reside in the area express distaste at the tourist attraction on behalf of the victims of crime. 'Busing in tourists to see [the Dancing Inmates]', local Mariana Reyes declares, 'rewards them for the actions that led to their incarceration' (Alesevich 2013). Although CPDRC inmates are presumed innocent by law, in practice their continued incarceration, often up to six years for a large population of inmates, amounts to guilt for many locals. And at the end of the day, many of the inmates' continued incarceration in this detention centre speaks only to the grave poverty most CPDRC inmates face.

The distinct viral power and subsequent prison economy generated by *Thriller* clearly serves the interests of the Philippine state. The inmates' dance is endlessly repeated on YouTube, amusing viewers and in doing so distracting them from the overall reality of Philippine prison life where many prisoners live in cruel, inhuman and degrading conditions with acute overcrowding and insufficient food. Furthermore, it reduces CPDRC inmates to a single, entertaining image that obscures the wider, more complex and ultimately unjust picture – that CPDRC inmates have been detained for up to six years awaiting trial, amid political and socio-economic power struggles, in a penal system that is abysmally slow. The inmates' captivating video performances as seemingly happy, cheerful and content Filipino prisoners is their double-edged sword. As we become increasingly conditioned to live in a 'Broadcast Yourself' society, where fame itself is enough reward, the resulting benign projection and banal mediation of the inmates through YouTube clearly undermines the integrity of this 'rehabilitation' programme.

INTERLUDE FIVE

Michael Jackson, the undead and the posthumous duet

Clad in a gold jacket, white T-shirt, and maroon trousers with a diamante-encrusted gold belt, Michael Jackson sings and moonwalks across the MGM Grand Arena stage with grace and ease, promoting his latest single, 'Slave to the Rhythm', at the 2014 Billboard Music Awards show (Jackson 2014). Jackson's signature vocal yelps are supported by a tight five-piece band, and sixteen backing dancers, who twirl across the stage before moving down to the audience, skipping through the Grand Arena's aisles. The official Vevo filmographers follow the dancers, relaying the event to viewers at home via YouTube's Michael Jackson Vevo partnership. The cameras switch over to shots of the audience, who appear enraptured by the multimodal, multidimensional performance. The camera pans to the right, and we see some members of the audience are moved to tears. Why? Because it is 2014 – five years after Jackson's death – and this crowd have the honour of witnessing Michael Jackson's first posthumous 'live' performance.

In the six months, and multi-million dollars it took to plan, choreograph and film this four-minute performance, the King of Pop's likeness was technologically re-produced using pioneering Pulse Evolution and Tricycle Logic programming to create a 'digital or synthetic human' (Kravets 2014). The creators sought to produce a performance in the style of 'classic Michael' (Gallo 2014), but without any input from Michael Jackson himself. A conflation of time-travel, advanced projection technology and pop mythology, this holographic Jackson appears as if in his thirties, moonwalking across the stage while, paradoxically, frozen in time. To meet the public's apparent substantial demand for continuing Jackson posthumous performances, Michael was re-made as a synthetic human by a team of employees that included the estate of Michael Jackson, his lawyer and advisor John Branca, various choreographers and associates (see Gallo 2014; Kravets 2014). Sitting in a boardroom, most likely, Michael Jackson 2.0 was re-built from scratch. Jackson's subsequent Billboard performance appears to us as an exercise in liminality – a porous (re-)presentation of past, present and future. Unbeknownst to Jackson himself, Michael Jackson died to bring us (the) new *live*.

Death no longer curbs live musical performance, it seems. Nor does it diminish interest, or expectations, for continuing performativity. Rather, the growing trend of incorporating hologram technology into large-scale concerts leads to a certain re-conceptualization of 'liveness' (Auslander 1999), and highlights the fact that 'everything that appears on stage has a pre-history: it originates in other places and times, and in this sense, is always-already *mediated*' (Kjus and Danielsen 2016: 322). Hologram performances, at the very least, raise deep concerns for artists whose likeness may be harvested and utilized posthumously. Since Tupac Shakur's holographic rise from the dead in 2012, scholars and journalists have started to ponder what this growing trend might mean for recording artists. In late capitalism, the 'dead are *highly* productive', announced Jason Stanyek and Benjamin Piekut (2010: 14, italics added). For what is truly 'late' about late capitalism may be the novel 'arrangements of interpenetration between worlds of living and dead' – what Stanyek and Piekut call 'technologies of the intermundane' (2010: 14). Jackson's posthumous performance of 'Slave to the Rhythm' highlights how such technologies lie between bio- and necroworlds, centred on social, economic, cultural and affective worlds where the living participate with the dead in an inter-handling, mutually effective co-labouring, of which music in particular has witnessed a growing market for the 'dead talent' (2010: 14–15). Michael Jackson's 2014 all-singing, all-dancing hologram reminds us that live music performances and their recorded counterparts always operate through the logics of 'remediation' (Bolter and Grusin 2000). Indeed Jackson's hologram and the CPDRC's *Thriller* illustrate the impressive productivity new technology affords and encourages, as we witness growing arrays of interpenetrations between the living, the dead and society's growing number of individuals – and the institutionalization of the socially dead.[1]

Dangerous Mediations hinges on these blurred boundaries between life and death, between freedom and captivity, between living life to the fullest and a diminishing, social death. Through this lens, CPDRC's *Thriller* performance is a sort of cyber-marriage between analogue (dance) and digital (online mediation), between media old and new. And following Jackson's death in 2009, CPDRC's *Thriller* becomes a posthumous duet between the inmates (living a social death) and Michael Jackson (deceased yet immortalized through his music). Death springs forth new life, in strange and sometimes estranged ways, and Jackson's untimely death becomes a fitting reminder for the continued life and legacy that remains imbued within his music.

CHAPTER FIVE

Thrilling

Remediating *Thriller*

Why **Thriller**? *Thrill the world legacy*

It's a Saturday evening coming up to Halloween, and I'm picking up groceries in my neighbourhood supermarket in Marikina, a smaller city in Metro Manila, when I stumble upon a crowd of zombies and Michael Jackson look-a-likes congregating outside my local mall. A small stage has appeared in the Riverbanks Mall outdoor amphitheatre, adorned with a 'Thrill the World Philippines 2012' tarpaulin banner, and framed by giant posters of Michael Jackson through the years – from his Jackson 5 youthful Afro, to the *Thriller*-era Jheri curls. The arrival of local camera crews only add to the air of anticipation. At almost 7.00 pm, it's already dark, yet the Manila climate retains its incredible humidity. Nonetheless, my neighbours – of all ages and genders – are wearing Halloween costumes alongside variations of red 'Thriller' jackets, single white gloves, white ankle socks, hats and sunglasses, as they moonwalk across the stage (Figures 5.1, 5.2 and 5.3). A Michael Jackson dance-battle is up first, followed by the best-dressed King of Pop competition, or so I'm told by one of the organizers Dee Margaux Santiago, CEO and President of the Michael Jackson Filipino Fans Club Worldwide. At 3.00 am, after hours of rehearsals in between the dwindling on-stage entertainment, the event culminates in a collective performance of *Thriller* filmed by local news agents TV5. Timed to be performed in unison with global 'Thrill the World' communities, everyone present is invited – indeed expected – to participate in the communal, transnational *Thriller* dance.

Thriller's legacy is perhaps best surmised in this annual *Thrill the World* event, an international dance phenomenon launched in October 2007 by

FIGURE 5.1 *Participants battle it out in the Michael Jackson Dance-Off, Thrill the World 2012, Marikina, Metro Manila, 27 October 2012.* © Photo: Author.

FIGURE 5.2 *A 'Smooth Criminal' era Michael Jackson fan.* © Photo: Author.

FIGURE 5.3 *A Filipino youth in his red, homemade 'Thriller' jacket.* © Photo: Author.

Canadian dance instructor and Michael Jackson fan, Ines Markeljevic.[1] Simultaneously functioning as a zombie fancy-dress party, charity fundraiser and an attempt to break the world record for the largest simultaneous dance to *Thriller*, the event seeks out a broader goal than dancing alone. Rather, *Thrill the World* strives to promote 'unity among all the peoples of the world, humanitarianism and environmental stewardship ... as Michael continues to inspire the world to do so' (Thrill the World ABQ, n.d.). Every October thousands of people, from Manila to Miami, congregate at their local dance studios, recreational parks and gymnasiums to dance the *Thriller* in thirteen minutes of corporeal unison. For some Americans taking part, *Thriller* has become akin to a national dance. 'I realised that "Thriller" is like the national choreography of the United States,' *Thrill the World* enthusiast Shawn Sides claims. 'I'm so excited that there's this choreography in the world that our entire nation recognises' (Croft 2008). As coordinator of the Austin, Texas branch of *Thrill the World,* Sides succinctly summarizes the power vested in Michael Jackson's *Thriller*: the *Thriller* dance is the most central feature of the music video because it triggers real, physical movement from audiences the world over.

Given the international impact of Michael Jackson and *Thriller*, and his especially active fan communities in the Philippines as the Manila 'Thrill the World' example above illustrates, it may seem nearly redundant to ask why the CPDRC inmates danced *Thriller* in the first place. A more appropriate question might be: why not? *Thriller* has enjoyed lasting influence across music and popular culture around the world, and so this chapter maps the exceptional cultural history of *Thriller* as it exists across multiple planes. Stretching from the single, the album, the short film, the dance and, of course, the legacy of Michael Jackson himself, I show that by performing, recording and uploading their mass-scale interpretation of *Thriller* on to YouTube, the CPDRC inmates were effectively guaranteed widespread attention. Emerging from the specific music and YouTube context discussed in Chapter 1, adding to that its distinct sociocultural Filipino heritage from Chapter 2 and connection to a long history of performances of punishment presented in Chapters 3 and 4, this chapter contextualizes 'Thriller' and develops Jackson's monster metaphors to shed a light on its power as a remediated text. To do this, I take up a discussion of *Thriller* from where Kobena Mercer left off – that is, I extend Mercer's analysis of Jackson's musicality and address what his essay could not cover. Overlooked in terms of academic discourse, with most writing focusing on his sensationalized 'crazy' lifestyle, multiple legal scandals and somewhat fluid gender, sexual and 'racial identity' (George 2010: 12), serious writing about Jackson's artistry, his music and his pioneering short films only started to appear after his death on 25 June 2009. As a singer, songwriter, dancer, actor, businessman and philanthropist, the King of Pop is widely acknowledged for his vast contributions to music, dance and fashion. Yet I follow Joseph Vogel's belief that a crucial part of Jackson's legacy that deserves attention lies in his 'pioneering role as an African-American artist working in an industry still plagued by segregation, stereotypical representations, or little representation at all' (Vogel 2012). This aspect of Jackson's legacy that I see CPDRC's *Thriller* pushing forward, as their YouTube videos counter stereotypical representations of prisoners as subjugated, and offer new perspectives on what it is to be imprisoned in our digitized, networked world. Indeed the many YouTube interpretations of *Thriller* that followed CPDRC's video together demonstrate the effectiveness of Jackson's artistry in creating a work that continues to be relevant to a twenty-first-century audience.

In what follows, I present an intertextual, cultural history of 'Thriller', taking into account the vast structural changes from the single to the song's music video adaptation, as well as the crucial choreographed sequence, which has until quite recently gone unnoticed by music scholars.[2] I offer a close reading of Michael Jackson's *Thriller* to better illuminate the ancestral line of CPDRC's viral video, and posit that CPDRC's *Thriller* from 2007 marks a music video milestone in the history of popular culture, similar in effect, to the impact Jackson's original 1983 *Thriller* had on shaping popular music and global culture. While the history of music video certainly pre-dates Michael Jackson – arguably as far back as the very first sound film, *The Jazz Singer* (1927), for just one absolutely crucial example – the impact of *Thriller* still reverberates today. Songs from *Thriller* are credited with the breaking down of colour barriers on radio and television, imbuing popular music with the visual in innovative ways like never before, perfecting the art of music video and, as a result, shaping subsequent MTV practice. The original and remediated *Thriller*s unite important issues surrounding the decline of the recording industries, shifting spans of attention, the ubiquitous fusion of the audio with the visual, the increase in user-generated musical events and an accelerating globalization. CPDRC's *Thriller,* and the subsequent remediated performances since, remind us that remediation is never a one-way street. This calls to mind Bolter and Grusin's assertion that immediacy and hypermediacy are part of the double logic of remediation. In the ensuing section, I survey the many ways 'Thriller' has been adopted and adapted by millions of people around the world since the release of the music video *Thriller* in 1983, to illustrate how CPDRC's *Thriller* is but one of a great many *Thriller* remediations that live online. From youth groups dancing on the streets of Manila to record-breaking zombie flash mobs in Mexico, the wide variety of mediated *Thriller*s examined are merely the tip of the proverbial iceberg among YouTube's colossal, ever-shifting archive. In the concluding section I comment on the apparent growth in both public and private practices of *Thriller* adaptations, which in tandem with advancing personal video technology, has resulted in a near endless number of *Thriller* remediations archived and available on a host of internet platforms.

Rewrite, restructure, remediate: From single to short film

Thriller, the music video, is widely understood as playing a crucial role in Jackson's global dissemination and record-breaking chart success.[3] Mercer's article on the music video's 'monster metaphors' of race and the audiovisual remains the first and only close reading of *Thriller* as music video, and successfully demonstrated the need for contextualized readings of Jackson's works. In what remains, I provide an audiovisual overview of *Thriller* building on from where Mercer left off. I further contextualize and highlight what I consider to be the primary tropes that enable *Thriller* to be easily and fluidly transformed and remediated by vast populations, as an auditory but for the most part, as an embodied, multimodal text. In 1979, Quincy Jones approached British songwriter and producer Rodney L. Temperton with an invitation to write some tracks for Michael Jackson's then forthcoming album *Off the Wall*. After this successful alliance, Temperton continued the collaboration and wrote the title track of *Thriller*, purportedly under Jones's strict specifications (George 2010: 107). Structurally, 'Thriller' is based on a four-to-the-floor bass riff that is repeated for most of the song (Figure 5.4), and functions as one of the main hooks that catches – and keeps – our attention on the track. Among the many digitized, compressed and remediated *Thriller*s that appear on YouTube and their often reduced audio quality (as discussed in the latter of this chapter), this bass riff is sometimes all that can be clearly deciphered. The incredibly catchy walking bassline, followed by three syncopated beats instantly evokes the funky, R&B bassline of Rick James's 'Give It to Me Baby'. Released the year before 'Thriller', James's main two-bar, four-note bass riff is repeated for most of the song (see Figure 5.5).

The energetic bass riff heard in 'Thriller' owes much to R&B, funk and soul traditions and can indeed be considered 'infectious', to borrow Barbara Browning's use of the metaphor (1998). The infectious rhythm of this riff is precisely what invites the body to dance, to move and sway to its beat and it has become the organism that travels through online social networks, spreading into communities and resulting in flashmobs (as we soon shall see).

'Thriller', which appeared as the fourth of nine tracks on *Thriller*, was the seventh and final single to be released from Jackson's *Thriller* album.[4] Quite a stark contrast following the September release of *Thriller*'s sixth single, the lighthearted 'P.Y.T. (Pretty Young Thing)', Jackson sought to make *Thriller* a completely different experience for the music industry. Most aspects of *Thriller*'s inception, production and dissemination mark it as exceptional in terms of previous music video and pop music practice. Since the single was released over a year after the album *Thriller*, the single arrived long after

FIGURE 5.4 *Bassline for 'Thriller'. Written by Rod Temperton, performed by Michael Jackson, recorded between 14 April and 8 November 1982, released 30 November 1982. © Temperton/Jackson/Epic/CBS Records.*

FIGURE 5.5 *Bass riff for 'Give It to Me Baby' by Rick James, released 20 February 1981. © James/Gordy Records.*

the album's success had been formally recognized and financially validated. Thus the music video for 'Thriller' was tasked with serving a vastly different purpose to *Thriller*'s first single 'The Girl is Mine'. *Thriller*'s exceptional chart success gradually – and inevitably – began to wane by the summer of 1983, some eighteen months after its release. And so Jackson set his sights on creating a third music video from the album to reignite public interest in *Thriller*, based on the tried and tested formula for boosting album sales following the release of *Thriller*'s previous two music videos. Up to this point, the album had been in the Top 10 charts for almost a year, produced a string of Number 1 singles as well as two immensely successful videos, 'Billie Jean' and 'Beat It'. *Thriller* was already deemed a colossal success in the eyes of the record company, who consequently refused to finance a third music video that was widely considered to be an unnecessary vanity project for Jackson.[5]

The soundtrack to Jackson's *Thriller* music video is an exemplar of a highly successful pop remix, acting as a precursor to the many *Thriller* remixes and remediations that would follow in the years to come. Together, Jackson and director John Landis's vision of *Thriller* pushed the boundaries by augmenting the song and extended the already longer-than-average pop single (five minutes, fifty-nine seconds) to make it a substantially longer thirteen minutes and forty-two seconds. This deviation from conventional pop music practice is just the beginning of understanding how *Thriller*'s audiovisual extension might validate Jackson's assertion for it to be called a short film rather than a traditional music video. The re-conceptualization of *Thriller* by way of a significant audio remix, stretching the single version to over twice its duration, means that consequently, in contrast to standard music video practice of that era, two distinct yet official audio-recorded versions of *Thriller* exist.[6] The two differing audio versions of 'Thriller' are often taken for granted; yet the effect of extending the song to over twice its original duration has, in itself, interesting sonic repercussions.[7] The original song is composed in a somewhat conventional, if elongated, pop song tradition: verse, chorus, verse, chorus, bridge, verse, chorus and a spoken section before the end. Meanwhile the original song is completely restructured and remixed to accommodate the short film. The shift in order of appearance and inclusion of additional incidental music in the second version confirm that the musical and sonic structure of *Thriller*'s short film is at odds with conventional music video practice up to that point, which traditionally served to advertise the song as originally recorded.

A closer examination of the restructuring of the song and inclusion of extra-musical sounds, as well as the additional incidental score, composed by renowned Hollywood film composer Elmer Bernstein, reveal how *Thriller*'s short film soundtrack functions in a variety of ways to additionally frame *Thriller*'s film-within-a-film meta-narrative. The inclusion of the distinctive sound of the Pacific Tree Frog's 'ribbit ribbit' at 0.22 minutes into the short film, for example, serves to sonically 'place' or situate the listener within a Hollywood setting, before the on-screen narrative plays out this sub-plot.[8] As a consequence, *Thriller*'s film-within-a-film is both visually *and* audibly discernible. Consciously or subconsciously, it is the sonic rather than visual qualities that signal to audiences the fact that *Thriller*'s opening scene is a Hollywood motion picture within a music video set-up. The short film opens with Bernstein's incidental music (or 'scary music' as it is credited at the end of the film), which includes excerpts most likely to be leftovers from his soundtrack to *An American Werewolf in London* (1981) – compositions that were not included in the final film. In particular, this so-called scary music clearly draws from the introductory motif from Bernstein's track 'Metamorphosis'.[9] Following the so-called scary music and dialogue, the 'song' begins with verse one, followed successively by verses two and three without hearing the chorus at all. The verses are then followed by Vincent Price's two verses of *Sprechgesang*, before stopping suddenly with Bernstein's incidental music returning at 8.02, until the signature 'Thriller' groove returns almost thirty seconds later. Suspense builds and builds throughout the short film, and finally, almost ten minutes in, we are finally rewarded with the very first iteration of the 'Thriller' chorus. It is repeated twice more consecutively, before further interplays between Bernstein's score, the 'Thriller' groove, and Price's extended evil laugh. In the following final credits the chorus is reprised thrice more. 'Thriller' is extraordinary because of this duality. While the song-as-single adopted a typical verse-chorus structure associated with pop songs, the accompanying short film 'rejects this normative sequence in its coherent pursuit of a fresh narrative' (Wiley 2012: 112).

All this is to say that *Thriller* broke the mould by establishing an utterly different function from music videos that had come before. In a sense, Jackson's *Thriller* pioneered the idea that a music video could be a veritable victory lap – a precursor to the short films and visual albums we are now accustomed to in the era of the Lady Gaga and Beyoncé's 'Telephone' (2010), Beastie Boys' 'Fight for Your Right' (2011), Kanye West's *Runaway* (2010) and Beyoncé's *Lemonade* (2016) to name a few. This reinforces Mercer's (1986) argument that the *Thriller* music video presented a short film commemorating the album's already-established success rather than serving as a faithful advertisement for the single, in contrast to the customs of music videos of the time. Freeing up the music video from these previous confines enabled *Thriller* to experiment with novel collaborations between the movie and music industries by bringing Landis and Jackson together as co-auteurs. The accompanying *Making of Thriller* documentary (dir. Kramer 1983) that was given ample airplay on MTV and Showtime, though motivated by financial necessity, served to set a new precedence in terms of synergetic, transmedia storytelling, allowing audiences to learn more about the filmmaking process and catch a carefully curated glimpse of Jackson himself. Taken together, the excessive range of *Thriller*'s multimedia outputs significantly raised the profile of what a music video was, changed future possibilities of what a music video could be and lay solid foundations for what remediated music video would become.

Choreographing Thriller: Parody, play and politics

At their most fundamental, music videos serve as moving images that move us, affectively and effectively. Embedded deep within popular culture's psyche, the *Thriller* choreography represents the 'most important communal dance of the last three decades' (George 2010: 107), and arguably the 'most performed choreography – by choreographers, professional dancers, and the general public alike – of all time' (Mkrdichian 2009: 2). Tony Award-winning choreographer Michael Peters, who had previously choreographed Donna Summer's 'Love to Love You Baby' (1975) and worked with Jackson in choreographing Bob Giraldi's visualization of 'Beat It', was invited to collaborate with Jackson on the subsequent short film. Central to this music film's success is the now infamous zombie dance sequence, created in a partnership between Peters and Jackson. In an interview originally broadcast in July 2009 on VH1, Jackson revealed the delicate approach required to create a dance for zombies and monsters that maintained an air of sincerity that did not descend into complete hilarity. Jackson explains how he playfully collaborated with choreographer Michael Peters, and together they imagined how zombies might move 'by making faces in the mirror'. He continues:

> I used to come to rehearsal sometimes with monster makeup on, and I loved doing that. So he and I collaborated and we both choreographed the piece and I thought it should start like that kind of thing and go into this jazzy kind of step, you know. Kind of gruesome things like that, not too much ballet or whatever. (Jackson qtd in Reid 2009)

The resulting original choreographic routine, in which Peters also featured as one of the zombie dancers, is notable for its unusual rhythm and complex combination of sequences. Ten years after its release, the dance is recognized as a 'sophisticated blend of musical theatre and pop values' (Dunning 1994).

Quincy Jones remembers his experience of making *Thriller*, and its impact over a year after the album's release:

> In my perspective, Michael and MTV rode it [the short film] to glory. At last, 14 months after *Thriller* came out, the video for 'Thriller' [the song]

came out – it had 10 cameras, nobody had seen anything like this. We were fearless! You have to know you're just a terminal being used by a higher power. It's not about us. (Jones qtd in Reid 2009)

Thriller was not about 'us' mere mortals. Jackson's insistence on producing a third, and initially considered excessive, video was then, perhaps, about something more – about conveying a 'higher' message that went beyond that of a vanity project. The original album version of 'Thriller', written entirely by Temperton, delivered somewhat vague pop lyrics centred around a literary pun on 'thrill' (Mercer 1986), while the sound and structure reified a somewhat standard verse–chorus convention. To convey a sense of authenticity and meaning through 'Thriller' then, Jackson was forced to use 'non-verbal vocalisations' – the hiccup, the beat-boxing, the pitched screams, the 'Hee-hees' – to bring the song to life, as Mats Johansson observed (2012: 271). Jackson's intertextual borrowings from African-American and soul music heritage facilitated an in-depth interpretation of Temperton's lyrics – his use of soul and Motown inflections, such as the frequent improvised vocalizations in between verses, and as an underlying countermelody to Price's *Sprechgesang*. As others have argued, the non-verbal vocalizations both pay homage to African-American vocal stylings, but also serve as a 'stylised form of blackness that doesn't threaten mainstream white audiences' (Campbell 2003: 22; Johansson 2012; Wiley 2012).

The film's multiple transformation sequences – the fantastical and realist metamorphosis from boyfriend to werewolf to zombie – and the film-within-a-film scenes, remind us how music videos function as very concrete acts of remediation. Music videos like *Thriller* borrow audiovisual cues from the silver screen and the stage, as well as vice versa, representing 'one medium within another', taking great pains and elaborate editing to create a sense of immediacy, liveness and apparently spontaneous style (Bolter and Grusin 2000: 9). Retrospectively, these scenes imply that the film's 'entire opening sequence was a film within a film (or rather, a film within the video)' (Mercer 1986: 44). As we listen to the production of meanings in the music track, the various voices involved in the process (Jackson, Temperton, Price, Quincy Jones) are audibly combined into parodic play, as Mercer suggests. One way of approaching this transition from the song to the visual, in addition to Landis's obvious directorial voice, is through discovering the meaning that Peters and Jackson's dance brings to *Thriller*. Hence it appears that creating a short, music film for *Thriller* was crucial because it allowed Jackson to root and represent the song kinaesthetically, as a form of embodied black tradition and culture, through carefully devised choreographic sequences that blend as many styles and genres as the music itself.

Parody and play are central concepts to understanding *Thriller*. As a form of indirect and double-voiced discourse, parodic voices work together while remaining distinct in their defining difference, as Linda Hutcheon (2000: xiv) explains. The logic of parody is fixed on an unambiguous self-consciousness, and in *Thriller* parody lies in dramatic dialogue, dated dress and playful acting style. Parody is also found in *Thriller*'s acknowledgement that there is no narrative as such, rather a 'simulacrum of a story in its stylistic send-up of genre conventions' (Mercer 1986: 44). While the film continues to provocatively play on the meaning of the word 'thriller', further meaning is construed if we consider the 1950s era that is being parodied in the film's opening. As the American Civil Rights Movement gained momentum, the 1950s is remarkable for being a period of extreme violence against black Americans, including the continued murder and lynching of black men.[10] To be a young, black man in 1950s America perhaps veered towards life-threatening rather than the thrilling – a fact that seems equally, appallingly, relevant at the time of writing, as news of increasing US gun violence and police brutality that disproportionately affect American men of colour at a truly alarming rate.

Thriller's opening homage to the 1950s therefore operates on two levels: first, as an audiovisual jibe on Hollywood thrillers, and second, a wordplay on the many meanings of 'thrill' across a range of social, cultural, historical, violent and/or romantic contexts. More crucially, though, everything about *Thriller*'s audiovisual experience is deeply political: it connects to a lived history whereby large populations of the US experienced the everyday anxiety of oppression, routine terror and quotidian horror. The original short film *Thriller* operates as a mode of meaning-making on many levels, understood as an affective, transcendental text by the ever-increasing volume of *Thriller* adaptations performed on street corners and inside bedrooms, and relayed to us on social media screens.

May I have this dance? Remediating *Thriller* in everyday life

Why do we dance? To celebrate, to mourn, to heal, to give thanks, to preserve cultural heritage, to assert individuality, to provoke or to entertain? For some, dance is a potentially humiliating activity and dancing to club hits like no one is watching is a 'high-risk guilty pleasure' (Miller 2014). For others, to dance is to show off one's physical fitness, coordination, a form of display for attracting and selecting a mate – 'a vertical expression of a horizontal desire', as the old adage goes. As a solo act or performance with friends, dance embodies 'an ideological way of listening; it draws in our attention ... to dance to music is not just to move to it but to *say* something about it' (Frith 1996: 224). In this section, I focus on subsequent *Thrillers*' many dancing bodies to investigate precisely what it is that this wealth of online remediated *Thriller* videos 'say'. As such, I demonstrate the various multifaceted ways in which *Thriller* has permeated and continues to circulate the current mediascape, primarily through its meaningful choreography. My approach here is to examine a series of subgenres of user-generated video treating each *Thriller* remediation as a brief case study. I pay particular attention to those *Thriller* remediations that sit on the fringes of society and those that have received minor attention from mainstream media, such as the subgenre of public 'flash mob dances' and 'home dance videos' that capture everyday activities of the domestic sphere. Providing a brief survey of one of YouTube's dance videos' many subgenres – that of the remediated *Thriller* performance – I argue that these videos construct social and cultural value, as well as display shifting forms of attention across social media practice and participatory culture. New media practices recall old media, as we know, and *Thriller* dance videos are no exception. On the surface, their roots lie in the fundamental act of combining music and dancing in public and domestic settings, whether solo, paired or in groups. The videos also call to mind basic forms of broadcast presentation such as television, or even MTV forms of music videos. However, on closer inspection and in contrast to traditional forms of broadcast media, YouTube's inherent 'conversational character' enables viewers to respond directly to the videos both with their own videos and more commonly with text comments (Burgess and Green 2009).

Social media, mobile communicative and technological affordances today enable large groups to coordinate, acting as a powerful tool in connecting significant numbers of people for various means and to varying ends. One trend that emerged from the mid-2000s of particular relevance to *Thriller* remediations is that of the so-called 'flash mob'.[11] The inventor of the flash mob's early prototype, the 'inexplicable mob', Bill Wasik, wrote that we face an inherent paradox at the turn of the twenty-first century, whereby our personal technology (laptops, smartphones, browsers, apps) does 'everything it can to keep us *out* of crowds' (Wasik 2011). Wasik's 2003 social experiments, combined with Larry Niven's science fiction imaginings of a 'flash crowd', led to the term 'flash mob' being coined by Sean Savage, a UC Berkeley graduate student who blogged about Wasik's experiments as they took place (Wasik 2011; Nicholson 2005). Wasik stressed the physical transformative power rendered through the act of flash mobbing, which he believed was intrinsically bound up with political expression:

> People intuitively understand that it is a powerful thing to very quickly and surprisingly transform a physical space, and one reason they keep coming back to the mobs is there is this feeling that something is being created that can't be ignored. (Harmon 2003)

Flash-mob dances became increasingly popular through a symbiotic relationship with advancing video-sharing technology. YouTube's arrival in 2005 helped firmly launch – through the power of documentation and online archiving – a more widespread movement as more and more online videos featuring mass ensembles of individuals dancing the hallmark *Thriller* choreography appeared online. Some of the larger mass dances are organized to be flash mobs in the strict sense, that is surprise events taking place in public, both in outdoor locations such as parks, playgrounds and town squares as well as indoor malls, supermarkets and sports arenas, much to the bemusement and/or great annoyance of passers-by.

Other large-scale *Thriller* performances are strictly coordinated with mainstream media in tow, and are performed to an expectant audience, such as the Los Angeles 'Thrill the World' *Thriller* performance (2009), the successful Mexican attempt to break the world record for the most people dancing to *Thriller* (with 13,957 officially registered dancers according to Guinness Worlds Records 2009), and the large-scale Chilean flash-mob protest against governmental education cutbacks (Diaz 2011). Many smaller-scale *Thriller* dances appear in private residences, while organized and publicized *Thriller*s occur in public and semi-private locations such as hospitals, retirement homes, underground trains, cruise ships, hotel lobbies, at wedding receptions and high school proms (see, for example, Camden Springs 2012; Children's Hospital Colorado 2012; Short 2013). These collective *Thriller* dances continue to draw crowds, and with the rise of citizen-journalists such events are frequently recorded, edited, deposited and viewed from digital platforms like YouTube. From Baku to Baguio and Bristol, and from San Francisco to Stockholm, these videos illustrate how *Thriller* has certainly become the most performed choreographed dance in the world.

'Thriller' in the mirror: Remediating dances of domesticity

Far from being an exclusively public, large-scale phenomenon, small-scale domestic performances of *Thriller* appear just as frequently in YouTube's back catalogue. This pervasive genre of intimate videos highlights the lived reality of the camera as prophesied (and glorified) in Vertov's *A Man with the Movie Camera*: the camera can be anywhere, with superhuman vision, and provide close-ups of any object. Adapting Richard Chalfen's term 'home mode' that refers to the amateur filmmaker's representation of the private world of the domicile, home mode footage comprises material made, if not necessarily within the home, then dealing primarily with 'the home' – the domestic and the familial (Pini 2009: 71). The category I designate 'home dance videos' are those recorded performances that are uploaded online, primarily to the user-generated site YouTube (and related platforms such as Vimeo, Vine, Instagram, Snapchat). In home dance videos, individuals (or small groups) play back pop songs in private, often domestic space, dance to them, record and actively share these performances with the wider world through dissemination on social media sites. These homemade videos construct a kind of 'ordinariness', as the home is displayed as a domestic yet theatre-like space. These awkward shots in front of kitchen cupboards, in dimly lit bedrooms or framed by chintzy curtains serve to construct a sense of liveness or co-presence, inviting interaction from the viewer's home to the dancers, even though, of course, none of these videos are actually 'live'. Set against YouTube's self-conscious self-referentiality, these videos – like many of their flash-mob counterparts – appear to us dark and grainy, habitually captured on camera-phones and low-resolution webcams. But unlike the large-scale *Thriller* performances, these videos are widely ignored outright (as comprehended by generally low view-counts, mostly in double digits) or quickly dismissed by the culturati as inconsequential, narcissistic and/or vulgar. They are not taken seriously because they are not seen as serious, or in a great many cases, remain utterly unseen at all.

When examined collectively, the broad overview of *Thriller* home dance YouTube videos reveals some noticeable shifts in cultural practice. Four broad categories of home dance videos emerge:

1. The solo, 'private', *Thriller* rehearsal;
2. The instructional, educational *Thriller* video;
3. The family, home-movie style *Thriller* video, featuring babies, children, grandparents and even pets;
4. Intergenerational *Thriller* gameplay videos, post-December 2010, after the release of the music video game *Michael Jackson: The Experience*.

Through enacting an aspect of *Thriller*, the domestic sphere is here transformed into a multi-functional space, however fleeting. Through a dance step, a fancy costume, or even a simple gesture, these videos capture something that goes beyond the domicile: the humble living room is transformed into a dance studio, a classroom, a playroom – a place of intimacy, of learning, of the extraordinary and the everyday experience. While these categories are not necessarily mutually exclusive nor intended to be exhaustive, they outline the various functions that *Thriller* dances, and *Thriller* dance videos, continue to play in the everyday lived experience. They trace a gradual shift in markedly different dance practices, especially through the introduction of *Thriller* in the music video game *Michael Jackson: The Experience*. Initially released in November 2010 for Nintendo DS, PlayStation Portable and Wii, these gamified *Thriller* dance videos usually depict one, two or three dancers facing a flat-screen television, dancing primarily with their arms – not unlike the chair dancers of Merrill Gardens Retirement Community – a trend that has undoubtedly introduced many younger audiences to Jackson's music, albeit through a significant adaptation of Peters' infamous choreography.

Together, these *Thriller* home dance videos directly call to mind Walter Benjamin's assertion towards the shift in characteristics of modernity, whereby the camera's close-ups serve to satisfy the desires of the contemporary 'masses to bring things "closer" spatially and humanly, which is just as ardent as their bent towards overcoming the uniqueness of every reality by accepting its reproduction' (1969: 223). These once live performances are recreated in YouTube's mass-media platforms, and distributed as mass media through YouTube, circumventing and manipulating time and space so that the past becomes the present, what was geographically distant is rendered intimate, but paradoxically, what was once large-scale is made miniscule. As such we can understand such remediated *Thriller* videos as directly illustrative of the technologies of new media as predicted by Benjamin (1969; see also Auslander 1999; Manovich 2001). These *Thriller* videos further highlight how the lived musical experience – that is, how art and music is practised in the everyday – finds its being, not in its unique presence, but in its omnipresence, and constant instantaneous availability.

Conclusion

Although the wide range of YouTube *Thriller* videos seem to promote an escape from reality, through the transcendental act of dancing to the song as well as their mediation and digital transmission, ultimately they demonstrate a very real sense of liveness as a concept of both presence *and* mediation, whereby the live and the mediatized co-exist in a close relationship. In the *Thriller* home dance videos, these self-conscious, coupled performances often break the fourth wall in one sense as we see the dancer set up the track, before physically stepping away from the record button. Habitually, the dancers speak directly to the camera's imagined audience at the beginning or end of the performance, verbally expressing thanks for watching, encouraging or demonstrating an appreciation for comments and feedback – communicating to everyone and no one through their moves. All the while the performances remain carefully framed within a home video framework, as these dancers are filming themselves in a domestic setting, often free from the full-length mirrors that professional dance studios have that would enable a clear study of their bodies and movements. Thus through introducing a gap between self and world, these *Thriller*s become a method of meaning-making that facilitate a detachment required for any relation to the self. 'Various technical apparatuses – from the quill to the webcam', Peters and Seier note, 'place the self at a distance and at the same time bridge that distance to the extent that they make it accessible, and accessible for alteration' (2009: 390). For these home video *Thriller* dancers, the playback of recorded video *is* their rehearsal; the screen serves as their domesticated, remediated mirror. A process of remediation takes place in the reconfigured home of *Thriller* videos, whereby something 'new' is gained and preserved from imitating, quoting and varying 'old(er)' work (Peters and Seier 2009: 394).

A song – any song – can mean more than one thing at any one time, and the range of *Thriller* adaptations presented here, CPDRC's *Thriller* included, offer three revelations. One, they are symptomatic of wider changes from public to private and private to public forms of entertainment by demonstrating the extensive affordances and domestication of surveillance and mobile technology when fused with popular music and dance. Within the variety of home *Thriller* videos, familial spaces transform into sites of collective engagement and collective embodiment. Filmed, photographed, written about and shared online, these *Thriller* dance remediations – whether performed in private homes or in state institutions like prisons and nursing homes – provide glimpses into the lives of others, the banal and the brazen. Two, the 'infectious' spread and circulation of these intertextual texts, when read collectively, produce new aesthetic and political forms that structure the very foundations of YouTube's cultural collection. Each remediation of *Thriller* – the song, the dance, the sartorial statement and so on – borrows the visual, choreographic and musical language from *Thriller*'s 'protein shell' in order to communicate, produce and reproduce new meaning-making. Examined together, *Thriller*'s active and ongoing reimaginings recharge it with a unique and unequalled value in today's society, as it becomes an intergenerational, truly globalized music *and* dance tradition. Three, experiencing each new remediation of *Thriller* attunes us to the process rather than the final product alone. In the case of the many online *Thriller* audiovisual remediations, what is ultimately activated is both a witnessing *and* participation in the process of their own construction.

INTERLUDE SIX

'It's more fun in the Philippines'

We are in the air a matter of minutes before the games begin.
    I should have expected as much. Before booking my flight from Manila to Cebu, I ran a quick, obligatory Google search for any possible alerts on Cebu Pacific airlines. Instead of finding news about their fleet, air safety or punctuation record, I found countless links to YouTube videos of the apparently famous Cebu Pacific singing and dancing cabin crew. Thus I am just a little disappointed that the flight attendants did not bop their way through the safety procedures before departure. I need not have worried. It's no less than ten minutes into the stratosphere when the hum of the plane's engine is almost drowned out by the amplified announcements and peals of laughter as the flight attendants ask for a show of hands from the guests on board, designating those eager to participate in their famous 'Fun Flights' parlour games.[1] Billed as a 'fun in the skies' pop quiz, it involves the skills of speed, general knowledge and particularly good hearing. Passengers are asked a question over the PA system, and the first to raise their hand with the correct answer wins a prize. Being hard-of-hearing rules me out of this competition, and I say goodbye to the prize-winning yellow pen emblazoned with Cebu Pacific's bright logo.
    An arm two rows ahead of me shoots up, fervently waving until the flight attendant makes her way down the aisle to verify his answer. With an atmosphere more akin to that of a children's birthday than a traditional

flight, the attendant gives an emphatic thumbs-up, signalling the contestant's correct answer, upon which the passengers on board break into a modest round of applause. It appears that none of my fellow passengers – even those clearly not participating in the game – seem to mind this mid-flight interruption. Those who've won prizes beam and pose for selfies featuring said prizes on their smartphones, appearing to enjoy the experience the most.

The business of 'fun' is a lucrative one, it seems. Such a novel modus operandi appears to reap rewards for this airline company – their website is now the most visited travel site in the Philippines. Chief executive of Cebu Air, Lance Gokongwei, explains that the reason for the airline's popularity is their 'lighthearted approach', for which he says Filipinos are uniquely known. He elaborates, declaring that '[t]here is a different sense of fun in the Filipino personality – singing, dancing – and the airline reflects this' (de Leon 2011). This 'lighthearted' approach chimes in nicely with the Philippine Department of Tourism international campaign unveiled on social media on 4 January 2012. Released from the official Department of Tourism Twitter account on behalf of Tourism Secretary Ramon Jimenez, the tweet read:

> Starting tmrw all Filipinos will hav a simple truthful ans 2 d question why should I go to the Philippines. 'It's more fun in my country.'

Less than an hour after the campaign was launched by virtue of Twitter, the hashtag #ItsMoreFunInThePhilippines became the top online trending topic in the Philippines and across the world, mediating the unique, lighthearted 'fun Filipino' activities – including singing and dancing – to the global Twitterverse.[2]

'*Maligayang Pagdating sa Pilipinas!*'

Welcome to the Philippines!

CHAPTER SIX

'Together in electric dreams'

Hybridity, nostalgia and imagination in CPDRC

> Today, after more than a century of electric technology, we have extended our central nervous system in a global embrace, abolishing both space and time as far as our planet is concerned. […] As electrically contracted, the globe is no more than a village. Electric speed at bringing all social and political functions together in a sudden implosion has heightened human awareness of responsibility to an intense degree. (McLuhan 1994: 3–5)

> Viewers are asking for more. We may be worlds apart, worlds may separate us, but we still can be connected through electric dreams. (Garcia qtd in *NPR* 2007)

Hot on the trails of *Thriller*'s viral popularity in July 2007, and as a special request from Byron Garcia, the CPDRC performed a dual-function presentation of 'Together in Electric Dreams' in October 2007. The song was chosen by Warden Garcia, first in honour of his sister Governor Gwen Garcia's upcoming 52nd birthday. Second, Warden Garcia wanted to choose a fitting musical tribute the inmates would perform to acknowledge, with heartfelt thanks, their internet audience (Riminton 2007). Garcia picked an emotionally rousing and nostalgic musical choice, and arranged for the inmates to perform stirring new choreography to Paul Oakley and Giorgio Morodor's 'Together in Electric Dreams'. Complete with handclaps, rhythmic shouts that punctuate the verses and an acrobatic middle eight, the performance reached a climax when hundreds of inmates ran into the yard

FIGURES 6.1 AND 6.2 *The flag-waving interlude from Randy Kofahl's YouTube video of CPDRC's 'Together in Electric Dreams' (2008). The close-up shows how the Philippine flag is twice the size and waved twice as high as the flags from other nations.* © *Randy Kofahl.*

waving colourful, handmade flags of the world – each flag made to symbolize the nationalities of their new fans from across the miles (Figures 6.1 and 6.2).[1] 'Together in Electric Dreams', originally released in 1984, is an electro-pop, new wave classic that at the time of its CPDRC debut had endured nearly a quarter of a century of continuing popularity in the Philippines, largely kept alive in the Pinoy pop psyche by appearing as an 'All Time Hit' staple in

Filipino karaoke playlists and videoke song chips, including the Wow Fiesta, Xtreme Magic Sing and Grand Videoke song packages. YouTuber Randy Kofahl's recording of CPDRC's 'Together in Electric Dreams', filmed at the August 2008 live show, reveals the continuing popularity of the electro-pop song as we hear the surrounding CPDRC audience heartily singing along (Kofahl 2008). The voices become particularly animated when Oakley's backing vocals echo back 'Time to go away' in the first verse, so that by the time the song reaches the chorus the off-camera audience can be heard singing along with gusto, replete with cheerful shouts of encouragement.

Though the inmates live behind bars, Warden Garcia firmly believes that Web 2.0 technology has united Filipino inmates with international audiences and fans, some of whom now travel off the beaten track to Cebu to see their performances for themselves. To capture Garcia's appreciation, which he conveys on behalf of the inmates, he specifically chose the saccharine love song, composed by the Human League frontman with the Italian producer's signature synth-pop sound. The song narrates a passionate, futuristic tale of love across space and time, speaking of friendships given and lessons in bravery. Oakley and Moroder's catchy chorus repeatedly celebrates that distance is no deterrent for real love, wistfully set against the strains of 1980s synthesizers, electric guitars and drum-machine beats:

> We'll always be together/However far it seems (Love never ends)
> We'll always be together/Together in electric dreams.

In an interview with *CNN News,* Garcia adapts Oakley and Morodor's sentimental lyrics extolling the virtues of electric dreams, distant friendship and eternal optimism and explains his reason for choosing this song for the inmates to perform. Although they may be worlds apart, he says, 'with the Internet, we all can be together in electric dreams' (Garcia qtd in Riminton 2007). Enchanted by Oakley and Moroder's song, Garcia imagines each of CPDRC's YouTube viewers as friends, reading their requests for encores as acts of love and a desire to 'be together', traversing prison walls and transcending geographical boundaries.

The 'electric dreams' of Oakley, Morodor and Garcia's imaginations can be traced to Marshall McLuhan's concept of the global village, as the above epigraph reveals. For McLuhan, the advances in electric communication (through his primary example of television) meant that all information was available to anyone, anywhere in the world, at the same moment in time.[2] Like Appadurai and many others, I too counter McLuhan's optimism, believing that McLuhan overestimated the communitarian implications of the new media order. Appadurai described how the world we live in now seems rhizomic (multiple, non-hierarchic), even schizophrenic, which calls for theories of rootlessness, alienation and psychological distance between individuals and groups on the one hand, and fantasies of electronic proximity on the other (1996: 29).[3] Such electric dreams, or nightmares, navigate across today's 'communities of sentiment', where it seems that *imagination* is the key to all forms of agency (Appadurai 1996: 31). In forms of work and forms of negotiation between sites of agency and globally defined fields of possibility, imagination now assumes a different function in today's sentimental community, and should be understood as a social practice. Imagination is imperative, for Appadurai, as it is:

> no longer mere fantasy (opium for the masses whose real work is somewhere else), no longer simple escape (from a world defined principally by more concrete proposes and structures), no longer elite pastime (thus not relevant to the lives of ordinary people), and no longer mere contemplation (irrelevant for new forms of desire and subjectivity). (1996: 31)

Modernity is hinged on media, and electronic media have served to globally extol that there are possible lives and potential opportunities for their imagined selves and their imagined worlds. As a form of social practice and a constitutive feature of modern subjectivity, the imagination is thus offered new everyday resources through such new forms of media as YouTube videos. Yet CPDRC's *Thriller* demonstrates the extent of the truth to Appadurai's findings. The inmates rarely, if ever, get to experience watching themselves dance to 'Thriller' or 'Together in Electric Dreams' on YouTube, since the inmates cannot legally access the internet. Instead inmates can only imagine possible worlds from an impossible place as they rely upon Garcia to hear about their YouTube fame, reception and view-counts whenever he relays the statistics in updates and announcements. Just as Benedict Anderson's post-print capitalism created 'imagined communities', CPDRC's *Thriller* demonstrates how such post-digital networked forms exceed the potential of print media, extending transnationally and internationally, from mobile screens to large-scale projectors. The inmates may never get the opportunity to witness first-hand the fruits of their labour. But their participation in new media bears witness to monthly visitors who flock to the facility and serve to cement the fact that their performances count for something; that they indeed *matter*.

Appadurai continues, describing in detail the remarkable Philippine attraction to American popular music and culture, and an emerging global system and the unique Filipino perspective filled with ironies and resistances often disguised as passivity and, above all, a bottomless appetite in the Asian world for all things Western. He articulates that:

> the uncanny Philippine affinity for American popular music is rich testimony to the global culture of the hyperreal, for somehow Philippine renditions of American popular songs are both more widespread in the Philippines, and more disturbingly faithful to their originals, than they are in the United States today. An entire nation seems to have learned to mimic Kenny Rogers and the Lennon sisters, like a vast Asian Motown

chorus. But *Americanisation* is certainly a pallid term to apply to such a situation, for not only are there more Filipinos singing perfect renditions of some American songs (often from the American past) than there are Americans doing so (1996: 29)

Compounding this Americanization is, for Appadurai, the fact that Philippine lives are otherwise out of synch with the referential world that gave birth to these American songs. Drawing from Frederic Jameson's concept of 'nostalgia for the present', Appadurai locates the globalized Filipino as inherently paradoxical – a nostalgia without memory – looking back to a world they have never lost, which in the rhizomatic spread of culture, entertainment and leisure is one of its central ironies. Of course Appadurai contends that such disjuncture and ironies can be historically accounted for, as it lays bare:

the story of the American missionisation and political rape of the Philippines, one result of which has been the creation of a nation of make-believe Americans, [who tolerated for so long a leading lady who played the piano while the slums of Manila expanded and decayed.] Perhaps the most radical postmodernists would argue that this is hardly surprising because in the peculiar chronicities of late capitalism, pastiche and nostalgia are central modes of image production and reception. (1996: 29–30)

The inmate-dancers in CPDRC's *Thriller* may be illustrations of Appadurai's 'make-believe Americans' or even Tadiar's 'third world place in first world drag', enchanting the masses with their lip-synched covers of American pop songs and diverting the public's gaze while most every other Philippine prison expands and decays. To push Appadurai's allegory a little further, perhaps Warden Garcia embodies a twenty-first century re-embodiment of the aforementioned First Lady Imelda Marcos, who was famed for serenading visiting politicians and singing on the campaign trails. In such an imagined parallel universe, do we see Governor Gwen Garcia in the role of former President Ferdinand Marcos?

New media technologies enabled Warden Garcia's imagination to be fired up in the first place, whether it was through watching a Hollywood movie or hearing an American pop song and deciding to use either (or both) as the basis for a novel approach to penology. What is clear is that the Dancing Inmates are *his* electric dream. By imagining visibly disciplined inmates, Garcia packaged his electric dreams as ideology: an ideology of rehabilitation mediated through the markers of global capitalism, namely American pop songs and celebrity culture. Garcia's electric dreams, when transferred to the inmates, become a fantasy that is collectively expressed yet ultimately serves as collective escapism.

The digital sharing of CPDRC's pop performances, as we can see, highlights Tadiar's claim for the Philippines as a third world space in 'first world drag' (2004: 2). The CPDRC performances, presented as an ironic and paradoxical example of embodied liberty within captivity, recall the American dream of life, liberty and the pursuit of happiness – despite the fact that these prisoners were never promised such fantasies in the first place. While displaying a complex extension of the US colonial education experience, witnessed through 1,500 inmates continuing to shake their hips in time to the disco beats of the Village People, and singing along to hits in a once colonial language – English – CPDRC's *Thriller* demonstrates how colonial culture is no longer the US alone. Instead, it is the invasive imperialist ideology of late capitalism, which continues to be manifested through US cultural terms.

YouTube and the thrill of transformations

Narratives of transformation play an important role in the overall case of the CPDRC's so-called music therapy programme. Such compelling narratives are, of course, not limited to music, and can be found across society as part of societal aspirations, whereby narratives of self-improvement through social mobility continue to play an important role. While transformative agency is a powerful narrative, one of the main critiques of such narratives, particularly in relation to reality-based TV programmes (including quasi-musical shows such as *X Factor* and the now international *Idol* franchise), is that they encourage the repurposing of myths and deliver false possibilities – often to society's most vulnerable people. Children and teenagers feature frequently in such reality narratives of transformation, and particularly in televised talent shows, where child singers and dancers often progress to the show's finale. A particularly controversial incident stands out from one of the Philippines' most popular noontime TV shows, *Willing Willie* (2011). Audiences witnessed noontime host Willie Revillame prod and force a distressed six-year-old boy to dance on stage in front of a live studio audience and TV cameras; Willie laughed as the little boy cried while gyrating to Dr Dre's 'The Next Episode' for a cash prize of 10,000 pesos. After the segment was uploaded to YouTube, the incident sparked national debate, resulting in the show's sponsors pulling out, and an investigation by the Commission on Human Rights, Classification Board and Social Welfare Secretary of State, and ultimately the show was suspended. Multiple videos of the boy's humiliating experience still circulate online on various video-sharing platforms, and certainly point to the dangers of continually mediating harmful recordings of our most vulnerable citizens – the young, the poor and the disenfranchised. Such television shows, much like viewing CPDRC's *Thriller,* present deep ethical challenges and highlight the politics of witnessing suffering. Media scholar Jonathan Corpus Ong has written extensively about the spectacular over-representation, mediation and perpetuation of poverty and suffering on Filipino television. Drawing from ethnographic interviews with upper-class and low-income audiences of noontime shows, including those hosted by Willie Revillame, Ong's research reveals an acute sense of solidarity among lower-class audiences as lower-class Filipinos actively seek out representations of everyday suffering that mirror their own in news and entertainment media. Upper-class Filipinos tend to evaluate such televised depictions of the poor, who willingly participate in such 'degrading and exploitative' TV shows, as victims without agency (2017: 100). However such televised entertainment shows are used by lower-class Filipinos not as an 'escape to fantasy worlds of opulence' but as a 'compassionate practice of recognition and redistribution for sufferers like them' (2017: 157).

The cultural tropes of music's transformative agency are attractive, affective and affecting. Yet the poor, the subaltern and the disenfranchised may be particularly susceptible to the irresistible rhetoric of the transformation trope, and as Ong's research shows, everyday representations of suffering and poverty are deeply entrenched in Filipino televisual media. As a related, but nonetheless different form of audiovisual media, CPDRC's YouTube videos deliver to (Filipino) audiences depictions of suffering, shared or other. Incarcerated men and women such as the CPDRC inmates – housed in a detention centre awaiting trial with limited options and alternatives but to participate in the dance as the songs fill the prison soundscape – have been indoctrinated in the thrill of transformation, without being allowed to question or refute its actuality. With the spotlight firmly on the exceptional, talented few, the discourse of transformation obfuscates the lives of the overwhelming majority – those who did not win the talent show, the inmates who were not granted access to Garcia's 'Ambassadors of Goodwill' touring troupe and instead eventually went to Manila to stand trial, were incarcerated elsewhere, never to be seen (dancing) again.

Captivated by the thrill of transformation, we fail to address the complexities of exactly what it is that is being transformed by this narrative. Based on the corporeal performances of the CPDRC inmates, judgements are made, time and time again, on how the dance programme has transformed the inmates from 'lowly criminals to celebrity criminals' (Garcia qtd in Riminton 2007). Questions remain regarding the elusive nature of fame itself, in addition to why (internet) fame is widely advocated among prisoners and deemed worthy of so much attention. Incarceration is frequently characterized by a bleak, mundane and near-invisible experience. To that end, the dancing programme augments aspects of the incarcerated experience for inmates and staff alike, partly through the structure and ritual offered by daily dancing, but more pertinently through the additional attention that live and mediated performances bring. Graeme Turner's coinage of the term the 'demotic turn' (2004, 2006) is useful here, when considering the conversion from ordinary people into media content. In CPDRC, 'ordinary' inmates have been transformed into 'celebrity' inmates through YouTube; the programme and its mediation offer a transformative space, a place where inmates can undergo a process of 'celebrification'– a now-familiar mode of cyber-self-presentation (Turner 2004, 2006). Turner refutes the idea that such celebrity-making processes are democratic, but rather such access to mass-mediated fame plays a fundamental role within the construction of cultural identities. The result of this transformation is a somewhat inevitable 'acceleration of the industrial cycle of use and disposal for the products of these trends' (Turner 2006: 155), which satisfies our contemporary appetite for consuming celebrity culture. Transformative spaces are intertwined with an often short (but nonetheless intense) moment of fame, delivered through an overly saturated media economy, and include a degree of tangible and intangible power. The digital, audiovisual transformation of criminal bodies through the intervention of music and dance, reflects a desire for instant gratification in transformative narratives, and a belief that non-invasive solutions to 'curing' criminal deviances and remedying socially constructed inequities can, and do, work. Much like 'the reveal' that forms the heart of many reality television shows such as the 'makeover' genre where audiences get to witness the physical, and often drastic, transformation of the subjects (and objects), we see through YouTube comments that CPDRC's *Thriller* conveys to audiences, in part, this 'Cinderella' effect. As many of the YouTube comments reveal, in addition to widespread internet reception, the dance performance functions as a public and publicized restoration of order, control, health and vitality to lives that were previously deemed socially deviant. In this YouTube discourse of transformation, both prison warden Byron Garcia and, to an extent, Michael Jackson are credited as heroic figures who brought salvation – and redemption – to the poor and suffering prisoners.

Performing hybridity and nostalgia

The embodiment of Western popular music and dance choreography by CPDRC's Filipino performers can be read as a literal performance of hybridity. Cultural hybridity lies beneath much postcolonial Philippine performances, as previously mentioned (see Lowe 1996; Castro 2011). José Buenconsejo (2010: v) articulates how cultural hybridity, specifically in the case of music of and in the Philippines, is:

> not simply about syncretism or mixing of different cultural forms and traits, as this seems to have been the grand, albeit naive, metanarrative about its nature, but is actually about *social meanings, performative*

ones, which gain more intelligibility when situated within highly-specific local historical contexts or within particular nodes of relationship that bind the local to the global or vice versa.

To think of CPDRC's *Thriller* in this way is to consider it as a performative practice imbued with social meanings precisely because of its interaction with peoples and across cultures that stretch beyond the borders of the Philippine nation. In our current system of globalized capitalism it can be difficult to separate what can be attributed to colonialism and what can be understood as homogeneous Western enculturation. While the performance of Western music of any kind in the Philippines by a Filipino may be partially read as an outgrowth of the colonial experience, for Castro it is simultaneously a performance where the 'native identity is not completely subsumed by the coloniser' (2011: 56). Castro goes further still, conceptualizing Filipino hybridity as a fundamental characteristic of modernism:

> From a nationalist standpoint, the adoption of Western music might better be unpacked theoretically as a potentially empowering mimetic act as much as an expression of hegemony. Even more symbolically potent, however, hybridity in composition and performance practice is the deliberate carving out of space for the native. It creates a partnership of equal grounding that, significantly, has been manipulated creatively by the native. Hybridity validates the claim of the native on Western music, not as an immutable universal product, but rather as birthright. Hybridity, as a nationalist and creative strategy, might even be constructed as a hallmark of Filipino modernism. (2011: 56)

This hybridity that is embedded deep within many Filipinos, is a powerful and empowering expression; for Castro it becomes 'birthright', as a result of such an international and imperial history. Certainly, hybridity is not an obstacle towards cultural homogenization. Rather, cultural theorist Stuart Hall sees in the aesthetics of modern popular music a certain alignment with 'the aesthetics of the hybrid, the aesthetics of the crossover, the aesthetics of the diaspora, the aesthetics of creolisation' (1997: 39). Others, such as Homi Bhabha (1990) and Paul Gilroy (1993) have suggested that hybridity is a powerful instrument with investigative potential, and hybridized cultures and identities may be subversive – especially in the context of formerly silenced 'subaltern' subjects. When considered in tandem with CPDRC's *Thriller*'s play on nostalgia, we get a sense of just how quietly subversive a work it has the potential to be.

Far from being an eternal concept, the concept of nostalgia originates from the late seventeenth century after Swiss physician Johannes Hofer coined the term – compounding the Greek *nostos*: homecoming, and *algia (algos)*: pain – to describe the pathological condition of homesickness among

Swiss soldiers fighting abroad. The medical origins of nostalgia manifested themselves in physical and psychological ways, with symptoms including despondency, weeping, melancholia and not infrequently, attempts at suicide. The meaning of 'nostalgia' changed and developed over the centuries, and by the eighteenth century nostalgia was associated with a longing for home (Boym 2001). By the nineteenth century, nostalgia accrued an artistic and literary association, and a century later, it acquired kitsch preconceptions (Boym 2001). Recently, scholars have demonstrated that such feelings of longing are not necessarily as 'natural, nor as pan-human, and therefore not necessarily as innocent, as one might imagine' (Rosaldo 1998: 72). I enlist Svetlana Boym's concept of nostalgia that emphasizes the importance and power of nostalgia's 'global culture' (2001: xvii). For Boym there are two nostalgic tendencies: what she terms restorative nostalgia (which involves attempts to restore the past, seeking to reproduce what they perceive to be the essence of lost and, in many cases, impossible objects) and reflective nostalgia (which reflects on how things were, and thrives in wistful longing). Using Boym's framework, we see that CPDRC's performance has prompted both reflective and restorative nostalgia: firstly, CPDRC's *Thriller* is situated within a restorative framework whereby Garcia uses the medium of *Thriller*'s song and dance to rebuild inmates' sense of self, to rehabilitate by projecting his longing for a humanitarian method of disciplining bodies through his favourite music. Secondly, *Thriller* operates as a reflective text in its ironic humour, revealing, as Boym states, that longing and critical thinking are not always opposed to one another, 'as affective memories do not absolve one from compassion, judgment or critical reflection', and thus I argue that the inmates' reflective nostalgia is indeed 'enamoured of distance, not of the referent itself' (Boym 2001: 41–50). CPDRC's *Thriller* taps into a digital archive of nostalgia (after McClintock 1995), and in doing so articulates nostalgia, accents hybridity, while all the time affecting forms of pleasure.

Lastly, CPDRC's *Thriller* functions on a visceral level, as a remediated reimagining of Michael Jackson's *Thriller* short film. In explaining his choice of *Thriller*, Garcia neatly calls upon *Thriller*'s poetics, stating that 'unless we stop breeding demons in jails, gruesome ghouls from every tomb will seal the doom of nations and civilisations' (Garcia 2007a). Produced in 2007 some two years before Jackson's death, and subsequent (re-)launch into the stridently nostalgic mainstream media, it would appear that Garcia consciously chose *Thriller* to be the 'language of the [inmates'] soul' precisely because of *Thriller*'s immense, international cultural capital. *Thriller*'s overwhelming and continued chart success – over 100 million worldwide record sales to date – has firmly embedded *Thriller* within popular culture's psyche, as a formally recognized historically and aesthetically significant work. A mere reference to a pop text of this calibre is irrefutably equipped to trigger a wave of globalized nostalgia; commanding 1,500 inmates to perform *Thriller*'s choreographic sequence, considered by many to be the 'most important communal dance of the last three decades' (George 2010: 107; also Mkrdichian 2009: 2), and sharing a recording of that performance on a public forum such as YouTube, was almost guaranteed to be effective.

In addition to receiving millions of views since it was uploaded in 2007 and becoming a tourist destination, CPDRC's *Thriller* influenced a range of media projects that have brought a steady stream of film crews and actors behind bars. Among these are Ron Fricke and Mark Magidson's non-narrative documentary *Samsara* (2011), which features a gracefully shot scene using 70-millimetre film where the camera floats above rows of hundreds of CPDRC inmates – impeccably presented in their orange uniforms – dancing and vocalizing together in the prison yard. Originally moving to the funky beats of MC Hammer, the film cloaks that recording with an original, hypnotic dance track by composer Michael Stearns, which only adds to the overall incongruous feeling. With multiple close-ups of dancer Crisanto Niere, only he is singled out in the film credits, listed as 'Lead Singer: CPDRC, Philippines'. The act in question is sandwiched between a scene depicting the lives of those living in one of Manila's unnamed riverside slums, and subsequently, we follow Filipino youths digging through the rubbish in Quezon City's enormous Payatas Landfill. As non-narrative documentaries go, the film relies on the viewer to make the connections between this triptych of contemporary Filipino life – conflating images of extreme wealth positioned next to extreme poverty. The inmates' musicking becomes a hybrid between Hollywood entertainment and the prison industrial complex.

Nostalgia and spreadable media

Other multimedia offspring based on the CPDRC inmates are *Prison Dancer* (2012), a Canadian enterprise that started out as an off-Broadway musical before becoming an original, twelve-episode web musical, and independent Filipino film *Dance of the Steel Bars* (2013). Starring Filipino actors Dingdong Dantes as a 'convicted murderer who denies his passion for dancing just to prove his masculinity', Joey Paras as 'transsexual who tries to contribute to prison reforms by teaching his fellow inmates dance exercises', and Irish actor Patrick Bergin as a wrongfully accused US retiree looking for redemption (Apolinario and Manicad 2013), the movie was filmed on location at the CPDRC and features large-scale, cinematic dance sequences performed by the real-life CPDRC inmates serving as film extras. Subsequent films based on the CPDRC Dancing Inmates are in progress at the time of writing, such as Emmy-Award-winning Filipina-American director Michele Josue's 'hopeful' film *Happy Jail* that narrates a tale of 'dance, love, and brotherhood [that] keep[s] the lives of CPDRC's inmates worth living' (Happy Jail Facebook page, 15 June 2017). It also spawned countless spin-offs in prisons around the Philippines (for example 'The Manila Dancing Inmates' video of the Black Eyed Peas' 'I Got a Feeling'). Building from Dawkins's meme metaphor and Jenkin et al.'s theory on spreadable media from Chapter 1, these many offshoots reinforce CPDRC's *Thriller* as a form of spreadable media in and of itself. Moreover, following Garcia's dismissal from CPDRC in early 2010, his prison music-dance-therapy programme spread throughout prisons across the Philippine islands. On paper, it was formally implemented as public policy in all Filipino prisons with the introduction of the Bureau of Jail Management and Penology (BJMP) new 'dance rehabilitation' legislature in March 2010.[4] Through the immense power of nostalgic rhetoric, CPDRC's *Thriller* has had very real life effects for this group of former inmates, the Ambassadors of Goodwill, who have achieved this intangible, YouTube fame through touring the Philippines under Garcia's strict tutelage, blurring the boundaries between freedom and servitude. CPDRC's *Thriller*'s mass circulation of nostalgia via YouTube displays the vast potentials of the site, where anyone, including Philippine prisoners, can achieve international attention and recognition. From this perspective CPDRC's *Thriller* viral video, released in 2007, marks a milestone in contemporary pop cultural history that echoes the impact of Michael Jackson's original 1983 *Thriller* in terms of influencing popular music and affecting participatory culture on a global scale for decades to come.

Reading CPDRC's *Thriller* as a work of nostalgia has some notable theoretical implications. In conceptualizing *Thriller*'s power in affecting pleasure, in seducing audiences to its nostalgic power, Slavoj Žižek's discussion of film noir proves useful. When we watch American film noir of the 1940s, Žižek suggests that although we can no longer identify with it, what fascinates us is a certain gaze of the 'other', a hypothetical, mythic spectator from the 1940s who was purportedly still able to instantly identify with the world of film noir. 'What we really see when we watch a film noir is this gaze of the other; our relation to a film noir is always divided, split between fascination and ironic distance – ironic distance toward its diegetic reality, fascination with the gaze' (Žižek 1989: 39). The function of the nostalgic object, for Žižek, is precisely to conceal the antinomy between eye and gaze by the power of fascination, and in nostalgia, the gaze of the other is pacified, domesticated, 'gentrified'. As a result, we experience the illusion of seeing ourselves seeing – of seeing the gaze itself (Žižek 1992: 114). CPDRC's *Thriller* functions through providing a variety of gazes: the gaze of the 1980s audience watching and reminiscing over the inmates *Thriller*; and the neocolonial gaze through combining the quintessential American pop song and 1980s archival choreography within the confines of a contemporary Philippine prison setting.

Further, in showing how this type of nostalgia is operative in the case of CPDRC's *Thriller*, the aggressivity of this particular kind of expression of cultural dominance speaks directly to Renato Rosaldo's understanding of imperialist nostalgia. Rosaldo highlights the ironic nature of imperialist nostalgia, that utilizes a pose of 'innocent yearning' to capture people's imaginations while simultaneously concealing its complicity, with often-brutal domination (1998: 34). Establishing a Filipino cultural identity after centuries of colonization and occupation is not without challenges, and indeed serves to highlight the inherent paradox faced by new mediated subjects. Digital media platforms have given a voice to postcolonial and subaltern subjects, while simultaneously problematizing the Filipino performers, presenting them as uniform, 'highly trainable', Orientalist stereotypes, powerless to personally participate in the digital swirl within which they operate. As such, this quasi-MTV style video, with hundreds upon hundreds of clearly marked Filipino prisoners at its core, becomes a metaphor for twenty-first-century postcolonial Philippine attempts to assert independence from the US.

Marshall Berman (1992) questions the acclamation of traditional society by claiming that the twentieth century has been prolific in constructing idealized fantasies of life, which are fundamentally designed to gloss over the violence, cruelty and brutality of modern life. I extend Marshall Berman's metaphor of 'idealised fantasies' that gloss over violence to say that CPDRC's *Thriller* re-creation of nostalgic fantasy is imperative to this pop music production, and is manifested threefold. First, CPDRC's *Thriller* reveals a longing for an idealized past and an imagined future: through enacting Garcia's projected nostalgia for a universal language of rehabilitation on criminal bodies, the inmates convey seemingly oppositional binaries through their portrayal of prison life as ostensibly harmonious. Calling upon such inherent oppositions – widely held presumptions about (Filipino) inmates, as well as assumptions about life in a detention centre (fuelled, in part, by popular media depictions) – CPDRC's *Thriller* dramatizes such juxtapositions and expectations. Second, this enforced performance of nostalgia can create a longing for autonomy as well as immunize inmate performers through the momentary liberty afforded through musical performance. Third, the (post/neo)colonial histories and geographical conditions that surround CPDRC's *Thriller* – as the Philippines in general – display a kind of cultural hybridization, further calling to mind what Anne McClintock calls 'neocolonial nostalgia' through combining American pop superstars and 1980s archival choreography within the confines of a contemporary Philippine prison setting. The YouTube audience of CPDRC's collective performances are, in a sense, bound together – connected to this imaginary space where American pop nostalgia articulates a liminal, exocytose community on the other side of the world. Their overall oeuvre is defined by irreconcilable contrasts and co-existing oppositions, such as the inmates' determined, libertarian act of Philippine flag waving to 1980s synth pop sounds of Phil Oakley and Giorgio Moroder.[5] Still, representations alone do not equate progress; despite the call for positive images of the other, I follow Kaja Silverman who notes that this can 'all too often work to resubstantialise identity, even at times to essentialise it'(1992: 154).

While I consider their performance to be entrenched in nostalgic rhetoric, this should not in any way *depoliticize* their performance. In reality, it does the opposite. To read the inmates' performance simply as an exploration of 1980s nostalgia, as it so often is, both inflates and reduces the significance of their YouTube video, which conveys and reproduces a complex ideology of neocolonial progress at the *expense* of other experiences. Their thrilling, nostalgic performances, that continue to be disseminated globally on digital screens, are politically productive *despite*, and precisely *because of*, the range of embedded nostalgic gazes we identify without necessarily noticing. My reading opens, but deliberately leaves unanswered, the nature of the relationship between performances of nostalgia and the neocolonial, and between the neocolonial and the political. Instead, at CPDRC these exist both in tension *and* harmony with the other.

INTERLUDE SEVEN

Thank you for the music

It's a hot, sleepy Thursday morning in January 2013. As with every Filipino city, the hum and hustle of traffic is never far away, but as I step out of the car and approach the main gates of the CPDRC facility, I swear there's also a distant melody in the air. Across the road from the main gates sit two street vendors, both snoozing in the shade, against their makeshift stalls selling local snacks and chilled fizzy drinks poured into small plastic bags and sipped through a straw, as I discover. Apart from the vendors, there's no one else on the street, save for a trio of sleeping dogs.

I introduce myself to the guard stationed at the gate, tucked behind a metal grill, who – after several searches through handwritten lists, a quick telephone call, and a rifle through my backpack – ushers me through to a waiting area, where the first thing I encounter is a large tarpaulin poster featuring a description of the CPDRC's ethos accompanied by several photographs of the Dancing Inmates (Figure 7.1). Against a bright orange background that perfectly matches the colour of the CPDRC inmate uniforms, the poster declares:

> People have, for ages, looked down on Prisoners, but the Cebu Provincial Government's focus on their rehabilitation has turned that around (…) From tilling their own gardens to dancing their way into worldwide popularity (…) Within the confines of these walls the inmates learned

to hope. They regained their self-esteem, and finally achieved what they imagined themselves to have: pride and honor.

The faint melody gradually becomes louder, but it's still hard to make out who, or what, is making the sound. I'm introduced to the Acting Provincial Warden, Algier C. Comendador – the most recently appointed replacement since Byron F. Garcia's departure from the CPDRC mid-2010. We shake hands, exchange introductions and he summons another guard to escort me to another part of the prison – he seems especially busy today. The new guard unlocks more gates to let me through. They clang shut as he re-locks them afterwards. We walk passed corridors where inmates are hanging out, outside of their cells. Guards and inmates do not seem to mind my intrusion to their daily routine: some smile, others wave and call out 'Hello Ma'am!' Indeed I don't feel like I'm intruding too much – the calm atmosphere, combined with the faint background music, make for a rather relaxed, almost inviting ambience.

Eventually I'm led up to the viewing tower above the prison quadrangle, and see that the yard – the dancefloor that I know so well from so many YouTube views – has transformed into a bustling, multi-functional workspace. Preparations for this coming weekend's public performance are well underway (Figure 7.2); freshly glued costumes and props lie out in the baking heat, and soon after my arrival, are presumed dry and tidied away. As I look around the yard, the source of this morning's soundtracks become

FIGURE 7.1 *A large tarpaulin sign extolling the CPDRC ethos greets you at the entrance/waiting area to the facility (2013).* © Photo: Author.

INTERLUDE SEVEN

FIGURE 7.2 *The prison yard transformed into a site of arts and crafts preparation for the upcoming Sinulog costumes. In the distant periphery (upper left) sits one of two groups of inmates gathered to sing – read: queue up to sing – karaoke (2013).* © Photo: Author.

apparent. Two small groups of inmates are gathered, at the opposites sides of the prison yard, seated and standing around a microphone and television set. A sharp dissonance, amplified by two opposing yet simultaneous karaoke soundtracks fills the air. On one half of the yard, someone is singing what sounds a lot like the popular Visayan song '*Mibalik ako*' ('I returned'), though it's rather hard to be sure because the sounds from the other half of the yard are drowning out the song's melody.

I turn to ask the guard a question. Before I can say anything, he reads my mind and laughs: 'Thursday's we have karaoke!' As if to support his assertion, a rousing chorus kicks off from the opposing karaoke machine across the yard. There is no mistaking this song, for I know it all too well. An inspired yet unseen baritone voice sings out with gusto lyrics that inimitably soundtrack the sweeping incongruity of the situation. I cannot help but hum along to his warble as it echoes over the jangly karaoke speakers:

> Thank you for the music, the songs I'm singing
> Thanks for all the joy they're bringing
> Who can live without it, I ask in all honesty
> What would life be?
> Without a song or a dance what are we? (Andersson and Ulvaeus 1977)

CHAPTER SEVEN

YouTube's penal spectators

> To speak of reality becoming a spectacle is a breathtaking provincialism. It universalises the viewing habits of a small, educated population living in the rich part of the world, where news has been converted into entertainment ... It assumes that everyone is a spectator. (Sontag 2003: 98–9)

CPDRC's *Thriller* functions as a form of penal spectatorship, introducing the wider public to the precarious world of incarceration in a destination that might otherwise be difficult to sell. Though prisons are public buildings, they are not frequented like state schools, hospitals, libraries or parks. Physical access to prisons is tightly controlled. As a consequence, 'many citizens never encounter the overpowering tangibility of imprisonment' (Brown 2009: 7). Through YouTube screens – large, small and smaller – citizens must confront current practices of punishment, and the entertaining mediation and institutionalization of contemporary imprisonment. These citizens may often be disconnected from the reality of prisons in everyday life, privileged in this distance, or 'comfortably distanced,' to use Michelle Brown's phrase (2009: 7). Brown describes how the distance or remoteness of the penal spectator functions both in shielding us from conceptualizing the democratic burden of punishment as a kind of cultural work, while simultaneously guarantees that such imagining of punishment is haunted by abstract potentialities of danger and insecurity (2009: 9–11). What is significant about CPDRC's *Thriller* in comparison to other mediated forms of punishment and prison spectatorship, for example the wealth of films and TV shows set in real and fictional prisons, is that YouTube's platform inherently invites some – but not all – members of the public to speak back. In this chapter, I ask what does the public say about a video like this?

Early YouTube videos such as CPDRC's *Thriller*, are imbued with an aura of immediacy. YouTube's screen – initially the reserve of personal computers and laptops, and later moving to smaller-screen formats with more mobile accessibility – speaks to an imagined, digital community that converse through clicktivism, textual and audiovisual comments. It is as much a testament to the evolution and mainstream acceptance of YouTube that since my initial research on the CPDRC videos almost a decade ago, the academe now recognizes the significance of this new medium (see, for example, Burgess and Green 2009; Snickars and Vonderau 2009; Strangelove 2010; Vernallis 2013). Often presented as remediated, intertextual texts soaked in nostalgic rhetoric, YouTube texts' apparent innocuousness affords them the potential to evoke real societal change, as well as very real dangers in concealing or even erasing the very markers of their production.[1] As a consequence, it is imperative that attention be paid to these kinds of media products, despite the fact that not all of these videos are necessarily as rife with complexity or social significance as the case study presented here. Building from the broad contextualization of the CPDRC video phenomenon provided in previous chapters, this chapter provides a close textual analysis of CPDRC's *Thriller*, including an overview of the range of YouTube comments left by the community.

Penal spectators: Categorizing CPDRC's YouTube comments

Delving into YouTube user comments is in itself a rather depressing, if not downright dangerous activity. Scratch below the top-rated one or two comments and you might reveal an underworld of grammatically incomprehensible rants. Decipher these and therein lies the potential to offer a curious, bottom-up insight into the reception of any given YouTube video, reveal a great deal about the YouTube community and give insights into wider sociocultural trends. Watching videos on YouTube does not require users to leave comments, to speak back, or engage in any kind of dialogue with others watching the same videos. As mentioned in Chapter 1, the majority of YouTubers and casual viewers do not 'speak back', as it were, as the well-known 90–9–1 principle shows. YouTube comments are gradually beginning to be researched as a form of reception studies, which may give insights into audience reactions to particular videos or highlight certain pertinent or recurring issues (see Lange 2007; Thelwall, Sud and Vis 2011). CPDRC's *Thriller* can be considered one of the earlier exemplars to gain YouTube 'viral video' status, and along with receiving millions of views, by 2014 the video had amassed over 70,000 user comments from YouTubers around the globe. Recent work by Way (2015) uses discourse approaches to studying communication and comments on YouTube and other social media, building on critical discourse analysis (CDA). CDA is a general description for inter- or multidisciplinary work that studies social issues or problems based not only on text and talk, but also non-verbal approaches to discourse including sound, music, gestures, film, imagery and so on, which is often centred on understanding core ideologies and strategies of dominance and resistance in social relationships (see van Leeuwen and Wodak 1999; Wodak 2001; Tolson 2010). Following this lead, I apply a discourse approach drawing from CDA to examine audience responses based on YouTube comments left under CPDRC's *Thriller*. A CDA approach enables prominent features of this kind of user-generated viral video to be foregrounded, producing pertinent observations on music video's 'second aesthetic' (Vernallis 2013) and contemporary penal spectatorship. A large sample of YouTube comments was needed to find typical and untypical characteristics and audience responses. I selected a random sample of 1,800 comments posted underneath the original video over a five-year period (2009–13).[2] I then analysed these to locate the most cited, recurring qualities of comments left under CPDRC's *Thriller*, to illuminate the ways in which YouTube users engage with the text and connect with other YouTuber comments.

The selected sample of YouTube comments focused solely on comments written in English for a number of reasons. First, the overwhelming majority of comments were written in some form of English, using established and vernacular English vocabulary. Second, although CDA explicitly states that translations are best avoided (Wodak 2001), it is problematic, of course, to discount comments not written in English. Still, the complete range of languages presented in the comments – from Taglish, Cebuano, Spanish, Portuguese and more – further complicates matters and makes accurate translations resource-intensive. As such, the decision to focus solely on English-language comments is a limitation of this research. To try and overcome any potential bias, I limited my analysis to a randomly chosen sample of 1,800 comments out of over 70,000 available comments (estimated total number of comments for the video as reported by the YouTube API by February 2014). Given the frequency upon which new user comments continue to be added to this video and older comments removed or disappeared, alongside the decision to focus on English-language comments only, this comment snapshot cannot claim to be completely exhaustive, nor wholly representative. Rather, this overview of YouTube comments provides a general indication, though limited and limiting as it may be, of the general YouTube reception to CPDRC's *Thriller*.

On a fundamental level, the act of YouTube commenting facilitates membership creation, maintenance and negotiation within this social network. As others have reported, posting comments enables users to express feelings of affinity for the video or video-makers, and can help users maintain connections with friends and relatives at a distance (Lange 2007: 376). Yet it is difficult to gauge what a typical YouTube comment looks like, since the level of frequency, details on who participates and how comments are made can vary wildly based on video genre, theme, style and a host of other variable factors. Thelwall, Sud and Vis's research provides some general findings on YouTube comments, stating that there is 'no typical density of discussion on YouTube videos in the sense of the proportion of replies to other comments: videos with both few and many replies were common' (2011: 616). They found differences in how YouTube audiences engaged with each other based both on video categories, with videos categorized as Music (among others) typically attracting the least discussion. There was also disproportionate engagement based on comment content as positive comments elicited few replies, while negative comments triggered much more discussion. Within the comments gathered from this video, there appears to be but a small chance that another YouTuber will read their comment, and an even slimmer possibility that someone will respond to it directly with another comment.[3]

From this fixed comment sample, noticeable trends and commonalities emerge. I subsequently grouped CPDRC's *Thriller* comments into thirteen classifications based on identifiable thematic parameters. It must be noted that these categories are not mutually exclusive, nor is it likely – across over 70,000 comments in total – that they are completely exhaustive. The (relative) anonymity, asynchronous, solipsistic, physically safe and escapist nature of YouTube comments (and the comments and interactions on many other Social Networking Sites), enables users to post comments on any topic.[4] In essence, the following categorization briefly illustrates the breadth and difference of marked responses to CPDRC's *Thriller*, summarized by the categories given in Table 7.1.[5]

Crucial to participatory culture's success is the deeply held belief of individual members that their contributions matter, and thus participatory cultures thrive when members feel a social connection with each other. Members of a participatory culture care, at least to some degree, 'what other people think about what they have created' (Jenkins et al. 2006: 7). To expand further, Jenkins et al. conceptualize participatory culture into four key facets (Jenkins et al. 2006):

1. **Affiliations:** memberships, formal and informal, in online communities centered around various forms of media (such as Friendster, Facebook, message boards, metagaming, game clans or MySpace).
2. **Expressions:** producing new creative forms (such as digital sampling, skinning and modding, fan video-making, fan fiction writing, zines, mash-ups).
3. **Collaborative Problem-solving:** working together in teams, formal and informal, to complete tasks and develop new knowledge (such as through Wikipedia, alternative reality gaming, spoiling).
4. **Circulations:** Shaping the flow of media (such as podcasting, blogging).

Table 7.1 Categories of YouTube comments left by CPDRC's *Thriller* audiences

	Category	General comment features
1.	Amusement	Generally positive feedback often laced with flippant humour
2.	Approval	Positive to overtly positive responses, often expressing a strong emotional response, a sense of immersion and/or connection
3.	Disbelief	Positive and negative remarks expressing scepticism over the dancers' status as inmates, to conspiracy theories that they are all paid actors
4.	Facetious/Sardonic Humour	Jokes frequently made about their apparent/imagined criminal acts; interactive comments that respond directly to other comments
5.	Homophobic	Expressing hatred of drag performance, disgust at transsexuality, and/or making specific remarks against the *bakla*
6.	Intertextual Citations	Comments citing their route to this video; many pop culture references and requests
7.	Michael Jackson Fandom	Extensive messages professing love, adoration, praise and longing from Jackson's fans
8.	Other	Vague, unidentifiable comments or expressions of concern for the inmates
9.	Philippines/Filipinos	Comments made from self-identified Pinoys and Pinays, within the homeland and across the diaspora; generally positive, encouraging, and on occasion, humorous
10.	Questions about Germany	Questions or disparaging remarks pertaining to the copyright restrictions in place in Germany (re: GEMA licensing) and to a lesser extent, Sony (the copyright holders)
11.	Questions posed to the YouTube community	A quest for further knowledge or a search for answers to aspects of the video content made to the collective intelligence of YouTube's participatory culture
12.	Racial/Racist	Subtle to overtly ignorant to categorically offensive and disparaging remarks specifically pertaining to the performers as Asian, Filipino or 'Other'
13.	Religious	A mixture of comments that contain religious verses, quoted verbatim, to comments that credit the performance to a higher power, and prayers for their souls

Using Jenkins et al.'s four categories as a framework, we can understand how YouTube videos like CPDRC's *Thriller* operate as a form of participatory culture as it combines aspects of affiliation (a community of users, some – but not all – identifiable by usernames and YouTube profile pages), expression (as a site for video-making), collaborative problem-solving and, of course, widespread circulation through its inbuilt, URL-sharing functions. Bearing in mind the popular 90-9-1 rule of internet participation, this list is not representative of all audience responses to CPDRC's *Thriller*; rather it primarily serves as a starting point to discuss the video's reaction among YouTube viewers, as well as providing a general sense of the video's reception through the structural features offered by YouTube's technological, communicative interface.

The 'You' in YouTube: Users, comments and performativity

The sheer quantity of comments left underneath CPDRC's *Thriller* – as illustrated by YouTube's API statistics published alongside the video's homepage – offer a crude measurement showing that users have on some level been affected by this video. At the very least the high number of YouTube comments point to this video hitting a collective nerve, to borrow Lange's phrase (2014: 63). Posting comments to videos enacts media circuits, illustrating and maintaining particular social network patterns, creating connections and negotiating relationships – both in supporting pre-existing relationships and those that would not exist as such without online media distribution (Lange 2007: 367). Yet motivations for posting comments are multifaceted. YouTube is an environment where participants often post comments to increase their social visibility, thus prompting a video-maker to examine the commenter's work and potentially developing their social networks (Lange 2007: 367). Conversely, however, comments that do not display affinity with the video may discourage the video-maker from interacting with the commenter (Lange 2007: 369).

YouTube comments on CPDRC's *Thriller*, of course, speak directly to the specifics of this video performance, citing themes relating to prison(s), criminality, Michael Jackson, the Philippines, and other features of significance. YouTubers who have taken the time required to engage in this additional level of social interaction – those that have created a YouTube/Google account and logged in in order to post a comment – tend to share their specific observations about the video, their reaction to it, and/or to detail how they came to find it. Some comment in a mixture of ways, bringing forth a range of responses, from entertainment to empathy – a 'there but for the grace of God, go I' attitude – to revulsion at the inmates' criminal status, posting comments to that effect underneath their YouTube videos.[6] An overview of the range of comments left under this video – and arguably any YouTube video – reveals the extent to which audience agency is critical to YouTube. Agency is central to YouTube's operations, and YouTube functions as a site of co-labour, regardless of whether this is acknowledged by uploaders or not. YouTube's supposed democratization of online audiovisual space is rooted in accessibility and agency; power appears to lie in the hands of 'any' of YouTube's users, as is so often celebrated in YouTube's 'Broadcast Yourself' ethos.

As a user-generated content (UGC) platform, YouTube's respondents quickly acquired the label 'users' (Livingstone 2004). Unlike the more 'passive' recipients of film and television before, Web 2.0 users were theorized as active internet contributors, and as José van Dijck explains, YouTube became the perfect case study illustrating the need for a more comprehensive understanding of user agency (2009: 42). Locating agency in YouTube users is complex. Resisting fixed, oppositional categories of 'active' versus 'passive', and 'professional' versus 'amateur', user agency encompasses different levels of participation, motivation, behaviour and thought processes involved in YouTube engagement. Some have questioned the democratizing potential of YouTube, in particular the idea that access to YouTube alone is an accurate measure of egalitarianism (Burgess and Green 2009). Van Dijck believes online participatory culture tends to exaggerate user agency, and underestimate the mediated environment when evaluating opportunities in new media technologies (2009). Others, like Jenkins, argue that 'audiences, empowered by these new technologies, occupying a space at the intersection between old and new media, are demanding the right to participate within the culture' (2006a: 24). For many like Jenkins, YouTube users are not unwitting, uncritical participants in a digitalized form of mass capitalism, but instead have a great deal of agency. Yet this user agency 'encompasses a range of different *uses* and agents' (van Dijck 2009: 46), and combines the composite roles of cultural, civic engagement facilitator with the economic function of producer, consumer and data provider, alongside a volatile position in the labour market (van Dijck 2009: 55).

As the categories of YouTube user comments illustrate, comments range from remarks laced in irreverent humour, calls to introduce this programme to prisons around the world (and especially in the US, the location where a significant number of YouTubers comment that they are based), to frequent statements attesting to being moved to tears – that the inmates' performance had elicited a fantastical form of emotional contagion. In particular, a significant number of comments express utter disbelief at witnessing such a vast number of apparently criminal bodies dancing to Michael Jackson:

Ex. 1. These people committed crimes?! (Aeroforce14)

Ex. 2. Only 5 inmates were shanked in the making of this film. (isaac12345johnson)

Ex. 3. if you can't afford a dance school kill someone and go to this prison! (Healthy 2808)

Ex. 4. I find it so hard to believe that these people are criminals. Society has painted criminals as evil people who are beyond redemption, monsters with no souls, but that's just not true. (aerdna14)

Ex. 5. lmao [laughing my ass off], luv da drag queen. But are they really inmates? Honestly ... killers, rapists, gangstahs dancing to Thriller. (Belkis Martinez)

The above YouTubers have utilized the comment section to register the apparent absurd incongruence of the Dancing Inmates, mocking the surrealist fusion of pop music and dance performed by those assumed to be 'killers, rapists, and gangstahs'. These kinds of comments reveal the extent to which perspectives about incarceration and social class are expressed and circulate as 'natural' or common sense within many communities, not least among YouTube's innumerable and often fractured communities.

Other YouTubers use the comment section to praise the dancers, but in effect their compliments are addressed to the imagined YouTube audience more so than the dancers themselves. While wishfully admonishing the video's highly compressed, pixelated digital image, one user comments that:

Ex. 6. The guy playing Michael Jackson is REALLY good! Wish this was better quality (Gary Thayer)

Meanwhile another YouTuber compliments the collaborative efforts of the inmates:

Ex. 7. This is the epitome of teamwork. (Frances Zapata)

Users like Thayer and Zapata appear to imagine, on some level, that the CPDRC's 'Michael Jackson' might find the opportunity to read such words of positivity and encouragement, however unlikely the reality may be.

Together, these comments suggest that these YouTubers are themselves engaging in performative acts, just as they are responding to the performative acts of the dancers they are watching. I approach CPDRC's *Thriller* as a performance, read the YouTube video and their live dance shows as performance texts, but also interpret the YouTube user comments as acts of performance too. What do I mean by this? Acknowledging that all human activity could potentially be considered as 'performance', Richard Schechner asserts that 'to perform' means different things depending on its contexts:

In business, sports, and sex, 'to perform' is to do something up to a standard – to succeed, to excel. In the arts, 'to perform' is to put on a show, a play, a dance, a concert. In everyday life, 'to perform' is to show off, to go to extremes, to underline an action for those who are watching. (2006: 22)

To use Schechner's framework, CPDRC's *Thriller* certainly operates as a performance text within the bounds of his description: the inmates perform by dancing, acting, clapping and singing along to well-known pop compositions. Christopher Small's concept of 'musicking' is also applicable here, as the inmates actively take part in musical performances on many levels by performing, listening, rehearsing and dancing (1998: 9).[7] For Small, music's primary, everyday meanings were based on building social, communicative relationships.

Indeed YouTubers are also entwined in acts of performance. YouTubers enact social, communicative relationships by taking to the comment section to give out praise, tease, insult or pass seemingly indiscriminate observations. These displays of communication construct meaning, for to perform is to convey something – a special form of communication between two entities. Performance suggests 'an aesthetically marked and heightened mode of communication, framed in a special way and put on display for an audience' (Bauman 1992: 41). YouTubers publicly build social relationships and their communications are visibly framed and on display for a global audience. Judith Butler, while primarily applying the concept of performativity in her analysis of gender roles, sees performativity as having little to do with radical choice and voluntarism but rather as rooted in repetition: it is that 'reiterative power of discourse to produce phenomena that it regulates and constrains' (1993: xii). Although the original video captured a rehearsal – the inmates practising rather than a finished production – the fact of this rehearsal's capture on camera, and subsequent upload onto YouTube, has led to the additional frame of putting on a show, however unfinished it may originally have been.

To fully comprehend a YouTube video such as CPDRC's *Thriller* as a performance, and arguably, a performing art, is not just to say that such a work is performed in itself, but crucially 'it is to say that through it we perform social meaning' (Cook 2003: 207). The notion of the performing self – the CPDRC Dancing Inmates' performance personae – is somewhat troubled in the case of CPDRC's *Thriller*, if we approach their performance as that of a musical performance. The inmates dance and move in time to the music, and at times, many appear to be singing (or mouthing) along to the song's lyrics, and clapping in time to the beat. If – *if* – we were to consider such actions musical performances, then, according to Philip Auslander, the direct object of the verb *to perform* is the representation of the self – to perform first and foremost one's own musical personae (2006: 102). Their recorded video remains both a documentary of a performance from another time and place while also serving as a performance that 'performs' each moment it is experienced (Auslander 2006). Michael Jackson's *Thriller* has today become a part of YouTube's chaotic back catalogue, an interpretive construct. *Thriller's* multiple interpretations, covers and remediations demonstrate that while history has privileged text over performance, texts alone do not and cannot ultimately exhaust the work's identity (Cook 2003: 207). Applying theories of performance to the act of YouTube commenting in the context of this video, we understand how commenting on CPDRC's *Thriller* is a productive action that serves as a form of communication, power and display. In the age of vast and often widely accessible digital archives, the possibilities of texts and performances are constantly being renegotiated, as old works are renewed, recirculated and reimagined time and time again.

Comments and/as expressions of identity

A significant number of YouTubers use this comment section to make public matters of national and racial identity. As a video that is made in the Philippines and features only Filipino bodies – and over a thousand Filipino bodies at that – many users take this as a point of departure to leave comments where they publicly identify as Filipino, and/or use this platform to share with the global YouTube community their Filipino perspective on the performance. Such YouTubers encompass Filipinos located in the Philippines, *balikbayan*, and some who identify as members of the Filipino diaspora. This aligns with findings on the importance of YouTube user comments as a creating platform for public discourse where minorities and those who feel marginalized in open spaces of discourse can interact. Lange's study of YouTube comments mentions that, as women and people of colour feel discouraged from participating on YouTube, vital public discourse may be threatened (2014: 62). Topics such as racism are important to minority YouTubers who seek acceptance in online forums; feeling comfortable enough to express the self publicly is indeed a foundational element of a functioning liberal democracy (Lange 2014: 63; Freelon 2010).

For the most part, these self-identified Filipino YouTubers display a sense of pride and identify a sense of humour in the CPDRC performance:

> Ex. 8. to anyone who isn't Filipino, understand that this is perhaps the most Filipino thing imaginable. I dunno how to explain it, but it completely does (Louieman)
> Ex. 9. Lots of talent, and crossdressers. Accurate depiction of the homeland right there. <3 (Ivan Opina)
> Ex. 10. that is why the philippines always win many international dance contest, thumbs up (Ralton Tamayan)
> Ex. 11. This is so cool #proudtobefilipino (HazzardousCurls)

From about 2012 onwards, some of these comments embedded extra metadata such as hashtags like #pinoypride and #proudtobefilipino, connecting their YouTube comments to a wider Filipino social media narrative that may connect with CPDRC photographs posted on Instagram, as well as extending across Twitter and other social networking sites.

Alongside issues relating to national identity, other forms of identity are also discussed. Some YouTubers comment that they interpret the dancers as a symbol of difference, choosing to leave a comment that specifically addresses the CPDRC's 'girlfriend' character. Some of these express a form of facetious humour while others convey an extreme and at times aggressive homophobia. For others, it is the inmates' status as Filipino that marks them as different. Some write to declare the spectacle as 'Asian' with little or no contextualization, while others again simply recognize its apparent 'Otherness':

Ex. 12. Asian Invasion.!!!!! (Tony Her)
Ex. 13. they need asians to do something like this (Simonsmsm)
Ex. 14. There probably in prison for Hacking or having Too many Kids. (danger2bad1)
Ex. 15. The definition of Filipino= STUPID! Stupid people dumb fucks! So dirty they contaminated the sea, the land and the air with their burning food everyday! Disgusting people. (Yoda Ydyxz)

Comments such as Tony Her's and Simonsmsm are vague at best. Meanwhile applying discourse analysis to danger2bad1 and Yoda Ydyxz's comments, we see examples of how YouTube users can express particularly racist, inflammatory and offensive discourse. Such comments may also be examples of 'flaming', 'flame trolling' or 'flame bait', the internet phenomenon where members of online forums post deliberately offensive, insulting or provocative comments intended to garner a hostile response or heated argument – quite often over topics the poster has no vested interest in. Across YouTube, comment sections have developed forms of social etiquette that can be riddled with trolls, haters, flaming and vast kinds of polarizing behaviour. Studies of flaming on YouTube found that although many YouTubers reported that they did not flame, it is perceived to be very common throughout the video-sharing site (see Moor, Heuvelman and Verleur 2010; Johnson 2009; Lange 2014). Motivated by frustrations, offence or misunderstandings – either from the video content or from other comments – some YouTube users also flame purely for entertainment at the expense of others, or sometimes are moved solely by the desire for attention. While the above four comments each contain multiple interpretations within YouTube protocol, on a fundamental level these comments reveal that the video has forced the CPDRC inmates into a global discourse that is often centred around and *about* them, and focused on their status as Filipino and/or criminal.

'Just good YouTube': Human jukebox, copyright contradictions and personal agendas

Of the comments that make clear intertextual references, approximately half of these are comments written by YouTube users to voice their musical requests. As user cmc42561 and user bigeyesxx publicly announce, in block capitals for added dramatic, demanding effect:

> Ex. 16. WE NEED A GANGNAM STYLE NOOOWWW (cmc42561)
> Ex. 17. CALL ME MAYBE! THUMBS UP IF YOU WANT TO SEE THEM DANCE TO THIS SONG!!! (bigeyesxx)

YouTubers like cmc42561 and bigeyesxx appear to envision that the inmates, their choreographer, or the prison officials will see their shout-outs for songs like 'Harlem Shake', LMFAO's 'Party Rock Anthem' or the latest Katy Perry or Miley Cyrus single. To these YouTubers, the captive but creative corps seem to serve global citizens like a kind of audiovisual karaoke machine, a digital jukebox or dancing cover band who will quickly, and gladly, pander to their rapid requests. Through YouTube's comment and mediation mechanisms, the CPDRC's penal performance transforms into a digitized penal spectacle.

While the comments shown above make explicit reference to the CPDRC's *Thriller* video, other YouTubers' posts appear to have their own agenda entirely. These users use the comments section as a form of public relations, promoting their own ideologies or beliefs. This is particularly evident in the case of 'Racial,' 'Religious' and 'Michael Jackson Fandom' categories. For example:

> Ex. 18. Yet he has no root in himself, but endures only for a while. For when tribulation or persecution arises because of the word, immediately he stumbles. Matthew 13:21 (YahGodIs)
> Ex. 19. Homosexuality is a sin. Like you didn't know ... (TruckTurner_Jesus_Has_Risen)
> Ex. 20. I LOVE YOU FOREVER MIKE <3 (Sıtkı Hıdış)

The language used in examples 18 and 19 is moralistic, and full of judgement. The above comments, in conjunction with the 'Racial' category, may make implicit or explicit reference to the video, but for the most part such comments often function as stand-alone statements rather than two-way conversations. YouTube's anonymous comment-based communication does not exist in real time; rather it is based upon back and forth interactions, thus most comments, such as the above, exist in a state of stasis. These patterns of commenting behaviour found under CPDRC's *Thriller* video chime with recent studies that also found that YouTube comments often do not deal with the events represented in the video, but rather seek to express fragments of issues fused with personal perspectives, framed in terms of established alignments and prejudices (Way 2015: 193). Example 20 is, however, indicative of another form of commenting – where CPDRC's *Thriller* acts as a forum for expressions of fandom for Michael Jackson fans, particularly after his death in 2009 (discussed in more detail in the next section).

A small but nonetheless significant number of YouTube comments take a surprising, particular issue with the video's lack of copyright in Germany, and take to the comment section to pose further questions about this to the YouTube collective.[8] GEMA and Germany's licensing laws operate distinctly differently to most other nations, and while there is not sufficient space to address this in depth here, this copyright issue is worthy of further investigation. In short, the video's restricted copyright belies several inherent paradoxes within YouTube operations. In 2007, Sony Music attempted to remove the audio from this copy-protected video soon after it first went viral by requesting that YouTube remove Sony's audio track. Upon realizing that they could maximize this opportunity to direct and convert YouTube views into actual paying customers of Jackson's back catalogue, Sony – like many other record labels – retreated. This undertaking becomes particularly ironic post-Jackson's death in 2009. To coincide with the posthumous DVD release of *Michael Jackson's This is It*, in January 2010 Sony flew a team of Jackson's choreographers, backing dancers, and an HD camera crew from Los Angeles to Cebu to film the Dancing Inmates in a promotional video for the film (Sony Pictures 2010). To go from issuing cease and desist warnings and removing audio in certain jurisdictions to then using the viral video's proletariat as free labourers in the production of a Hollywood bonus feature, it is evident that major record labels operate to the beat of their own drum when it comes to the mechanics of YouTube's music-like videos. Comments about music copyright and YouTube flag up their ever-changing relationship, as the fluctuating status of CPDRC's *Thriller* illustrates.

To return to the YouTube comments, others use the German copyright restriction as a springboard to make disparaging remarks about Germany, German and/or Sony Music (who some view as the culprit behind the restricted access):

> Ex. 21. 'Video can be viewed worldwide except in Germany.' More proof that the German's don't have a sense of humour. (Xavi Bob).

For other users, this video simply surmises the good in YouTube's extensive oeuvre. Numerous commenters note how this video is experienced simply as a positive part of an otherwise ordinary, everyday YouTube viewing. As YouTuber pokemaniac408 observes:

> Ex. 22. this is just good YouTube (pokemaniac408)

Comments such as these suggest how videos like CPDRC's *Thriller* primarily function as a form of entertainment, however fleeting. While some users take to the comments to credit the source that recommended the video (such as 'Thumbs up if Reddit/Glee/Vitamin Water ad sent you here'), many other comments highlight the fact that what users encounter with and experience of this video appears to be entirely random, with expressions of surprise, shock and disbelief occurring frequently. Perhaps these YouTubers searched for the original Michael Jackson *Thriller* video, and CPDRC's *Thriller* appeared as an option in the 'Results' category. Perhaps it was generated through YouTube's internal recommendation algorithm after watching a video-clip on prisons, or it automatically played as part of YouTube's inbuilt, mechanized, promoted playlists. Or perhaps they searched for a video to learn the *Thriller* dance. Whatever their reason or route to locating CPDRC's *Thriller,* these comments demonstrate that a substantial number of YouTubers are motivated to join in the community discussion.

Applying critical discourse analysis to the array of comments together, it becomes striking that the reactions to, and interactions with, CPDRC's *Thriller* are not at all straightforward, nor are they entirely predictable. It also highlights several issues regarding the problematic study of YouTube comment threads, not least in terms of methodology, and crucial issues around language and translation. By working with a random sample of comments drawn from an impossibly large – and unstable – number of comments, this analysis offers just one perspective on the breadth and range of YouTube user responses via text-based comments and communications. This viral video's YouTube comment board covers a wide-range of thematic threads and accommodates a vast array of socially emotive interaction, from the banal to the brazen. Yet like much of YouTube's cultural fate, for the most part such videos, once watched, return to the virtual archive – most likely soon forgotten, disappearing into YouTube's digital sinkhole.

Music and/as national pride

From the beginning, YouTube was synonymous with audience-driven entertainment – thanks, in part, to its remarkable feedback loop that gives content creators near-instant commentary on what content was deemed successful, and what content was utterly forgettable. Over the past ten years it has given birth to a cultivated entertainment culture that operates outside of, yet constantly in dialogue with, traditional audiovisual media ecosystems. An early study of YouTube by Hanson and Haridakis (2008) explored the primary motivations for using the site based on Papacharissi and Rubin's internet motives scale. Hanson and Haridakis identified four key factors that attracted users to YouTube: (1) leisure entertainment, (2) interpersonal expression, (3) information seeking and (4) companionship. The critical discourse analysis of comments left underneath CPDRC's *Thriller* thus far support these elements to varying degrees. However, the majority of user comments point to the video's affective potential. Taken as a whole, the range of comments left underneath CPDRC's *Thriller* convey a range of different pleasure activators from amusement, empathy and wonder. Following Michael Jackson's unexpected death in 2009, the video appears to trigger emotions of pride and loss for Jackson's fans. A substantial number of YouTube users take to the comments to cite their admiration and/or love for Michael Jackson, using the video's online platform as a forum to express seemingly 'knowing' insights into what and how Jackson would have experienced these videos. Pleasure, for these Jackson fans, appears to be derived from an assumed alignment between the Dancing Inmates' performance and Jackson's music, sense of humour and humanitarian outlook. The comments reproduced in Table 7.2 indicate a small sample of comments that affectively display expressions of entertainment and pleasure.

The ideology behind packaging embodied discipline (and/or rehabilitation) as pleasure and (mass) entertainment is inextricably bound up with issues of bodily agency. But what pleasures are being activated in

Table 7.2 A sample of CPDRC's *Thriller* YouTube comments expressing being entertained – through an incitement of pleasure, emotion and/or amusement – from watching Garcia's original CPDRC *Thriller* video

Good community service, entertaining the internet. (Mary L)
Amazing Philippines People! Very Entertaining. Show your best in the World. (jenise david)
i got goose bumps. (merlin1997ish)
I need to schedule a vacation to the Philippines and see this place. This is just beyond awesome. (Zen53GT)
please tell me Michael Jackson knew about this. I think the entertainment of this video alone would have made his life that much better:P (1cjl2)
Happiest criminals in the world. (cruchb3rry)
This was pretty awesome, made me laugh. Then I realized they have all done horrible things ... -.- (7keno7)
I can hear Michael's boyish laugh saying how great this is. He would have loved it!!! I know I enjoyed watching it!!! (Cyndi L)
When I was link six (I am 12 now) I saw my mom watching this with her friends laughing and she said 'Aye boys! If you don't dance you get no slop for the week!' I was very confused!! LOL (MythStalker. Productions)
fantastic michael would be so proud of you guys. (...) this is therapy for these guys that is what music is for, to bring hapiness and hope. (Isabelle Speed)

CPDRC's *Thriller*? And is this a sustained pleasure derived from CPDRC's YouTube cover of *Thriller* that continues to captivate hundreds of millions of viewers, incite vigorous debate and inspire original creative output in a wide range of unexpected ways years after it first went viral? On the one hand, the perceived success of the CPDRC's *Thriller*, along with the thousands of YouTube comments that convey pleasure and entertainment in witnessing the inmates' performance, supports Garcia's claim for keeping the body fit in a manner deemed pleasurable. On the other, perhaps rather than pleasure being activated in the inmates' embodied performance, Garcia may instead be referring to his perceived pleasure, and by extension, the YouTube audience's pleasure. Key to this pleasure activation is the video's YouTube dissemination, which gestures towards the video's perceived success in its intimate relationship with various forms of nostalgia and hybridity, intertwined with the early twentieth-century US colonialization of the Philippines and subsequent post/neocolonial states.

CPDRC's *Thriller* also taps into another kind of pleasure in the form of pride, or more specifically, national pride. As we have seen from a number of YouTube comments, several users take to the comment board to express various iterations of Filipino pride – a form of cultural identity that exists across and beyond country borders, from both national and diasporic publics. The Philippine islands are imagined in these comments both as a concept and as a concrete object of sorts, one where the CPDRC performance is interpreted as (re-)creating, (re-)inventing and (re-)inforcing the myth of a Philippine nation as somehow capturing the very essence of a people. Among these YouTube comments we see how ideas of culture, nationhood and nation states invoke Benedict Anderson's 'imagined communities' (1983), addressing an imagined Filipino 'community' or virtual collective. And yet such ideas and identities are hardly natural no matter how they may be perceived. The blurred, fluid and fluctuating boundaries of a Philippine national identity are both contested and sustained within these comment threads, where Filipinos living in Cebu, Crete or Canada publicly perform their symbolic ties to the homeland. More specifically, such comments and discourse detail the tensions within Filipino communities and highlight that these communities should not be homogenously constructed or imagined.

The performance text further invites us to question the tactics of popular culture consumption and globalized cultural convergence. Garcia, along with many Filipinos and non-Filipinos alike, expresses pride – and pleasure – in seeing Filipino prisoners gain national attention and cultural recognition through YouTube's digital visibility:

> I wanted something to thrill the world. I just found it so hilarious, so melodious. What an irony. They're right here in this jail, considered the

rejects of society, and yet these rejects are now making our province and our country proud. (Garcia qtd in Hunte 2007)

Garcia, quoted here from an interview with *ABC News,* imbues the CPDRC performances with a sense of regional and national pride; pride at having publicly reformed the so-called 'rejects of society' into pleasing entertainers, and a satisfaction in bringing Cebuanos to the intra-national and international stage. Through their musical performances and practices, the inmates have become representatives for and of the Philippine nation, which carries a weight that surpasses the realms of most prison sentences.

Music and musicians as cultural ambassadors

Throughout this book I have suggested that music, musical sounds and musicking activities can be imbued with potent, positive meaning and serve as progressive symbols radiating a powerful public image. Music – and by extension, musicians, performers and music entertainers – can be tasked with the official and unofficial functions of cultural diplomacy, standing in as cultural ambassadors for nation and/or brand. The American Jazz Ambassadors, for example, helped promote social and political objectives during the Cold War and associated periods of rampant anti-Americanism, while today the US State Department continues to invest in a form of musical propaganda through hip hop diplomatic and philanthropic initiatives (Salois 2015).[9] In Christi-Anne Castro's vivid account of the University of the Philippines Madrigal Singers' (the Madrigals) international successes in the field of music, she highlights the extra-musical meaning that becomes infused in their performances as they become musical representatives of and for the Philippines. The Madrigals are regularly billed as ambassadors of the Philippines and, as a result, 'it is possible for audiences to transitively interpret musical success as a symbolic triumph for the Philippine nation and for Filipinos as citizens and expatriates of that nation' (2011: 158). Castro carefully dissects this metaphor with an important revelation, explaining how this seeming leap is not actually as large as one might think especially when we consider how sports teams in international meets neatly stand in for their respective nations. She continues that once we set up this interpretive framework, it becomes:

> easy to fill in a variety of metaphors that relate the activities needed for successful singing with the positive attributes of a national body. As such, it seems a natural enough leap that a successful performing group might be adopted by the state and nationalised in order to support and even control the network of meanings that arise from music and

its performance. The Madrigals are particularly effective at promoting certain national ideals because of their repertoire and performance practice. They are young and vigorous performers, ideal for representing a new society. (2011: 158–9)

Through this lens it becomes rather straightforward to see how young, dynamic performers – athletes, dancers and opera singers alike – can serve to project a specific international image of the Republic of the Philippines, or indeed a great many nation-states. The idealized Philippine nation is thus reflected, in the case of the Madrigals, during their international concert tours each year, to audiences that have included a variety of presidents, prime ministers and popes. Through hundreds of hours of rigorous rehearsals, meticulous appearance and detailed choreographed movements, the Madrigals present themselves as immaculate cultural ambassadors of the Philippines with an impeccable award-winning background to support, and indeed sanction, this image.[10]

As this section's opening quotation from Garcia details, the CPDRC's performance achievements share a rather similar sense of international recognition. They are simultaneously tasked with bringing a very real sense of cultural pride to the Cebu province and to the Philippine nation. While the Madrigal Singers project a particular identity that is beneficial to the Philippine government – that of world-class prestige, flawless appearance, musical excellence and virtuosity that inherently give the Philippines a sense of pride according to Philippine Ambassador J. Eduardo Malaya (Gov.ph 2012) – they are simultaneously internationally recognized as ambassadors for the wider region and for promoting 'dialogue and understanding among peoples in Southeast Asia' (UNESCO 2009). A cursory glance through the comments on CPDRC's *Thriller* articulate the extent to which, for many YouTubers, the Philippine inmates stand as representatives of the world's largest continent: an 'Asian Invasion', as YouTuber Tony Her exclaims.

Both the Madrigal Singers and the CPDRC inmates enjoy thousands of YouTube video uploads. Both 'acts' boast hundreds of thousands to millions of video views. The viral popularity of both performance troupes demonstrates the international extent of their fame, while YouTube's imagined level playing field renders both groups as strangely equal, despite utilizing disparate musical texts and operating from vastly different contexts. The Madrigals tour the international concert circuit 'in the flesh' at least twice a year, while the CPDRC performances circulate through a distinctively digital yet nonetheless similarly international circuit. Intended purposes aside, through YouTube, both troupes serve as international representatives of their city, their country and for some YouTubers, are transformed into ambassadors representing the entire continent of Asia. Through certain YouTube comments, Filipinos are essentialized and re-imagined, animated and propagated as an imaginary community of 'Asians'.

The ambassadors of goodwill

> I wanted something to thrill the world. I just found it so hilarious, so melodious. What an irony. They're right here in this jail, considered the rejects of society, and yet these rejects are now making our province and our country proud. (Garcia qtd in Hunte 2007)

Due to the international popularity of the videos, by the end of 2007, eight Filipino prisons had begun adapting Garcia's dance as rehabilitation. In March 2010, the Philippine government passed legislation to implement the dance programme in all prisons across the Philippines, placing Byron Garcia at the helm of the new 'Ambassadors of Goodwill' programme. This new programme featured twelve former dancing inmates, now released from CPDRC and touring the Philippine islands with Garcia, who sometimes appeared alongside in the dual role of programme creator and a kind of troupe 'manager', promoting the CPDRC rehabilitation programme in other Philippine prisons and on daytime television shows (see Awit 2010; Rosales 2010). The dancing inmates received numerous internet accolades, from placing number five on *Time Magazine's* Top 10 Viral Videos of 2007, to making the shortlist in the 'Best Caper' category of the top 100 media moments from 2000 to 2010 (Geier et al. 2009). Garcia's actions have been singularly recognized and rewarded by international, external sources simultaneously. In April 2011, Garcia won the Second Annual Disruptive Innovator Award at the 10th Tribeca Film Festival in New York.[11]

Although neither the CPDRC facility nor the Philippine government have released official CPDRC recidivism statistics, the authorities claim that recidivism has been reduced since the introduction of the dance performances. For those CPDRC inmates who were eventually released or acquitted, a modest number of these former inmates formed the 'Ambassadors of Goodwill' troupe. This group have carved out a performance niche in the Philippine market: teaching dance to inmates in other prisons and detention facilities throughout the Philippines, of which there are over 1,300. The Ambassadors, backed by the Philippine government's Bureau of Jail Management and Penology (BJMP), are described by Garcia as former Dancing Inmates who have:

> bonded together to spread the message of peace, love, compassion and repentance to all jails in the Philippines in line with Mr. Byron Garcia's crusade on spreading his 'Music and Dance Therapy' to all jails nationwide. BJMP chief Resendo M. Dial said the memorandum of agreement is a collaborative effort between BJMP and Garcia to institutionalise music therapy in jail facilities nationwide. Music therapy which includes therapeutic dancing and singing becomes the centerpiece component for BJMPs inmate development program. (Garcia 2010)

Garcia uploaded a YouTube video charting his 'crusade' to institutionalize his 'Music and Dance Therapy' programme, capturing on film the press announcement where the official memo is signed into action on 26 March 2010 against a soundtrack of Michael Jackson's 'Heal the World' (1991). The remaining video shows footage of the Dancing Inmates performances as they 'spread the message of peace, love, compassion and repentance' in pilot projects held at three of the Philippines' largest jails: Manila City Jail, Quezon City Jail and Makati City Jail (Garcia 2010).

In effect, this memorandum legitimizes the Dancing Inmates programme, as the Ambassadors of Goodwill bring song and dance to Filipino prisons across the nation. Composed of up to twelve of the key dancers from the original *Thriller* video, including Crisanto Niere and Wenjiel Resane, Garcia established the Ambassadors troupe after his sudden and mysterious departure from the CPDRC in 2010.[12]

Media reports indicate that Garcia used his influence to gain releases for some select inmates so they could perform in his troupe; in one such interview Garcia explains how he negotiated their release for a variety of crimes, leading to assertions that the twelve released Ambassadors were the most talented dancers and arguably his 'favourites'. Asked to explain the Ambassadors' commuted sentences in media interviews, Byron Garcia stated that 'only one or two were in for minor offences, two of three were in for murder, and the rest were in for drugs' (Colors 2010). The interview with *Colors Magazine* revealed a highly questionable but unconfirmed report of bribery and corruption extending beyond the CPDRC walls, as one of the 'murderers in the dance troupe is Giovannie Nemenzo. Unconfirmed reports say that the families of his victims received a 25,000 peso settlement for his release' (2010). While multiple unconfirmed reports abound, it is hard to distinguish fact from fiction with regards to the origins of the Ambassadors of Goodwill.

What is undisputable, however, is that the Ambassadors have enjoyed modest levels of media publicity since their release. Clad in their remodelled orange jumpsuits emblazoned with white peace signs affixed to their backs, the troupe appeared on Filipino public broadcast television, including the popular noontime show *Eat Bulaga*, where they danced for a live studio audience and the millions tuned in on television, and went on to participate in the show's games for monetary prizes. Still, upon closer inspection, the fantasy of freedom in a life outside of the CPDRC is not quite as it seems. In 2010, the Ambassadors of Goodwill lived in a small boarding house that was owned by Garcia. Located in Cebu, the boarding house was a three-minute walk from their rehearsal space. Garcia thus transferred his role from prison warden to that of paternal, benevolent landlord who allegedly allows them to live there rent-free (Colors 2010). The ex-Dancing Inmates must keep a log and rehearse six days a week in order to make 2,400 Philippine pesos a month – the equivalent of GBP£1 a day.[13] After several attempts to reach Garcia in person in Cebu in 2012, 2013 and 2017, and despite successful communication with him over social media, at the time of writing Garcia declined to be interviewed for this book.[14]

Music is certainly considered a communicative form, and often compared with language for its ability to communicate on multiple levels (Castro 2011: 6). On a fundamental level the CPDRC inmates, through their performative fusions of pop song and dance that are digitally circulated, communicate with us – the YouTube audience. The seemingly universal qualities of music are reiterated by Byron Garcia across a variety of media platforms, and most often take form in his repeated pronouncement that 'Music is the language of the soul' (Garcia 2006), and communicates with the inmates in a variety of implicit and explicit ways (see Figure 7.3). Since 2006, their continuing performances both live in the prison yard and on digital screens around the world, are parallel to and 'bound up with the audience's perception and expectations, which shape and are shaped by technological change' (Auslander 1999: 158) This technological change echoes what Philip Auslander terms the 'technology of reproduction' (1999: 159). As exceptional as the first viewing of *Thriller* seems for many audiences,

FIGURE 7.3 *The view of the CPDRC's music room, which overlooks the prison yard. Painted onto the walls is the text: 'Music is the Language of the Soul!' (attributed to Sir Byron F. Garcia) and in smaller font, underneath: 'Dancing is a Form of Positive Expression'.* © Photo: Author.

and I count myself among them, the truth is that the endless repetition of the CPDRC's pop dance videos on a barrage of social networking sites like YouTube, Dailymotion, Facebook, Instagram and Twitter, transforms the exceptional into the mundane to the extent that such performances become part and parcel of a perfectly ordinary, and ultimately banal online experience.

Nonetheless, the symbiotic relationship between the live and the technologically transmitted remains inextricably linked. Attempts to curtail the live performances and recordings of the dance performances in 2010 caused over half of the inmates to refuse to participate (see Israel 2010b). The legacies of colonialism and Althusser's Ideological State Apparatuses of subjection run deep. The inmates' physical movements embody their remoulding as social subjects, and thus what is normally invisible in the outside world, this shaping of human subjects, is made visible within CPDRC and beyond through globally disseminated YouTube videos. Still it is important not to ignore the potential benefits that may be experienced through participation in a large-scale exercise activity, particularly in a culture where dance plays an imperative cultural and historical role as a form of sacred devotion, personal expression and celebration (see McNeill 1995; Williams 2013).

Through their choreographed reinventions and repertoire of iconic pop songs, the CPDRC inmates have demonstrated several facts. Their dance performances establish that although a person may be incarcerated, the transferable, permeable nature of pop music and dance enables inmates to remain a part of their community. Problematic as it all is, the Dancing Inmates clearly play an active role in challenging and/or shaping perspectives of their island and country by participating in a new site for tourism performances and mass media entertainment. The CPDRC performances 'show how even though they are in prison, they are still useful', as one Cebuano respondent states. The prisoners' status as social waste has been confronted head on, and in fact, their apparent societal usefulness becomes a recurring motif in discussions with my Cebuanos informants. Albeit because of society's voracious appetite for consumption, the cost appears to be that the inmates ultimately become 'conspicuously consumed' themselves (Adams 2001: 106).

The limited engagement that YouTube culture generally fosters underpins the stereotype that Philippine performers – and by extension Filipinos – are 'chameleons', a mutable talent that unconsciously imitates the original (Diamond 1996: 141). The self-image of the Philippines, as a meeting point between East and West, as well as its multiple colonizations, differentiates the Philippines from other Asian countries (Castro 2011: 6). For these reasons, the Philippines more than any other Asian nation 'seems to have been plagued with doubts about its cultural identity from both Asian and Western perspectives' (Diamond 1996: 141). This relates directly to the

CPDRC performances, as the 'technical aspects and the stereotypes about mimicry surrounding *Thriller*'s reception provide a window into how its choreography constitutes modernity, naturalises empire, and reinforces limited cultural engagement' (Perillo 2011: 613). As Lockard observed in his study of popular music in the Philippines, popular culture has the power and ability to manipulate minds but it can just as easily be turned against authorities as a weapon (1996: 170). The choice of primarily Western (in particular American) pop music soundtracks for the dance programme is not surprising, given the vast, continued impact of the US imperialist project on the Philippines and Filipino people. What is significant in the production, uploading and digital sharing thereafter of CPDRC's *Thriller*, is how the Philippines is imagined – constructed, even – as a site for international, intercultural encounters and exchange. Pop songs, mass media technology, and a prison warden with an overtly active imagination, as they are in CPDRC's *Thriller*, enabled stereotypes of the innately musical Filipino to perpetuate with startling results.

Coda

Dangerous mediations, prisoners of love and other considerations

We currently face a crossroads. Music today has the power to cross the secure, high walls of prisons and detention centres, dismantling any perceived mythic boundaries between freedom and captivity, and between local and global music cultures. Digital technology has further shifted the mobility of what can be considered presence, and what might be the present. Multiple histories of musical performance can be present in mediated forms. The actuality of the live – of witnessing performance, of participating in an intense communal activity – has not been hampered by the rise of digital media, for the qualities of liveness and mediation are never in opposition. Audiovisual cultures – sonic histories and visual contextualizations – are today continuously preserved as history due to increasingly accessible technological devices that enable any performance to be recorded, disseminated and archived with the press of a button. The rise of YouTube accentuates the fundamental importance of audiovisual and digital literacy within our increasingly mediated environment, and how likely it is to shape our future. It becomes obvious that audiovisual platforms like YouTube necessitate clear comprehension across the entire population. As TED curator Chris Anderson intimates, the rise of online video is driving a significant worldwide phenomenon that he terms 'crowd-accelerated innovation', a self-fuelling cycle of learning that goes beyond age, race, nation and discipline. In his own words, delivered with more than a pinch of bright-eyed TED fervour, Anderson declares that 'it's not too much to say that what Gutenberg did for writing, online video can now do for face-to-face communication' (Anderson 2010). While there is much to celebrate about YouTube's egalitarian promise, Anderson and many new media scholars disregard the many real and dangerous potentials embedded within digital video.[1] Simultaneously others encroach into an overly negative spectrum, which is equally reductionist and ultimately unhelpful. With YouTube's presence in society now firmly planted for over a decade, and we witness its variety of spin-offs, by-products and related developments, the social impact of YouTube upon private individuals and large conglomerates becomes increasingly apparent, and so it becomes essential to pay close attention to how such media and music affect, and reflect, contemporary society.[2] CPDRC's extensive and widely viewed YouTube oeuvre represents an underlying shift in popular music and media representation, on a fundamental level. While international audiences may or may not consider CPDRC's *Thriller* video to be a mainstream cultural text, what is clear is that some of the Filipino public measure the CPDRC performances as equal to if not *above* Hollywood films, as demonstrated by this exemplar of the Philippine bootleg DVD trade (Figure 8.1).

FIGURE 8.1 *Bootleg DVD featuring* Cebu Dancing Inmates Gangnam Style *and a pirated copy of American police thriller drama* End of Watch *(dir. David Ayer, 2012) on sale from a street vendor stall in Marikina, Metro Manila, 20 October 2012.* © *Photo: Author.*

This DVD, and others like it, illustrate how there is a market – albeit a black market – for the CPDRC performances that exists *offline* as well as on. It furthermore beautifully illuminates how digital and analogue worlds intermingle and collide in the everyday world. Incongruously (or, rather, congruously?) paired, a scene of dancing inmates led by Wenjiel Resane flanks a cop drama starring Hollywood actor Jake Gyllenhaal on the cover of a Filipino DVD. The existence of this bootleg DVD forced me to reconcile that the ways in which YouTube videos are consumed – the attention they command and their perceived value – are of great significance, as they raise important questions regarding affect, participatory culture and everyday new media practice. Not limited by internet connectivity, YouTube videos have become part of daily life in ways far beyond what we might initially imagine, thus raising important questions regarding popular music, the self and embodied media technology practice across the world. YouTube's outcome is not unidirectional, but dialectical. And so it enables expansive dialogue between spatially disparate communities. This relationship between digital and analogue communities – indeed between freedom and incarceration – is difficult and uneven, truly affecting the lives of those who live both online and off.

CPDRC's pervasive online existence and widespread popularity highlight how in YouTube's open-access, highly networked globalized media market, digital music video may be read as expressing cultural, ideological, historical and political self-identities. As a site of much contestation, YouTube is both critical and mundane, lofty and of the every day. A sociocultural harbinger, it is precisely in YouTube's mutability – its ability to deliver meaning and pleasure – that YouTube's seductive power lies. CPDRC's *Thriller*, and its many repeated and varied remediations, has become embedded into public consciousness. However, it is seldom given the same social and cultural significance as other mass-mediated content, primarily because it is framed within and inextricably linked with its hosting platform YouTube. YouTube's ubiquitous mediation far exceeds the boundaries of the domestic and public spaces, but falls into the multiplicity of in-betweenness – a state of chronic hyper-attentiveness, of distributed subjectivity – that characterizes so much of how we fill small pockets of time in today's mediated environment. As YouTube develops and appears to move ever further away from its DIY, user-generated origins, and much of its recent content seems polished, higher definition and almost like TV or film, we are simultaneously reminded that hundreds of thousands of YouTube videos, such as CPDRC's *Thriller*, would not – could not – exist anywhere else.

An alternative trajectory of CPDRC's *Thriller's* origins demonstrates the vital role YouTube's real-time, user-generated communities contribute to the platform's success. Indeed, if not for the specific near-instantaneous feedback loop built into YouTube, CPDRC's *Thriller* might never have happened in the first place. On 27 April 2007, YouTube user 'TakingBackFlow' left a comment under Byron Garcia's video of the CPDRC inmates' performance of Queen's 'Radio Gaga', with the simple request: 'Do thriller!' Garcia read this comment and replied two days later with 'ok, will do!' (Figure 8.2). The interplay, and interconnectedness, between music and YouTube's communicative platform is paramount, and worthy of attention within popular music and music industry studies, new media and audiovisual theory. Though we may never know the 'true' origins or impetus behind this video, in an increasingly mediated culture where images and information flow freely, affecting and inspiring even the most unlikely citizens, perhaps no such singular truth exists. Thus, themes of interconnection, agency and power that run through this work have served as frameworks in my textual and contextual reading of CPDRC's *Thriller*.

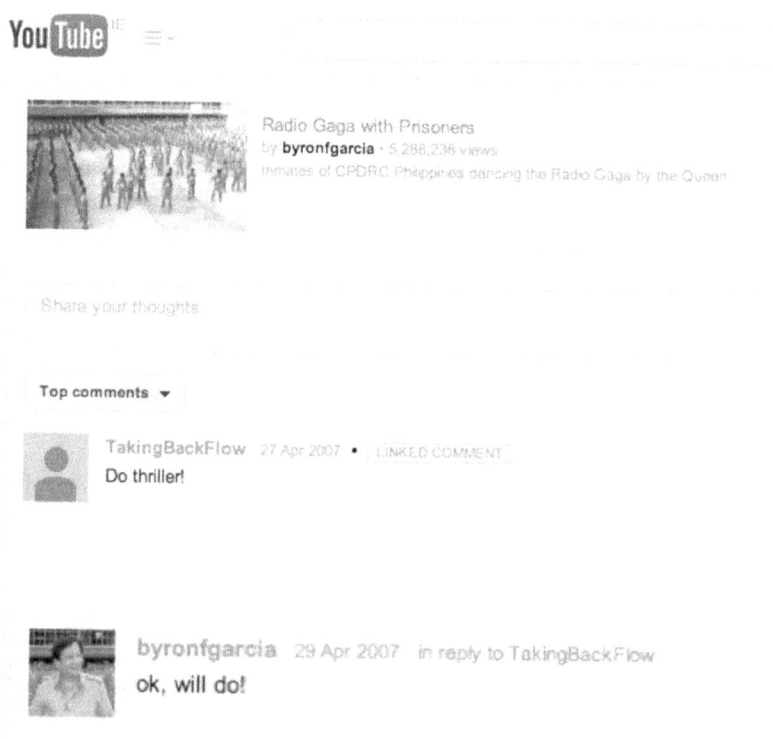

FIGURE 8.2 *'Do thriller!' commands YouTuber TakingBackFlow; 'ok, will do!' replies byronfgarcia. Could this be the original inspiration for CPDRC's* Thriller?

Postscript

On 9 May 2016, anti-establishment candidate Rodrigo Duterte won the Philippine presidential election, becoming the 16th President of the Philippines. The campaign trail that led to this point was a lesson in penal populism; Duterte singled out the problem of illegal drugs embedded in a language of crisis, to which he would provide drastic but necessary solutions by declaring an all-out war on drugs (at the expense of individual liberties). Duterte – a trained lawyer, prosecutor and former long-standing Mayor of Davao City in the Philippines' southern island of Mindanao – took every opportunity to publicly boast of his brutal approach to abolish drug pushers. During the campaign he not only admitted his direct links to the Davao death squads that claimed the lives of over 1,000 people since the 1980s, but used these associations as a platform to promote his presidential campaign: most notably his promise to reduce crime by killing thousands of criminals. Such extrajudicial killings were put into action as soon as Duterte was sworn into office on 30 June 2016. There are, of course, conflicting figures regarding the number of lives Duterte's war on drugs has claimed, varying from figures released by human rights organizations and by Philippine government bodies. Taking the latter as a point of departure, by 31 January 2017 over 7,000 deaths were linked to Duterte's war on drugs, according to official figures from the Philippine National Police – a figure attributed both to deaths during police operations and vigilante-style killings (Bueza 2017). A year later, the death toll had surpassed 12,000 people according to figures released from the Human Rights Watch *World Report 2018*.

In an attempt to find some answers to questions left unanswered from my 2012–13 visits to CPDRC, following the rise and election of President Rodrigo Duterte while writing up this book in 2016, I decided to return to Cebu for one last visit. I found Cebu in the summer of 2017 a city changed, transformed utterly in the intervening years. The city *sounded* different; downtown, the bustling nightlife I had come to know a few years previously, with characteristic sounds of karaoke sailing through the air, was replaced with an almost eerie silence in some quarters, and almost devoid of the large gatherings of people I had grown accustomed to in my previous trip. This may be, in part, due to the new House Bill 1035 – an anti-noise pollution bill that bans the 'use of karaoke, videoke, and other equipment used to amplify sound' in residential areas between 10.00 pm and 8.00 am (House of Representatives 2016). Filed in 2016, the anti-karaoke bill was based on a similar ordinance President Duterte had successfully imposed as mayor of Davao City. Duterte's presidency seemed to be affecting every facet of Filipino life. Details of Duterte's declared 'war on drugs' had been pouring through my news feed, exposing stark figures of rapidly rising fatalities and incarceration rates throughout the Philippines. I returned to Cebu to assess for myself if, and if so how, Duterte's policies had affected the everyday experiences of the Dancing Inmates of CPDRC, as it swells beyond capacity to cope with the sheer numbers of new detainees. Tragically, those who end up in prison are lucky to be alive.

Little did I know that my planned trip to Cebu and the CPDRC, that had been months in the making, was to be preceded by a major, publicized debacle. A few weeks before I was due to arrive in Cebu, the Philippine Drug Enforcement Agency in Central Visayas (PDEA-7) launched a surprise Greyhound operation inside the facility. Arriving around 1.00 am on 28 February 2017, the 289 PDEA officers ordered all 3,600 male inmates of CPDRC to assemble in the famed prison yard, remove their clothes, sit naked and cross-legged on the quadrangle floor while the inspection took place (CNN Philippines 2017). Declaring the operation justified and the strip-search tactics necessary to ensure the mutual safety of all involved, the PDEA recovered a number of bladed weapons, packets of *shabu* (crystal methamphetamine), mobile phones, laptops, cash and other contraband, which led to the dismissal of the then acting CPDRC warden Gil Macato. However, in the days and weeks that followed, photographs depicting rows and rows of naked CPDRC inmates were posted in news media, both on and offline, triggering alarm from human rights advocates, politicians and civilians. The Presidential Palace released a statement in March stating that while the strip-search was justified, photos of the naked inmates were a clear violation of their rights, and the Commission on Human Rights were sent to investigate the reports of CPDRC inmates who felt ashamed and traumatized after discovering photos of their naked bodies published in national media (Vestil 2017).

Thus my return to Cebu coincided precisely with the mounting tensions surrounding security, human rights abuses, government policy and unfavourable media coverage of the CPDRC. The Cebu Capitol government hired three former military and police officials to help manage the CPDRC's ever-growing inmate population. And by May 2017, the furore had reached such heights that a congressional enquiry was initiated by the Deputy Speaker of the House of Representatives of the Philippines (and our former mayor of Cebu) Gwendolyn Garcia. Despite multiple letters, phone calls and visits to the Capitol Building and the CPDRC, my requests for access to conduct interviews with inmates and staff inside the CPDRC went unanswered or were refused by the new Acting Warden Roberto Legaspi – primarily on the grounds that they could not ensure my personal safety within the prison at this time. CPDRC's population had doubled from what it had been in my previous visit, and with this severe overcrowding came reports from CPDRC resident doctor, Dr Mario Joyag Jr, of a rising number of inmates suffering from respiratory infections, hypertension and other illnesses. For reasons that became increasingly understandable, it was clear that my research project was rather low on the administrations' long list of priorities. As my trip drew to an end, I had to admit defeat and accept that gaining entry to the facility was not possible at this time and in this current climate.

Still, I continued to make multiple attempts by phone and email to secure an interview with Byron Garcia in the run up to and during this trip, as I had done so on the previous visit, but again to no avail. Coming towards the last few weeks of my time in Cebu, I made a last-minute bid to reach out to Garcia for an interview via social media. On 6 June 2017, I found Byron Garcia's personal Facebook page, and chanced my arm by writing him a message inviting him to discuss his role in the CPDRC Dancing Inmates programme via Facebook Messenger. He replied later that day, completely overlooking my request to meet, but instead giving me some insight into his continued perspective on CPDRC's operations. He wrote:

> There is no program anymore, it ended when I left CPDRC, I guess they continued with the dancing minus my philosophy. CPDRC now is rocked with controvecies [sic] mainly due to drug prolification [sic] and human rights violations. It is not the same CPDRC anymore. The systemic overhaul I did in 2004, was completely overturned again and went back to the sick and corrupt jail culture with the incoming administration of Governor Davide in 2013.
>
> When we were able to maintain a jail occupancy to capacity of 1600 inmates for 9 years, it took the new administration 2 years to overcrowd it with close to 3000 inmates to date.

According to Garcia's account, his particular philosophy on responsive rehabilitation through music and dance was cast aside under the city's new administration, and the progress achieved under his – and his sister's – tenure, was simply undone. Much like *Thriller,* however, Garcia chose to end our brief conversation with a cliffhanger of sorts. He continued:

> It's all history now. But the concept is still in my mind and my heart, If and when another opportunity will come, you can expect a rebirth.

There was never going to be a happy resolution to this story. Instead *Dangerous Mediations* ends much like it began, with more questions, and with Garcia painting the picture of someone waiting in the wings for the change in political powers necessary to grant him his platform to reintroduce the world to his music and dance philosophy. I replied right away, thanking him for his message and reiterating that I would like to talk more about this in person if he would agree to meet anytime, anywhere in the days and weeks that followed. Alas this ended the conversation. Subsequent messages went unanswered, and it seemed this was all Garcia wished to say on the matter. In a state of mild apprehension, I instead await the inevitable 'rebirth'; whatever shape and form it will take remains to be seen – and heard.

Prisoners of love

Still feeling a little dejected after failing to gain access inside the CPDRC on this trip, before I left Cebu I stopped in with some old contacts and a family friend – Sister Jacinta Tapales and her fellow sisters at the Carmel Monastery in Mabolo, Cebu. I had visited the sisters during my previous visit in 2013, stayed in touch via post and email in the intervening years, and promised to call in when I was next back in the city. This order of Catholic nuns, like others enclosed religious orders, have chosen to live their lives behind bars. They reside in cloisters separated from the outside world by high walls and locked gates to prevent distraction from hours of daily prayer and contemplation. Though they may be symbolically cut off from the external world immediately surrounding them, they are rather active online, with many of the sisters owning smartphones, and with access to the order's office computer to check their email accounts and Facebook pages. Their days are busy. The sisters spend as many as seven hours a day in prayer, five hours working in the gardens, kitchen, laundry and other areas on site, leaving only an hour leisure time in the evening.

I received an invitation over email to meet with the sisters during their one hour of leisure, and a date was fixed one evening in June 2017. Located on a busy downtown street, I entered the convent grounds through the tall metal gates manned by uniformed security guards – not an unusual sight in any Filipino city – and I was led into one of the convent's reception rooms by one of the lay volunteers who worked for the church. She instructed me to take my seat behind the metal grille that sliced the room into two halves. I sat on one side of the room, sweating profusely in the humid weather in my light summer dress, and was soon joined by about twenty Carmelite sisters clad in thick brown and white habits as they assembled into the other side. As with my last visit some years before, the sisters appeared to range in age from youthful twenty-something novices to those well into their eighties. I had prepared a list of research-related questions to ask the sisters about Cebu, about music and dancing. But a few minutes in, I quickly realized I was the one being interviewed here as I fielded questions about my research, my visits to CPDRC, my trips to Cebu Capitol, what Filipino food I had tried (*Lechon? Biko? Puto Maya with Sikwate?*), and what Cebuano fruit I liked best (easy: ripe mangoes). The conversation flowed with ease as I explained my book project on the CPDRC inmates to them, and they responded with intrigue and even more questions. Just when I thought the conversation was wrapping up, we veered back to a discussion of Cebuano culture, music and dancing.

'We have some dancers here, you know,' the Reverend Mother quipped, looking around at her fellow sisters who smiled and giggled. 'Would you like to see?!'

CODA

Before I knew what was happening, a group of nuns stood up, chairs were pushed back creating a space in the middle of the parquet floor. Some sisters hurried out of the room, only to return with a CD which was quickly placed into the stereo system. An upbeat track, full of bells and whistles, filled the reception room as a cluster of six nuns took to the impromptu dancefloor. The group of mainly younger sisters broke into a clearly well-choreographed routine to the song 'I Love Cebu', cheered on by the non-dancing sisters seated around them. Composed by Russel Alegado, the song received much airplay in the region following its win in the Best Upbeat/ Dance category at the 34th Cebu Popular Music Festival in 2014, and has gone on to become a *Sinulog* favourite. The other nuns – the elderly and infirm – sing along to the chorus of the recorded track, singing 'I love Cebu, *bahandi ka ning dughan ko*' ('treasure in my heart'). No sooner had this number ended than a second track began. The sisters quickly segued into a second dance, this time hula dancing to the 1930s *hapa haole* number 'My Little Grass Shack in Kealakekua, Hawaii' (Figure 8.3). Witnessing a group of six full-habit nuns dancing a hybridized Filipino-Hawaiian hula behind a metal grille was as surreal an experience as they come, as the sisters sang along to the song's romantic lyrics: 'I'm just a little Hawaiian a homesick island boy, I want to go back to my fish and poi, I want to go back to my little grass shack in Kealakekua Hawaii.'

Their smiles were infectious, as the dancing nuns giggled throughout the impromptu performance. As the song ended, the seated sisters and I clapped heartily as the dancers caught their breath and pulled up their chairs. I

FIGURE 8.3 *The Carmelite Sisters of Cebu's Filipino-Hawaiian dance, June 2017.* © *Photo: Author.*

thanked them profusely for sharing their dances with me, complimenting their ability to learn such routines in an enclosed order, and chatter ensued. 'We are also in prison!' one of the nuns piped up, to which the other sisters replied in fits of laughter. 'Yes, we are behind bars too!!' another joins in. 'But we are prisoners of love!' replied the Reverend Mother, and the entire room laughed again.

'We are prisoners of love.'

The Reverend Mother's use of the phrase 'prisoners of love' is telling. Their performance, while apparently spontaneous and completely voluntary, was yet another performance behind bars. Though their enclosed lifestyle was deliberately chosen, they too lived in a prison of sorts – describing themselves as 'prisoners of love'. And like the CPDRC inmates, despite the nuns' vocation and exclusion from the outside world immediately surrounding the convent walls, they too were plugged into the musical, media and cultural worlds around them. The phrase 'prisoners of love' is used by economist Nancy Folbre (2014) to discuss how the specific characteristics of care work and the unique relations between vulnerable people and their caregivers can make those involved in providing caring work 'prisoners of love' – motivated by the emotions of love and care rather than appropriate financial remuneration. This kind of emotional labour and physical body work that leads to prisoners of love situations tends to disproportionately affect women, migrant workers and people of colour, who often perform such care beyond the rationalized schedules of bureaucracies of which they are employed. The Philippines' history is filled with exporting such caring bodies and emotional labourers in the form of nurses, health care assistants, au pairs and domestic labourers to help fill the shortfall in healthcare and undertake much of the 'dirty work' required in the Global North (Dyer, McDowell and Batnitzky 2008). The notion of prisoners of love was further articulated as I went back over my field notes gathered over multiple visits to Cebu in 2012–13 and 2017. Reflecting on the various dances behind bars that I witnessed in Cebu – both the Carmelite nuns' private performance behind the convent walls and the CPDRC inmates' rehearsals and public performances during the monthly live shows as well as those recorded and shared with the global audiences – it became clear that both dancing troupes are framed by remarkably similar situations and historical contexts.

Both performances articulated the interconnected histories between Cebu, the Philippines and the US, between public and private, between freedom and captivity that are made luminous through music, for better or for worse. The developments in music technology, online social networks and contemporary imprisonment call for new theoretical frameworks and new forms of criticism suited to seeing beyond the surface content of cultural expressions to understand and analyse these new conditions of production. Writing over two decades ago, George Lipsitz (1994: 6) details how 'shared cultural space no longer depends upon shared geographic place'. CPDRC's

CODA

Thriller brought to light how one prison can become a new discursive space, one that allows for recognition of new networks and affiliations, while responding to the 'imperatives of place at the same time that they transcend them' (Lipsitz 1994: 6). Behind bars or not, music is an integral and constantly present aspect of today's new discursive spaces, where moments of agency can be – and indeed are – asserted.

*

As I set out in the opening pages, *Dangerous Mediations* listens to three key issues; all of these issues are raised with a view to offer more recognition and understanding of the complexities of YouTube. The first thread on 'musical mediations of power and subversion' is explored to different extents throughout this book. In Chapter 1, I suggest that CPDRC's digital mediation is interwoven with offline practices and argue that CPDRC's YouTube mediation is not antithetical to older forms. Instead, they sit together on a spectrum of communication and act as a cultural interface imbued with messages to be shared across physical and digital platforms. The fourth chapter continues this thread on musical mediations of power and subversion by placing CPDRC's *Thriller* in the wider context of prison music practices the world over. In certain contexts, I show that CPDRC's *Thriller* can be read alongside a history of subversive uses of music, specifically in places of detention.

My second strand on 'prison, subjectivity and spectacular entertainment' is picked up in Chapters 3 and 4. Here I stress that although contemporary prisons have evolved from places of punishment in many quarters, in the era of late capitalism, some of these places – like CPDRC – have been transformed into productive spaces of spectacular entertainment, leisure and tourism. Chapter 7 follows on from the penal tourists physically visiting CPDRC presented in Chapter 3, and moves online by looking at the YouTube reception of CPDRC's *Thriller* by what I call YouTube's 'penal spectators'. Through YouTube screens, these spectators confront aspects of the practices of punishment but often remain disconnected from the reality of prisons, instead viewing CPDRC's *Thriller* from a privileged distance. In reflecting on the digital divide, we see how the ramifications of this play out in a myriad of ways in CPDRC's *Thriller* – in the video itself, but also in the comments left underneath. As I have shown, in CPDRC's *Thriller* we see how punishment has returned to a public act that doubles as a sociocultural forum. Such pop performances function to unite communities and provide social rituals where community members can reflect on social and moral values. Indeed, YouTube videos like this function as a digital panopticon, where a form of online justice is performed by (potentially unwitting) members of the public.

Finally, the theme of 'music and mediation in postcolonial Philippines' is investigated in the second chapter, which opened with the paradox of Filipino stereotypes as the world's happiest, and most musical, people. I argue that

CPDRC's location – in the Philippines, and specifically in Cebu – brought with it a rich legacy of a particular kind of sonic colonization through audiovisual technologies that is significant and has lingering consequences that play out in performances like CPDRC's *Thriller*. This history of colonization through song helped construct and advance such stereotypes, which I argue play a crucial role in establishing and uncritically accepting CPDRC's *Thriller* as a form of banal entertainment. Another such lingering consequence of the US imperial project over the Philippines is found in the heavy roster of American music that remains top of the pops in Filipino culture, so Chapter 5 takes to task the elephant in the room regarding CPDRC's viral success: 'why *Thriller*?' To which I respond, reflecting on Jackson's monumental impact in the Philippines and beyond, 'why not *Thriller*?' The messages imbued in the original *Thriller*'s audiovisual experience are deeply political, connected to a lived history of oppression, terror and quotidian horror. Jackson's *Thriller* operates as a mode of meaning-making on many levels, understood as an affective, transcendental text by the ever-increasing volume of *Thriller* adaptations performed on street corners and inside bedrooms, and relayed to us on social media screens. In Chapters 5 and 6 I intimate that *Thriller* is a form of 'spreadable media' that has spawned countless remediations, which I dissect to reveal its inherently sticky features that animate it as an intergenerational, globalized song *and* dance tradition.

Taken together, the chapters in *Dangerous Mediations* seek to lend empirical weight for progressive approaches to interpreting new media texts and practices. Looking ahead, the affective approach and reflective vision proposed in this book signifies that critical readings of today's new media texts are imperative if we are to make sense of the wealth of user-generated content appearing on YouTube and other video-sharing platforms. By way of conclusion, I want to ask: can we now see – or perhaps *hear* – history differently? At the very least, going forward, *Dangerous Mediations* challenges you to heedfully approach the ever-increasing number of new music video-like works that appear on YouTube and other video-sharing sites (including those still to come).

The utopian possibilities of YouTube – and of music's transformative power within prison systems – are not without merit. *Dangerous Mediations* demonstrates how CPDRC's *Thriller* enabled the inmates of CPDRC – an overlooked and marginalized group in most conceptualizations of the global cultural industry – to become agents of cultural resistance. Simultaneously, however, the interconnectedness of music, YouTube and prison cultures brings with it a host of paradoxes: the easier it is to mediate the music, movements, sounds and experiences of the self and others, the more difficult it is to be truly seen and heard among the clatter and clash on social media. These kinds of on and offline mediations have the potential to be dangerous for us all, with untold consequences. The phrase 'dangerous mediations' is productive, I hope, for it highlights the significance of certain historical moments, colonial contexts and postcolonial discourses that are often hidden at first glance, but are nonetheless crucial to making such mediations possible.

Although this book chooses CPDRC's *Thriller* as its focus, there may well be applications for other audiovisual works, digital media and performances in detention. *Dangerous Mediations* represents only a preliminary step in the journey towards a more socio-critical musicology that I advocate as essential in our current digitally mediated environment. Alongside other scholars and activists working in these and related fields, I hope that together we can interrogate the interactions of pop music, mediation and the many forms of imprisonment that continue to exist today.

APPENDIX

Table of CPDRC Dancing Inmates YouTube videos uploads by Byron F. Garcia (as of 23 march 2011)

Date	YouTube video title/song title	Artist and/or composer	Views
08/12/10	'I Gotta Feeling' by The Quezon City Dancing Inmates	Black Eyed Peas remix	4,932
08/12/10	'I Gotta Feeling' by The Manila Dancing Inmates	Black Eyed Peas remix	5,768
29/11/10	Ambassadors of Goodwill Montage – Former Inmates	Michael Jackson remix	62,027
27/02/10	'This Is It' (remix) Promotion with Sony Pictures	Michael Jackson w/Payne, Daniel, Dres	41,696
29/11/09	'Grease [sic] Lightning'	John Travolta	178,199
04/11/09	'Queen Medley'	Queen & Styx	866,550
26/07/09	'Dangerous'	Michael Jackson	2,151,651
18/07/09	CPDRC Guests: 'And I'm Telling You I'm Not Going'	Alvin/Beyoncé Knowles	81,981
03/07/09	'Sorry Sorry'	Super Junior	5,009,280
28/06/09	'Ben', 'I'll Be There', 'We Are the World'	Michael Jackson	5,456,886
01/06/09	'Jai Ho' Remix	Sukhwinder Songh	3,090,474
27/04/09	'Tell Me', and 'Lies' Remix	The Wonder Girls & Big Bang	739,312
30/03/09	'Nobody'	The Wonder Girls	3,221,538
16/03/09	(Comedy Sketch)	Ai Haruna	13,179
13/03/09	'Just Can't Get Enough'	Depeche Mode	51,693

Date	YouTube video title/song title	Artist and/or composer	Views
05/02/09	'Pump It'	Black Eyed Peas	28,462
02/02/09	'My Sharona'	The Knack	17,464
16/01/09	'CPDRC Song' (with dance routine)	Byron F. Garcia	29,230
09/10/08	'CPDRC Song' (photo montage, no routine)	Byron F. Garcia	163,470
27/07/08	'Macarena' (Jon Secada Remix)	Los del Rio	253,276
28/06/08	'Low'	Flo Rida	2,349,431
28/04/08	'I Need a Hero'	Bonnie Tyler	2,023,306
02/04/08	'Gloria'	Laura Branigan	1,350,415
10/03/08	'My Sassy Girl'	Korean Sun Dance Troupe	8,768,443
23/02/08	'Soulja Boy'/'Can't Touch This' Remix	Soulja Boy & MC Hammer	11,255,922
22/01/08	'Mabuhi ang Sugbuanon'	Unknown	42,826
22/01/08	'Sinulog 2008, Homage to Santo Niño'	Big Brass Band Medley	53,896
21/12/07	'Jump'	Pointer Sisters	2,759,780
15/11/07	'The Haruhi Dance'	The Melancholy of Suzumiya	1,139,986
15/10/07	'Canon in D, Rock Version'	Joel Oporto (Pachelbel remix)	727,725
07/10/07	'Gregorian Chant' a.k.a. 'Sadness'	Enigma	1,484,731
07/10/07	'Do the Hustle'	Van McCoy	2,977,980
07/10/07	'Rico Mambo'	The Breakfast Club	1,271,908
25/09/07	'Music is the language of the Universe'	n/a	80,451
12/09/07	'Do the Hustle/In the Navy/The March'	KC & the Sunshine Band/Village People	209,031
08/08/07	'Thriller'	Michael Jackson	163,868

Date	YouTube video title/song title	Artist and/or composer	Views
01/08/07	'CPDRC Concepts'	n/a	46,776
17/07/07	'Hail Holy Queen'	Deloris & Sisters	1,459,397
17/07/07	'Thriller'	Michael Jackson	48,164,350
30/04/07	'Dayang Dayang' & 'Sister Act'	Aishwarya Rai	943,354
29/04/07	'I Will Follow Him'	Deloris & Sisters	4,075,724
26/04/07	'Jumbo Hotdog'	The Maskulados	1,230,092
24/04/07	'Radio Ga Ga'	Queen	4,713,079
02/10/06	'Bebot'	Black Eyed Peas	7,466,571
01/10/06	'Algorithm March'	Itsumo Kokoara	2,374,223

GLOSSARY

Anito (Filipino) Deity; idol

Bakla (Filipino) A term that once specifically referred to effeminate and/or cross-dressing males (a gender-based observation); however, today's use of *bakla* often conflates effeminacy, transvestism, homosexuality and/or the concept of the third gender

Balikbayan (Filipino) Refers to Philippine nationals who permanently reside abroad. It may also refer to those of Filipino descent who acquired foreign citizenship/permanent status abroad

BJMP Bureau of Jail Management and Penology, Philippine government

Cebuano (Filipino) Pertaining to people, language or culture from or of the Cebu region of the Philippines; the Cebuano people form the second-largest Filipino cultural-linguistic group

Clicktivism The use of social media and other online methods to support, promote and facilitate a cause including petitions, protests, boycotts, crowdfunding and circumvent news/media blackouts

CPDRC Cebu Provincial Detention and Rehabilitation Center, Cebu, Philippines

Hataw Sayaw (Filipino) 'Sayaw' means 'dance'; 'hataw', while literally translated as 'to strike or beat', when used in the context of dance as in 'hataw sayaw', pertains to 'dance show' or to 'dance your best'. The phrase 'Hataw na!' is slang for 'Bring it on!'

Ilocano (Filipino) *Ilocano* or *Ilokano* pertains to people, language or culture from or of the Ilocos region of the Philippines; Ilocano people are the third-largest ethnolinguistic group in the Philippines

Jeepney (Filipino) A converted jeep, originally left over from US military vehicles, used as a popular mode of public transport in the Philippines

Mabuhay (Filipino) Greeting; 'Long Live', literally means 'Live', from the word 'Buhay' which means 'Life'

OFW Overseas Filipino Workers account for an estimated 10 per cent of the population of the Philippines. (Related to Arroyo-Macapagal's term OFI: Overseas Filipino Investors)

Palabas (Filipino) Spectacle

Peso (Philippine Peso) Official currency of the Philippines, designated ₱ or PHP

Pinay Feminine version of the informal demonym *Pinoy,* referring to Filipino people, both in the Philippines and overseas

Pinoy Informal demonym referring to Filipino people, both in the Philippines and overseas. Though the term is strictly masculine, it is often used to denote Filipinos regardless of gender

Preso (Filipino) Inmates; prisoners

Pro-am Professional-amateur. Refers to an intermediate, indeterminate status between amateur and professional, usually in relation to sport, but increasingly used to refer to online (inter)activity

Sinulog The most popular annual cultural and religious fiesta held in Cebu

UGC User-Generated Content

Users In the context of YouTube, users are all those that 'use' the site – from the very active to the more passive

Visayan (Filipino: Bisaya) Pertains to people, language or culture from or of the Visayan region of the Philippines; Visayan people are the largest ethnolinguistic group in the Philippines (an estimated 33 million as of 2010)

YouTuber Although it generally designates anyone who watches YouTube, more specifically a YouTuber is one who makes and uploads original video onto the site, and/or otherwise actively contributes to the YouTube community (through acts including, but not limited to, commenting, sharing, liking, disliking videos)

NOTES

Introduction

1 The title 'Dancing Inmates' was officially bestowed on them by Warden Byron Garcia, cited in multiple media reports as well as Garcia's composition 'CPDRC Song' (Garcia 2008a).

2 I acknowledge that the works of Attali and Foucault (as well as others like Butler, Bhabha and McClintock that follow) were written quite a while ago. However these authors have produced some groundbreaking theorization on topics that are central to my thesis, including panoptical power, gaze, performativity, postcolonial theory and cultural hybridity, and, as such, aspects of their writing are imperative to developing a historical context for *Dangerous Mediations*.

3 I point towards such quotations taken from Henry David Thoreau's journal entry as: 'When I hear music I fear no danger, I am invulnerable, I see no foe. I am related to the earliest times and to the latest' (1857), to Friedrich Nietzsche's well-cited avowal that 'Without music, life would be a mistake' (1889), to more recent quotes such as Maya Angelou 'Music was my refuge. I could crawl into the space between the notes and curl my back to loneliness.' (1997). The internet seems persistently rife with the circulation and recirculation of such bite-sized quotations, collecting and archiving them in personal blogs (see Cybermidi Music and Midi Blog's 'Top 50 Music Quotations' (http://www.cybermidi.com/news/index.php/blog/music/top-50-music-quotations) and commercial franchises alike (see GoodReads 'Quotes about Music', http://www.goodreads.com/quotes/tag/music).

4 The rise in mainstream media's reporting cases of music and torture in the post-millennial era is attributed, in part, to the publicly disclosed US military use of music as an interrogation technique in internment camps in President George W. Bush's 'War on Terror'.

5 Upon the discovery that Barney the Purple Dinosaur's 'I Love You' theme song was being used to torture Iraqi inmates, media frenzy ensued, largely deriding any notion that the use of music, especially a children's nursery song, could be understood as a form of torture. For more details of the media's response to music torture, see Cusick (2006: 155) and Johnson and Cloonan (2009: 161–94).

6 The Philippines is the 39th largest economy in the world as of 2013 (World Bank 2013).

7 In line with the Philippines' increasing technological, media and socially networked culture, recent *TIME* research has placed Makati and Pasig City (part of Metro Manila) as the 'Selfiest City in the World', with 258 selfie-takers per 100,000 people (Wilson 2014).
8 Internet World Usage Statistics (IWS) data state that as of June 2016 there were 54 million internet users – representing a 52 per cent penetration per IWS; the Philippines presently boasts the fastest growing app market in Asia.
9 I am grateful to Ricardo D. Trimillos for pointing me towards *katakata*. See *Cultural Center of the Philippines (CCP) Encyclopaedia of Philippine Art*, Volumes 1, 2, 5, 7 and 9 (1994).

Interlude One

1 The synthesized groove is followed by Price's *Sprechgesung* and not the first verse of the song, thus the sequence of Price's narration immediately alerts an informed listener that this is the soundtrack of *Thriller* the short film, as opposed to the album version of 'Thriller'. See Chapter 5 for further details on the different versions of *Thriller*.

Chapter 1

1 Of course, such complaints regarding online sound quality are in no way limited only to YouTube, and rely heavily on the type, and quality, of playback technology used.
2 Early computer interfaces and web design often attempt to manipulate their two-dimensional surfaces to appear three-dimensional through skeuomorphism, which is still prevalent in many computer interfaces, for example web pages appearing as magazine pages; computer word processors designed to look like a notepad; computer desktop material stored in office-like 'files' and 'folders'.
3 Many contemporary music videos pay homage, consciously or subconsciously, to famous choreography and dance sequences like Fred Astaire's 'Top Hat, White Tie and Tails' from *Top Hat* (dir. Sandrich, 1935). Meanwhile Buñuel's surreal style is most famously seen in his collaboration with Salvador Dalí in the silent short film *Un Chien Andalou* (1929); several scholars have pointed to this film, along with the work of the surrealists, as greatly influencing the art of contemporary music video (see Austerlitz 2007; Richardson 2012; Rogers 2013).
4 The music video channel, VH1, was launched in January 1985, aimed at an older viewer demographic.
5 Many excellent texts trace the history and development of music video, including Goodwin (1992), Frith, Goodwin and Grossberg (1993), Vernallis (2004; 2013) and Korsgaard (2017).

6 The final tally of producing *Thriller* is often disputed; however, a *Billboard* article from 2009 cites Ron McCarrell, VP of marketing for Epic record label, who states *Thriller* was made at a cost of $1 million. See also Inglis and Hearsum (2013: 485). The specifics and impact of Michael Jackson's *Thriller* are discussed in depth in Chapter 5.

7 Over the past several years, interactive televisions have become more affordable in many regions, with most new television appliances serving dual functions as Web browsers, media streaming and interactive devices with built-in memory cards.

8 Google acquired YouTube in October 2006 for over US$1.65 billion.

9 This service 'elevates' YouTube's most popular users – those who have built up consistently large and loyal audiences through the creation of 'engaging videos' – to become YouTube Partners, whose content has 'become attractive for advertisers' (YouTube 2007a). The present YouTube Partner Program, according to YouTube's statistics, enables thousands of 'partners' to earn revenue into the six figures – although which currency these six figures is in is never actually specified. Popular content is highly sought after by YouTube, and financially rewarded, either through the Partner Program and/or advertisements, leading to the founding of several YouTube studios such as Machinima and Zephyr. Such YouTube production studios have evolved to fill a niche in the market, inheriting and reproducing in many ways the cultural gatekeeping practices from television and film.

10 As YouTube announced via their official blog: 'Over the past few weeks, you may have noticed that we've been working with select partners to improve YouTube's presentation of advertising on their videos in a manner that brings you creative, compelling content and should also increase revenue flow to artists and content owners' (YouTube 2007b).

11 Although research has produced various degrees of difference dependent on the Web 2.0 community in question, the standard distribution rates set out by Jakob Nielsen in 2006 serve as a general indication for participation ratios: 90 per cent of users are lurkers who never contribute, 9 per cent contribute intermittently, while 1 per cent account for most user contributions – in short, most online communities follow a 90–9–1 rule. Lurkers, within YouTube and internet culture more generally, are defined as those who actively follow by reading and observing online activity but do not contribute.

12 Indeed many user-generated YouTube videos, like definitions of pornography, can be considered to possess a certain 'I know it when I see it' quality (after Justice Potter Stewart, Jacobellis v. Ohio 1964).

13 For example, the non-musical channels in this Top 10 list include YouTuber PewDiePie, a Swedish videogame commentator, who often features musical jingles during his videos, while YouTube channel Machinima (a portmanteau of 'machine' and 'cinema') hosts thousands of original videos including trailers and reviews, which occasionally cover music and/or extra-musical content (such as Machinima's review of MTV's Video Music Awards 2013).

14 I borrow Richard Grusin's evocative description of YouTube as a promiscuous medium here. For Grusin, YouTube's promiscuity lies in the fact that any

YouTube video can so 'easily be embedded within virtually any digital medium' (Grusin 2009: 60).

15 The video is also censored by virtue of the places where YouTube itself is banned, access is limited, or irregular. In 2015, for example, YouTube could be accessed by citizens in the majority of nations around the world, from Fiji to Finland. Certain regions and countries enjoyed localized versions of YouTube (i.e. Australia, Canada, Japan, several European countries and in the US). YouTube was previously blocked but subsequently lifted in 2015 in Armenia, Brazil, Libya, Russia and Turkey, to name but a few. Other countries, like Saudi Arabia, experienced a limited block in 2015, while YouTube remained banned outright in China, Iran, Myanmar, Pakistan and Sudan. The wide range of levels in which YouTube is accessible certainly problematizes any concept of rendering YouTube as a homogenous, inter- and transnationally equal, mass media platform.

Interlude Two

1 The low-fi quality of CPDRC's *Thriller* indicates two cultural shifts. One, rapid progress in technology has dramatically altered our normative experiences of user-generated screen media over the course of the decade following this video's release, from advances in personal video recording devices and computer graphics cards, to better access to affordable internet and increased bandwidth. Two, it demonstrates that developments in technology are unevenly and unequally disseminated, on local, national and global levels.

Chapter 2

1 A long line of colonizers followed the Spanish, with the United States' imperial forces in power until independence in 1946 (albeit a brief, but nonetheless disturbing period of Japanese occupation during World War I), only for Martial Law to be declared under the Marcos regime (1972–1981).

2 I'm grateful to Karen Tongson who pointed out this reference – and much more besides – in her presentation 'Thriller in Cebu' at the 2008 Modern Language Association Annual Convention (MLA), San Francisco, CA.

3 US General Jacob Smith's instructions to the US military before the Balangiga massacre on the Visayan island of Samar during the Philippine–American War (1901), which led to the death and torture of thousands of Filipinos. The effects of the Balangiga massacre resonate loud and clear today; the town's three church bells were taken as war trophies by the US army in 1901 and have been exhibited on US army and air force bases since then. Despite multiple requests at recovery from the citizens of Balangiga, various Philippine presidents, and interjections from the Catholic Church, the US government refuse on the grounds that the bells are property of the US government.

4   There is no European empire-building during the same period as the US imperial projects; as the US neo-imperialist project was developing, what remained of European empires began to unravel.

5   There is an exception to the near-invisibility of Filipinos in international media of late. In the wake of the devastating Super Typhoon Yolanda/Haiyan that killed over 6,000 Filipinos in November 2013, a barrage of images of Filipinos circulated across an array of international screen media, from televisions to large-scale billboards, mediating Filipino tragedy in light of the natural disaster. At the time of writing there are small but increasing signs of opportunities for the representations of Filipinos in music and media culture, including the Broadway and West End productions of disco-opera *Here Lies Love* (David Byrne and Fatboy Slim 2013–14), based on the life of former Philippine First Lady Imelda Marcos, and the 2014 US tour of the rarely performed Filipino opera *Noli Me Tangere*. Sung in Tagalog with English subtitles, Felipe de Leon's opera featured a large cast and crew of Filipino, Filipino-American or Asian heritage. For a more detailed discussion on the politics of *Here Lies Love* see Mangaoang (2019).

6   See Fuentes' (1995) film for further details of the 1904 World's Fair. In one particularly distressing scene from Fuentes' compelling mockumentary, the crowds gawked at the Ifugaos 'exotic ritual', unaware that the displaced people are actually mourning their fellow tribe members who froze to death on the journey to Louisiana.

7   Such overt generalizations are, again, widely perpetrated in popular media, where Filipinos are cited as the world's best fishermen, nurses and service providers.

8   Other nations have experienced similar 'innate musicality' attests. Musical stereotypes assigned to Icelandic and Irish peoples, for example, form part of both nations' colonial (or in the case of Iceland, crypto-colonial) discourses. In addition, in the case of both Iceland and Ireland – and unlike the Philippines – such stereotypes are contemporarily supported by a disproportionally large global musical presence in relation to both Iceland and Ireland's populations and economic situations. For accounts of the relationship between Iceland's musical, sonic output and geographical, national identity see Hall et al. 2019. Related discourses exist regarding musicality as an inherent feature of 'race', particularly surrounding the Irish and their 'natural proclivity for music and song', and can be traced back to the Norman invasions of the twelfth century, but reached their peak during the Victorian era, at the height of the British colonialization of Ireland (McLaughlin and McLoone 2000: 181; see also Fitzgerald and O'Flynn 2014; O'Flynn and Mangaoang 2019).

9   Rose Fostanes sang the Frank Sinatra song 'My Way' in the *X Factor Israel* final episode, an interesting choice given the controversial associations with this song in Filipino karaoke culture. The so-called 'My Way killings' were a series of deaths that followed a half-dozen people who performed this song in Filipino karaoke bars between 2000 and 2010, leading many karaoke bars in the Philippines to ban the song completely (see Michaels 2010).

10 It must be noted that any such discussion of a supposedly innately Filipino 'musicality' may be read as 'Western musicality', for that is often what is

being acknowledged in these situations. Thanks to Christi-Anne Castro for conversations about the 'musical Filipino' myth (Personal correspondence, 19 December 2012).

11. The Visayan region is a group of islands occupying the central part of the Philippine Archipelago, and includes the islands of Panay, Samar, Negros, Leyte, Cebu and Bohol. Cebu City faces neighbouring Bohol island on the eastern harbour, which serves as an international port for domestic ships and inter-island vessels, and Cebu's busy international airport connects Cebu to domestic and international destinations on a daily basis.

12. The early Cebuano *balitao* song and dance was initially performed to the accompaniment of the *subing*, a Filipino bamboo flute, and subsequently accompanied by a guitar made from a coconut shell (*buko*).

13. Instead the Philippine Commission and Chairman of the Philippine Exhibition Board, W. P. Wilson, opted to heat and insulate the Filipino nipa huts (see Delmendo 2005).

14. Drawing from Foucault's 'order of discourse' and Bahktin's 'heteroglossia', Bhabha's poststructuralist perspective of third space theory is not unproblematic. To choose just one critical voice, geographer Matthew Sparke (2005) argues that Bhabha's third space theory obscures politically important issues surrounding reterritorialization in the legal battles of First Nations.

Interlude Three

1. Such ghoulish groans, heard here as they are in the original *Thriller* video, were made to be diegetic markers as the ghouls break into a wooden house to descend upon the girlfriend.

2. I refer specifically to the short film's narrative ending, at twelve minutes, to differentiate from the literal ending with credits that feature an extended repeated clip of Jackson and the zombies dancing the *Thriller* chorus, followed by an additional dance sequence of three body-popping zombies who return to their tombs in style. Compared to both of *Thriller*'s short-film endings, CPDRC's ending proves to be a major contrast.

3. Garcia first introduced this type of edited, fade-to-black ending in his video of the inmates dancing to 'I Will Follow Him' from Hollywood film *Sister Act*, uploaded three months before *Thriller* (Garcia 2007c).

Chapter 3

1. The Suroy-Suroy Sugbo is one such tourism initiative undertaken during Gwendolyn Garcia's government; her legacy focuses on her role in the development of Cebu as one of the country's premier tourist destinations.

2 This audience nationality analysis is speculative, drawn from interviews at CPDRC in January 2013 and June 2017. Prison visitors were not required to state their nationality on any entry forms, so it was during conversations with staff and inmates at CPDRC that the particularly high numbers of South Korean and German tourists visiting the prison performances was relayed to me.

3 Photographs of Garcia and the inmates with an array of visitors are presented in the photo-montage video 'CPDRC Song' (Garcia 2008a). Official 'CDPRC Inmate' merchandise is on sale too, with proceeds reputedly helping to defray the cost of incarceration, and after Garcia's dismissal in 2010, funds raised went into a co-operative prisoner health fund. Some CPDRC merchandise has made its way onto online markets too (for example, CPDRC inmate T-shirts appear on eBay from time to time).

4 The role of music in placing these TV dramas appears to be of some significance. All three prison television shows use vivid soundtracks that combine pre-existing pop songs and originally composed material, with composer Ramin Djawadi's Main Title for *Prison Break* receiving an Emmy nomination (2007), and the *Oz* soundtrack peaking at #1 on the Billboard Soundtrack chart and #8 on the Top R&B/Hip Hop Albums (2001). Most recently, the original theme song 'You've Got Time' was written by Regina Spektor exclusively for *Orange is the New Black* (2013). The song starts with a jolt with the sounds of metal cell-doors slamming, followed by lyrics describing US incarceration: 'the animals, trapped, trapped, trapped 'til the cage is full'.

5 Even with the increase in capacity, tickets to the six annual Angola Rodeo are frequently sold out, and patrons complain about the long queues of traffic on the highway leading to the facility. Figures for 2009 show that the rodeo produced $2,463,822 in revenue, with proceeds purportedly covering rodeo expenses and supplementing the Louisiana State Penitentiary Inmate Welfare Fund.

6 For a nominal fee, one can be treated like an actual prisoner while staying overnight from 9 pm to 9 am at Karosta Prison in Liepāja, Latvia.

7 Though operating on humanitarian grounds, I point to the actions of charitable groups such as Prisoners Abroad, a UK group who care for incarcerated Britons in foreign prisons. Part of their remit assists British tourists holidaying in foreign countries to visit a British inmate. Being a 'prison tourist' – visiting a stranger in prison without personal solicitation – is especially well received by the British embassy in Thailand, who help facilitate British tourists to visit Britons incarcerated in Thai prisons (Hopkirk 2005).

8 Recent studies have shown that increasing numbers of employers use Internet search engines and social networking sites to vet potential job candidates, and are influenced based on their online presence. For example, 2013 research by Harris Interactive found that 43 per cent of hiring managers who research job applicants through social media have found information that has caused them not to hire a candidate (Harris Interactive 2013).

Interlude Four

1. Thanks to Hannah Bulloch and Piers Kelly for their YouTube diligence with this particular video excerpt.
2. The filmic grain and vignette of the documentary shot on 16 mm original print, and the narrated voiceover complete with an opening orchestral melody – grainy, warbling and softly distorted – harks back to its original format as an early phonograph cylinder or gramophone recording. The film was released by Pizor's own production company, Imperial Distribution Corporation. Formed in 1931, the corporation was founded by Pizor to distribute and produce documentary films, low-budget Westerns, melodramas and short subjects; *Manila – Castilian Memoirs 1930s* and the Port O'Call series was just one such enterprise.

Chapter 4

1. Lyrics from Rorschach's 'Pavlov's Dogs' (Gern Blandsten), as appears on their LP *Remain Sedate* (1990).
2. Psychological torture, or 'no touch torture', includes such categories as isolation (solitary confinement), sensory assault (loud music, bright lights, shouting), sensory deprivation (hoods, goggles, gloves), desperation (indefinite detention, sense of futility), debilitation (food, water, sleep deprivation), spatiotemporal disorientation (confinement in small places, natural light denied) and degradation (verbal, religious, sexual, nudity, overcrowding). See United Nations *Convention Against Torture and Other Cruel, Inhuman, or Degrading Treatment or Punishment*, 1987.
3. Despite the fact that the US signed the United Nations prohibition of torture agreement (1984), and a multitude of international protests held at US embassies around the world against the US state-sanctioned use of torture, the use of EIT continues.
4. There is not space in this overview to examine the present reality that publicized practices of humiliation, discipline and executions continue around the world. Lashing, whipping and caning are enforced in some former British territories and in many Islamic countries under Sharia law, and self-flagellation is publicly practiced among some Roman Catholic extremists in the Philippines and Mexico. Despite an apparent move towards more 'humane' executions, methods including beheading, firing squad, hanging, stoning, gas chambers and (botched) lethal injections remain in use in various countries. In tandem with the rise in user-generated content servers and citizen journalists, graphic images from executions and other state enforced violences all too frequently and freely circulate through the mediasphere, only for such media to be cleaned up by low-paid content moderators often located in the Philippines. The hidden, manual labour that moderators must undertake to ensure that obscene, violent, illegal and abusive content is removed from our

online experience on platforms like YouTube reveals another inherent danger in today's contemporary media culture, and points to the trauma suffered by such workers who are disproportionately located in developing countries like the Philippines (see Chen 2014).

5 See Table 7.1 for more details on the video's YouTube responses.
6 Born digital, as the term suggests, refers to material or industries that originate in digital form, for example websites that are inherently digital to newspapers and sound recordings, which are increasingly digitally presented.
7 Choreographer Gwen Lador explained her view that teaching the inmates to dance was easier than getting the routines accurately timed. 'They know how to dance but they have trouble coordinating with that the music, especially if the music is new to them,' says Lador. 'You have to practice. You have to count for them' (Journeyman Pictures 2007).
8 Inmate Leo Suico features prominently in several interviews and video documentaries on the prison; before Garcia took over CPDRC, Suico was addicted to drugs that were smuggled into the facility. As a former member of law enforcement, he was chosen by Garcia to 'keep everyone in check' and help Garcia introduce a 'new system of discipline' (allegedly) grounded on 'Christian principles' (Journeyman Pictures 2007).
9 It is worth reproducing here Byron Garcia's elucidation from his YouTube page explaining the impetus behind this particular performance of 'Mabuhi ang Sugbuanon' in his YouTube video titled: 'Mabuhi ka GWEN'. Garcia writes: 'My innocent plan for my sister to dance with the inmates on her birthday would somehow set another world record. It was a unique way of celebrating her birthday. The dynamic Governor Gwendolyn Garcia celebrated her birthday in dance – not with a dance instructor – but with prison inmates. It was like a scenario of a swan dancing with lions, a peacock prancing with wolves or a princess romancing with a beast. This is yet a phenomenon that no official of the land has ever done worldwide, ever since. For where in the world has there ever been a government official danced [sic] with 1,500 hardened criminals? A criminal by any name is still a criminal, a prisoner by any name is still a prisoner and a governor by any name is still a governor' (Garcia 2008b).
10 Their performance to 'I Need a Hero' was decorated with homemade banners adorned with pictures of Mahatma Gandhi, Albert Einstein, Pope John Paul II, Mother Teresa, Nelson Mandela, Dalai Lama, Martin Luther King Jr, Rosa Parks, Aung San Suu Kyi and Anne Frank.
11 Gwendolyn Garcia was suspended from office in December 2012; permission to visit the CPDRC facility in December 2012–January 2013 was granted by then Acting Governor Agnes Magpale.
12 While conditions in the majority of Philippine prisons remain severely overcrowded, and dilapidated, one of the Philippine's oldest penal facilities – located on the island of Palawan – has implemented a 'humane' re-education, retraining and rehabilitation programme (Agence France-Presse 2014). One of the world's largest open prisons, Iwahig prison's approach is made possible because of the prison's vast 64,000-acre plot encompassing coconut groves, fish ponds,

corn plantations, vegetable plots, forests and mangroves. These facilities teach inmates life skills they can use once they return to society, as they tend to rice paddies (wielding machetes), learn to farm and be self-sufficient from the land.

Interlude Five

1. For literature on the origins of the term social death, see Orlando Patterson's *Slavery and the Social Death: A Comparative Study* (1985).

Chapter 5

1. The international viral popularity of CPDRC's *Thriller* released in July 2007 helped pave the way for events such as this to take place. The organizer of the inaugural Australian *Thrill the World* event in 2008, Andrew Curnock, was directly inspired to join after watching CPDRC's *Thriller* (Feeney 2008).
2. Musicological undertakings fall beyond the remit of Mercer's essay, and additionally, writing in 1986, the vast and international impact of *Thriller*'s choreographed sequence might not yet have been apparent. It is also important to note that Mercer's essay came before Jackson's physical appearance began to notably change in terms of skin colour and plastic surgery, although Mercer does – almost prophetically – point out how Jackson's appearance in promotional photography for 'Thriller' appears increasingly non-black.
3. *Thriller*'s rotation on MTV was fundamental in MTV's development as a mainstream, household media technology. See Chapter 1 for more details on MTV and the audiovisualization of popular music.
4. The single 'Thriller' went on sale on 12 November 1983 in most countries, and 23 January 1984 in the US.
5. To finance this enterprise, then, new transmedia approaches were required. Director John Landis's associate George Folsey Jr conceived of the idea of filming the filmmaking process, which could be pre-sold to cable television as an hour-long documentary called *The Making of Thriller*, thus raising enough capital to make *Thriller* itself. The plan was executed and a bidding war between cable companies ensued, resulting in MTV and Showtime paying $250,000 each to the rights to air *The Making of Thriller* documentary.
6. Although two audio versions of *Thriller* exist, the album/single version is more likely to receive radio/airplay, while the audio from the short film tends to be reserved specifically for dancing. For just one mainstream example, see the *Thriller* dance sequence in the Hollywood film *13 Going on 30* (dir. Winick, 2004).
7. A noteworthy exception to this general 'two-Thriller' oversight is Wiley 2012.
8. The use of the Pacific Tree Frog's (*Hyla regilla*) distinctive croak, often described as a 'ribbit ribbit' sound, has a long history in Hollywood soundtracks dating back to the early talkies. Despite the frog's existence only

in the US, the Pacific Tree Frog has become the quintessential sound signifier of frogs in screen media, regardless of the film's geographical setting. Kudos to Derek Foott for sounding out this frog sound.

9 The opening 0–0.50 seconds of Bernstein's 'Metamorphosis' is clearly referenced in *Thriller* from 2.10 to 3.07 of the so-called scary music.
10 The brutal murder of 14-year-old African-American Emmett Till in 1955, and acquittal of his murderers, speaks to the injustices black Americans faced during the Civil Rights Movement.
11 'Flash mob' first appeared in the Oxford English Dictionary in 2004, and is defined as 'A large public gathering at which people perform an unusual or seemingly random act and then disperse, typically organized by means of the Internet or social media'.

Interlude Six

1 Cebu Pacific (CEB), the primary low fare air carrier serving the Visayas region as well as domestic and international destinations, pride themselves on their innovative and creative approach to airfare, stating that aside from the price and service, the brand promise of a 'Fun Flight' experience that includes upbeat, on-board games serves to differentiate CEB from its competitors and thus attract more customers.
2 As mentioned previously, Filipinos – those in situ and the Philippine diaspora – represent a very active and sizeable percentage of social networking activity (see Dimacali 2010).

Chapter 6

1 A video of this performance never appeared on Byron Garcia's YouTube channel, although it is referenced in many news reports (see NPR 2007; Riminton 2007). Video performances of 'Together in Electric Dreams' are available through CPDRC visitor's recordings, such as Kofahl 2008.
2 Despite many queries regarding the accuracy of McLuhan's media prophecy, and subsequent criticisms as a technological determinist, his concepts are still useful in this case study.
3 Appadurai explicitly references Deleuze and Guattari's *Capitalism and Schizophrenia* project here.
4 It is difficult – if not impossible – to accurately assess the exact number of views the original posting of CPDRC's *Thriller*, plus every mirror (those videos that have been reproduced on YouTube, as well as those reposted elsewhere, on Dailymotion, Vimeo, Facebook and so on), but a conservative estimate puts the collective views at 100 million.

5 The homogenous rows of orange-clad inmates moving in unison to the Village People's disco anthem 'YMCA', espousing – at face value – the virtues of brotherhood, and the Young Men's Christian Association, while the song is widely understood as a celebration of male homosexuality. Videos of this performance are no longer available on YouTube as of May 2015.

Chapter 7

1. Examples of YouTube videos that have played a significant role in affecting socio-political change include social activist videos such as *Kony 2012*, videos from the Arab Spring 2012, the Obama 'Yes We Can' viral campaign, and so on. Other YouTube videos have enacted music industry change, such as Psy's 'Gangnam Style' (2012) which broke the 1 billion YouTube views record (and at the time of writing, the 3 billion mark), the effect of which pushed record companies to count YouTube views in chart listings.

2. The original set of 1,800 comments was copied, pasted and saved 'old-school' style on 4–6 February 2014. Following the release of open source data scraping for YouTube comments, the full set of comments available through the YouTube API on the '"Thriller" (original upload)' video was downloaded using YouTube Comment Scraper (http://ytcomments.klostermann.ca) on 2 May 2017. It must be noted that in the intervening three years, the number of comments had dropped significantly from over 70,000 to 43,936 – whether deleted by individual YouTubers themselves or removed by YouTube for contravening their usage policies. This is a significant limitation to this kind of research.

3. There is insufficient space here to adequately discuss the rate, and range, of changes that have been made to YouTube's (read: Google's) privacy settings in recent years. In short: while it was once possible to believe near-anonymous comments on YouTube videos (it was never truly 'open' like some other comment-communities), since 2012 YouTube have officially implemented changes to their commenting system, now actively prompting – almost forcing – users to link their YouTube accounts with their 'real names'. The probability of a YouTube comment being responded to is greatly enhanced if the comment is seen as a 'flame', 'flamebait' or 'troll' as numerous studies have shown (discussed in more detail in the paragraphs that follow).

4. 'Every cool, new community feature on YouTube involves a certain level of trust. We trust you to be responsible, and millions of users respect that trust. Please be one of them,' YouTube's Community Guidelines announce. These terms of service ask users to 'respect the YouTube community' and not to 'cross the line' by sharing material that is sexually explicit, violent, hateful, harmful, threatening or in breach of copyright. User comments, however, are less regulated, and no clear regulations about comment content exist on the Community Guidelines (YouTube n.d.).

5. **Note:** All YouTube comments reproduced throughout this book appear *sic erat scriptum*, as originally published on YouTube, with the username – also

reproduced exactly as it appears in the source text – identified in the brackets immediately succeeding each comment.

6   I choose this saying purposely to draw on Dwight Conquergood's essay 'Lethal Theatre: Performance, Punishment, and the Death Penalty', which uses this phrase in its discussion of the reactions of medieval spectators at the scaffolds (2002: 351).

7   For Small, music's primary, everyday meanings were based on building social, communicative relationships. It should be noted here that the inmates who appear to be visibly 'singing along', may be silently mouthing the words, and not singing. One of the key features of this YouTube video, as I will later demonstrate, is the fact that Jackson's soundtrack serves to cloak the inmates' individual utterances, silencing them.

8   The first sentence of the video's 'About' section states: 'Video can be viewed worldwide except in Germany.' In addition, a pop-window appears a few seconds into the video and announces: 'Audio of this video has been claimed by Sony Music Entertainment. They lifted the ban except in Germany.'

9   Mark Katz's applied work with the Next Level Hip-Hop Diplomacy programme addresses music and/as social empowerment, as discussed in Salois 2015.

10 A quick example: the Madrigals' careful medley of ABBA songs performed in concert in 2010 (Jacob 2010). Note the Madrigal Singers' immaculate dress, hair, make-up, precise gestures and subtle choreographed movements.

11 'For iconoclasts who disrupt the status quo, Tribeca's Disruptive Innovation Awards remind us that "when your only tool's a hammer, every problem starts looking like a nail"' (Hatkoff 2011).

12 There are several theories regarding Byron Garcia's departure from the CPDRC in February 2010. Although Garcia would not confirm nor deny, anecdotal sources alongside several media reports suggest that Garcia was dismissed from his post at the same time it came to light that visitor donations made to the CPDRC inmates were unaccounted for. This public enquiry into the CPDRC's accounting practices coincided with his sister's campaign for another term as Governor of Cebu, to which she felt it best not to review her brother's contract pending investigations into the missing donations (see Israel 2010a and 2010b).

13 To illustrate this point further, according to government statistics from the Philippine National Wages and Productivity Commission, the average minimum wage in Central Visayas in 2012 was increased from P305 to P327 (approximately £4.14 to £4.48); the Ambassadors' monthly wage of P2,400 is approximately a quarter of what the average monthly minimum wage worker in the area receives.

14 See the Coda for further details on communications with Garcia.

Coda

1   It is worth quoting Anderson's words directly here, as they are representative of the overtly sanguine new media optimists: 'very happily, here's one class

of people who really can't make use of this tool. The dark side of the web is allergic to the light. I don't think we're going to see terrorists, for example, publishing their plans online and saying to the world, "Please, could you help us to actually make them work this time?"' (Anderson 2010). Since 2010, if not before then, it has become increasingly apparent just how voracious the 'dark side of the web' is – both the dark internet or Lost Net (internet sites that are no longer accessible through conventional methods), Deep Web and Darknet (underground websites and file-sharing networks that are hard to locate).

2   Such developments refer specifically to the increasingly advertisement-saturated YouTube environment – by 2014, 25 per cent of embedded ads on YouTube videos are now un-skippable.

REFERENCES

Adams, Jessica. 2001. '"The Wildest Show in the South": Tourism and Incarceration at Angola'. *TDR/The Drama Review*, 45 (2), 94–108.
Agence France-Presse. 2014. 'Murderers Wander with Machetes at Idyllic Philippine Prison'. *Inquirer.net*. (Online) June 22. http://newsinfo.inquirer.net/613299/murderers-wander-with-machetes-at-idyllic-philippine-prison#ixzz35LCN1FCS.
Alesevich, Matt. 2013. 'Meet the Dancing Inmates of Cebu, Philippines: Where Getting Locked Up Abroad Is a Laughing Matter'. *South East Asia Backpacker*. 20 April. http://www.southeastasiabackpacker.com/dancing-inmates-cebu.
Anderson, Benedict. 1983. *Imagined Communities: Reflections on the Origin and Spread of Nationalism*. London: Verso.
Anderson, Chris. 2010. 'How Web Video Powers Global Innovation'. *TED Global 2010*. (Online) https://www.ted.com/talks/chris_anderson_how_web_video_powers_global_innovation.
Andersson, Benny and Björn Ulvaeus. 1977. 'Thank You For the Music'. *The Album*. (Album) Polar Music.
Apolinario, Cesar and Marnie Manicad, dir. 2013. *Dance of the Steel Bars*. 'Drama' Portfolio Films International. https://danceofthesteelbars.com.
Appadurai, Arjun. 1996. *Modernity at Large: Cultural Dimensions of Globalization*. Minneapolis: University of Minnesota Press.
Associated Press. 2008. 'Guantanamo's Auditory Assaults Fail to Win Raves'. *The Denver Post*. December 9.
Attali, Jacques. 1985. *Noise: The Political Economy of Music*. Translated by Brian Massumi. Minneapolis: University of Minnesota.
Auslander, Philip. 1999. *Liveness: Performance in a Mediatized Culture*. New York: Routledge.
Auslander, Philip. 2006. 'Musical Personae'. *TDR: The Drama Review*, 50 (1) (Spring), 100–119.
Austerlitz, Saul. 2007. *Money for Nothing: A History of the Music Video from the Beatles to the White Stripes*. New York: Continuum.
Awit, Jujemay G. 2007. 'Cardinal Urges: Know More than Inmates' Dances'. *Sun Star Cebu*.(News) 7 October.
Awit, Jujemay G. 2010. 'BJMP Hires Byron as Jails Consultant'. *Sun Star Cebu*. (News) 25 March.
Banlaoi, Rommel, C. 2004. 'Globalization and Nation-Building in the Philippines: State Predicaments in Managing Society in the Midst of Diversity'. In *Growth and Governance in Asia*, edited by Yoichiro Sato, 203–214. Hawaii: Asia-Pacific Center for Security Studies.

Bauman, Richard. 1992. 'Performance'. In *Folklore, Cultural Performances, and Popular Entertainment*, edited by Richard Baumann. Oxford: Oxford University Press, 41–49.

Baym, Nancy. 2010. *Personal Connections in the Digital Age*. Cambridge: Polity.

Bayoumi, Moustafa. 2005. 'Disco Inferno'. *The Nation*. 26 December. http://www.thenation.com/article/disco-inferno#.

BBC News. 2003. 'Sesame Street Breaks Iraqi POWs'. *BBC News*. (Online) 20 May. http://news.bbc.co.uk/2/hi/middle_east/3042907.stm.

BBC News. 2007. 'Philippine Jailhouse Rocks to Thriller'. *BBC News*. (Online) 26 July. http://news.bbc.co.uk/1/hi/6917318.stm.

Beer, David. 2008. 'Making Friends with Jarvis Cocker: Music Culture in the Context of Web 2.0'. *Cultural Sociology*, 2 (2), 222–241.

Beller, Jonathan. 2006. *Acquiring Eyes: Philippine Visuality, Nationalist Struggle, and the World-media System*. Quezon City: Ateneo University Press.

Bending, Lucy. 2000. *The Representation of Bodily Pain in Late Nineteenth-Century English Culture*. New York: Oxford University Press.

Benjamin, Walter. 1969. *Illuminations*. Translated by Harry Zorn. New York: Schocken Books.

Bergh, Arild, Tia DeNora and Maia Bergh. 2014. 'Forever and Ever: Mobile Music in the Life of Young Teens'. In *The Oxford Handbook of Mobile Music Studies Volume 1*, edited by Sumanth Gopinath and Jason Stanyek, 317–334. New York: Oxford University Press.

Berman, Marshall. 1992. *All That Is Solid Melts into Air: The Experience of Modernity*. New York: Penguin.

Bhabha, Homi K. 1990. *Nation and Narration*. London: Routledge.

Bhabha, Homi K. 2006. 'Cultural Diversity and Cultural Differences.' In *The Postcolonial Studies Reader*, edited by Bill Ashcroft, Gareth Griffiths and Helen Tiffin, 155–157. New York: Routledge.

Bigelow, Kathryn, dir. 2012. *Zero Dark Thirty*. (Film) Columbia.

Bloom, Greg and Michael Grosberg. 2012. *Lonely Planet Philippines*. London: Lonely Planet Publications, 11th Edition.

Bolter, Jay David and Richard Grusin. 2000. *Remediation: Understanding New Media*. Cambridge, MA: MIT Press.

Born, Georgina. 2005. 'On Musical Mediation: Ontology, Technology and Creativity'. *Twentieth-Century Music*, 2 (1), 7–36.

boyd, d. 2007. 'Why Youth (Heart) Social Network Sites: The Role of Networked Publics in Teenage Social Life'. In *MacArthur Foundation Series on Digital Learning – Youth, Identity, and Digital Media Volume*, edited by David Buckingham. Cambridge, MA: MIT Press, 119–142.

Boym, Svetlana. 2001. *The Future of Nostalgia*. New York: Basic Books.

Brøvig-Hanssen, Ragnhild and Paul Harkins. 2012. 'Contextual Incongruity and Musical Congruity: The Aesthetics and Humour of Mash-Ups'. *Popular Music*, 31 (1), 87–104.

Brown, Michelle. 2009. *The Culture of Punishment: Prison, Society, and Spectacle*. New York: New York University Press.

Brown, Michelle. 2012. 'Empathy and Punishment'. *Punishment & Society*, 14 (4): 383–401.

Browning, Barbara. 1998. *Infectious Rhythm: Metaphors of Contagion and the Spread of African Culture*. New York: Routledge.
Buenconsejo, José. 2010. 'Introductory Notes on Philippine Music Hybridity'. *Humanities Diliman*, 7 (1), v–viii.
Bueza, Michael. 2017. 'In Numbers: The Philippines' "war on drugs"'. *Rappler*. (Website) 23 April. https://www.rappler.com/newsbreak/iq/145814-numbers-statistics-philippines-war-drugs.
Bull, Michael. 2013. 'Sound Mix: The Framing of Multi-sensory Connections in Urban Culture'. *SoundEffects*, 3 (3), 26–46.
Bureau of Education. 1902. *Second Annual Report: Department of Public Instruction*. Reprint, Manila: Bureau of Printing, 1954.
Burgess, Jean. 2008. '"All your chocolate rain are belong to us?" Viral Video, YouTube and the Dynamics of Participatory Culture.' In *Video Vortex Reader: Responses to YouTube*. Institute of Network Cultures, Amsterdam, 101–109.
Burgess, Jean and Joshua Green. 2009. *YouTube: Online Video and Participatory Culture*. Cambridge: Polity Press.
Burkitt, Ian. 2008. *Social Selves: Theories of Self and Society*. London: Sage.
Burson-Marsteller. 2016. 'Executive Summary'. *World Leaders on YouTube: Full Study*. March 2016. Accessed 12 June 2017. https://www.burson-marsteller.com/what-we-do/our-thinking/world-leaders-on-youtube/world-leaders-on-youtube-full-study/.
Butler, Judith. 1993. 'Critically Queer'. *GLQ: A Journal of Lesbian and Gay Studies*, 1 (1), 17–32.
Butler, Judith. 1997. *The Psychic Life of Power: Theories in Subjection*. Stanford: Stanford University Press.
Cabanes, Jason Vincent and Kristel Anne F. Acedera. 2012. 'Of Mobile Phones and Mother-Fathers: Calls, Text Messages, and Conjugal Power Relations in Mother-away Filipino Families'. *New Media and Society*, 14 (6), 916–930.
Callaghan, Patrick. 2004. 'Exercise: A Neglected Intervention in Mental Health Care?'. *Journal of Psychiatric and Mental Health Nursing*, 11 (4), 476–483'.
Camden Springs. 2012. 'Seniors Thriller Dance – Camden Springs Retirement Community'. YouTube video. 31 October. https://youtu.be/wCdPij1tVlM.
Campbell, Eric. 2007. 'The Philippines – Dancing Prisoners'. *ABC News*. 30 October. (Online) http://www.abc.net.au/foreign/content/2007/s2102280.html.
Campbell, Melissa. 2003. 'Saying the Unsayable: The Non-verbal Vocalisations of Michael Jackson'. *Context*, 26 (Spring).
Campomanes, Oscar. V. 1995. 'The New Empire's Forgetful and Forgotten Citizens: Unrespresentability and Unassimilability in Filipino American Postcolonialities'. *Critical Mass*, 2 (2), 145–2000.
Cannell, Fenella. 1999. *Power and Intimacy in the Christian Philippines*. Cambridge: Cambridge University Press.
Cashin, Andrew, Emily Potter and Tony Butler. 2008. 'The Relationship between Exercise and Hopelessness in Prison'. *Journal of Psychiatric and Mental Health Nursing*, 15 (1), 66–71.
Castro, Christi-Anne. 2010. 'Subjectivity and Hybridity in the Age of Interactive Internet Media: The Musical Performances of Charice Pempengco and Arnel Pineda'. *Humanities Diliman: A Philippine Journal Of Humanities*, 7 (1), 1–23.

Castro, Christi-Anne. 2011. *Musical Renderings of the Philippine Nation*. New York: Oxford University Press.
Chen, Adrian. 2014. 'The Laborers Who Keep Dick Pics And Beheadings Out Of Your Facebook Feeds'. *Wired*. (Online) 23 October. https://www.wired.com/2014/10/content-moderation/.
Cheng, William. 2016. *Just Vibrations: The Purpose of Sounding Good*. Ann Arbor: University of Michigan Press.
Children's Hospital Colorado. 2012. '"Thriller" Dance at Children's Hospital Colorado – Halloween 2012'. YouTube video. 31 October. https://youtu.be/PXcki1Cda-k.
Cloud, David S., Carla Anne Robbins and Greg Jaffe. 2004. 'Red Cross Found Widespread Abuse of Iraqi Prisoners'. *Wall Street Journal*. (Website) 7 May. https://www.wsj.com/articles/SB108384106459803859.
CNN Philippines. 2017. 'Palace: Strip-Search Justified, Photos of Naked Detainees a Rights Violation'. (Online) 6 March. http://cnnphilippines.com/news/2017/03/06/Cebu-inmates-strip-search-Abella.html.
Colors. 2010. 'Thriller: Phililppines'. *COLORS Magazine*. (Online) Accessed 23 June 2013. http://www.colorsmagazine.com/stories/magazine/78/story/thriller.
Conquergood, Dwight. 2002. 'Lethal Theatre: Performance, Punishment, and the Death Penalty'. *Theatre Journal*, 54 (3), October, 339–367.
Constantino, Renato. 1970. 'The Mis-education of the Filipino'. *Journal of Contemporary Asia*, 1 (1), 20–36.
Cook, Nicholas. 2003. 'Music as Performance'. In *The Cultural Study of Music: A Critical Introduction*, edited by Martin Clayton, Trevor Herbert and Richard Middleton, 204–214. New York: Routledge.
Cook, Nicholas. 2013. 'Beyond Music: Mashup, Multimedia Mentality, and Intellectual Property.' In *The Oxford Handbook of New Audiovisual Aesthetics*, edited by John Richardson, Claudia Gorbman and Carol Vernallis, 53–76. New York: Oxford University Press.
Cooper, Matthew. 2013. 'Why the Philippines Is America's Forgotten Colony'. *National Journal*. (Online) 15 November. http://www.nationaljournal.com/magazine/why-the-philippines-is-america-s-forgotten-colony-20131115.
Counsell, Colin and Laurie Wolf, eds. 2001. *Performance Analysis*. New York: Routledge.
Croft, Clare. 2008. '"Thriller" Still Brings Out the Zombie in Many'. *Austin 360*. (Online) 22 October. http://archive.today/E6Zy1.
Cusick, Suzanne G. 2006. 'Music as Torture/Music as Weapon'. *TRANS-Revista Transcultural de Música*, 10, article 11. http://www.sibetrans.com/trans/article/152/music-as-torture-music-as-weapon.
David, Clarissa C., Jonathan Corpus Ong and Erika F. T. Legara. 2016. 'Tweeting Supertyphoon Haiyan: Evolving Functions of Twitter during and after a Disaster Event'. *PLoS ONE*, 11 (3), 1–19.
Dawkins, Richard. 1989 [1976]. *The Selfish Gene*. London: Oxford University Press.
de la Costa, Horatio. 2005 [1946]. 'Jewels of the Pauper'. In *Jesuit Missions*. Reprinted in Aguilar C. *Crossing Over 5*. Quezon City: RBSI.
de Leon, Felipe Padilla. 1973. 'Poetry, Music and Social Consciousness'. *Philippine Studies*, 17 (2), 266–282.

de Leon, Sunshine Lichauco. 2011. 'Making Flying Fun'. *Forbes*. (Magazine) 26 May. http://www.forbes.com/global/2011/0606/features-cebu-pacific-lance-gokongwei-flying-fun.html.

de Quiros, Conrado. 1990. 'Bracing for Balikbayans'. *Flowers from the Rubble*. Pasig, Metro Manila: Anvil Publishing, 139–141.

Deleuze, Gilles. 1992. 'Postscript on the Societies of Control'. *October*, 59 (Winter), 3–7.

Delmendo, Sharon. 2005. *The Star Entangled Banner: One Hundred Years of America in the Philippines*. Quezon City: University of the Philippines Press.

Denisoff, R. Serge. 1988. *Inside MTV*. New Brunswick, NJ: Transaction Publishers.

Devereux, Eoin, Aileen Dillane and Martin Power. 2011. *Morrissey: Fandom, Representations and Identities*. Bristol and Chicago: Intellect.

Diamond, Catherine. 1996. 'Quest for the Elusive Self: The Role of Contemporary Philippine Theatre in the Formation of Cultural Identity'. *The Drama Review*, 40 (1), Spring, 141–169.

Diaz, Diego. 2011. 'Thriller Masive Por la Educación en Chile'. YouTube video. 24 June. https://youtu.be/WgLy4gwir3Q.

Dickason, Deane H. 1934. *Castilian Memories: Manila*. Documentary (Film) USA, Imperial Pictures Inc.

Dimacali, T. J. 2010. 'Philippines Still Text Messaging Champ – US Study'. *GMA News Online*. 18 August. http://www.gmanetwork.com/news/scitech/content/198832/philippines-still-text-messaging-champ-us-study/story/.

Ding, Yuan, Yuan Du, Yingkai Hu, Zhengye Liu, Luqin Wang, Keith W. Ross and Anindya Ghose. 2011. 'Broadcast Yourself: Understanding YouTube Uploaders'. *Proceedings of the 2011 ACM SIGCOMM Conference on Internet Measurement*. New York: ACM, 361–370.

Diokno, Pepe, dir. 2008. *Dancing for Discipline*. (Film) Rock Ed Philippines and The Asia Foundation.

Duffett, Mark, (ed.) 2014. *Popular Music Fandom: Identities, Roles and Practices*. New York: Routledge.

Dunning, Jennifer. 1994. 'Michael Peters, a Choreographer Of "Dreamgirls," Is Dead at 46'. *The New York Times*, 1 September.

Dyer, Sarah, Linda McDowell and Adina Batnitzky. 2008. 'Emotional Labour/Body Work: The Caring Labours of Migrants in the UK's National Health Service'. *Geoforum*, 39 (6): 2030–2038.

Elequin, Eleanor T. 1986. 'An Appreciation Of Filipino Philosophical Outlook Through Filipino Popular Lyrics'. In *Philippine World-view*, edited by Virgilio G. Enriquez, 81–99. Quezon City: University of the Philippines Press.

Fast, Susan and Kip Pegley. 2012. *Music, Politics, and Violence*. Middletown, CT: Wesleyan University Press.

Feeney, Katherine. 2008. 'Zombies to Thrill the World – and Brisbane'. *Brisbane Times*. 24 October.

Ferguson, Niall. 2003. 'An Empire in Denial: The Limits of US Imperialism'. *Harvard International Review*, 25 (3), Fall, 64–69.

Fernandez, Doreen G. 1981. 'Philippine Popular Culture: Dimensions and Directions the State of Research in Philippine Popular Culture'. *Philippine Studies*. 29 (1), 26–44.

Ferran, Lee. 2007. 'Boogie Behind Bars: Inmates Dance the Days Away'. *ABC News*. 14 August. http://abcnews.go.com/icaught/story?id=3415920&page=2#.UcdMz-DAUSY.

Fitzgerald, Mark and John O'Flynn, eds. 2014. *Music and Identity in Ireland and Beyond*. New York: Routledge.

Folbre, Nancy. 2014. *Who Cares? A Feminist Critique of the Care Economy*. New York: Rosa Luxemburg Stiftung.

Foresight Future Identities. 2013. *Final Project Report*. London: The Government Office for Science.

Foucault, Michel. 1977 [1975]. *Discipline and Punish: The Birth of the Prison*. Translated by Alan Sheridan. London: Penguin Books.

Foucault, Michel. 1982. 'The Subject and Power'. *Critical Inquiry*, 8 (4), 777–795.

Foucault, Michel. 1991. 'Governmentality'. In *The Foucault Effect: Studies in Governmentality*, edited by Graham Burchell, Colin Gordon and Peter Miller, 87–104. Hemel Hempstead: Harvester Wheatsheaf.

Freelon, Deen G. 2010. 'Analyzing Online Political Discussion Using Three Models of Democratic Communication'. *New Media & Society*, 12 (7): 1172–1190.

Frith, Simon. 1996. *Performing Rites: On the Value of Popular Music*. New York: Oxford University Press.

Frith, Simon, Andrew Goodwin and Lawrence Grossberg, eds. 1993. *Sound and Vision: The Music Video Reader*. London: Routledge.

Fuchs, Christian. 2010. 'Social Software and Web 2.0: Their Sociological Foundations and Implications'. In The *Handbook of Research on Web 2.0, 3.0, and X.0: Technologies, Business, and Social Applications*, edited by San Muruhesan. S. New York: Information Science Reference, IGI Global.

Fuentes, Martin, dir. 1995. *Bontoc Eulogy*. (Film) Corporation for Public Broadcasting.

Fullmer, Mark. 2012. 'Literacy in the Facebook Era: A Pedagogical Approach to Internet English and Filipino Education'. In *Pagsubay*. Tacloban: Eastern Visayas Statue Univeristy.

Gallo, Phil. 2014. 'Michael Jackson Hologram at Billboard Music Awards: How It Came Together'. *Billboard*. (Online) 18 May. http://www.billboard.com/articles/events/bbma-2014/6092040/michael-jackson-hologram-billboard-music-awards/.

Garcia, Byron F. 2006. 'Speak Out: The CPDRC Experience'. *Sun Star Cebu*. 7 July. Sun Star Publishing.

Garcia, Byron F. (byronfgarcia). 2007a. '"Thriller" (original upload)'. YouTube video. 17 July. https://www.youtube.com/watch?v=hMnk7lh9M3o.

Garcia, Byron F. (byronfgarcia). 2007b. 'About Me' section on byronfgarcia's YouTube channel. http://www.youtube.com/user/byronfgarcia.

Garcia, Byron F. (byronfgarcia). 2007c. 'I Will Follow Him – Sister Act'. YouTube video. 29 April. https://youtu.be/2CPg9GWBoL0.

Garcia, Byron F. (byronfgarcia). 2008a. 'CPDRC Song'. YouTube video. 9 October. https://youtu.be/x-hinTjCD64.

Garcia, Byron F. (byronfgarcia). 2008b. 'Mabuhi ka GWEN'. YouTube video. 22 January. https://youtu.be/7Waaq8cb39Q.

Garcia, Byron F. (byronfgarcia). 2009a. 'Dancing Inmate's Michael Jackson Tribute'. YouTube video 27 June. https://www.youtube.com/watch?v=OK25cfzdTTg.

Garcia, Byron F. (byronfgarcia). 2009b. 'Grease Lightening'. YouTube video. 29 November. http://www.youtube.com/watch?v=KACFo5V73ro.

Garcia, Byron F. (byronfgarcia). 2010. 'Ambassadors of Goodwill—Cebu Dancing Inmates'. YouTube video. 2 April. https://youtu.be/C0AW5sh6iBk.

Garcia, Krista. 2016. 'A Profile of Internet Users in the Philippines'. *Rappler*. (Website) Accessed 28 May 2017. https://www.rappler.com/brandrap/profile-internet-users-ph.

Gehl, Robert. 2009. 'YouTube as Archive: Who Will Curate This Digital Wunderkammer?' *Internatinoal Journal of Cultural Studies*, 12 (1), 43–60.

Geir, Thom, Jeff Jensen, Tina Jordan, Margaret Lyons, Adam Markovitz, Chris Nashawaty, Whitney Pastorek, Lynette Rice, Josh Rottenberg, Missy Schwartz, Michael Slezak, Dan Snierson, Tim Stack, Kate Stroup, Ken Tucker, Adam B. Vary, Simon Vozick-Levinson, and Kate Ward. 2009. 'The 100 Greatest Movies, TV Shows, Albums, Books, Characters, Scenes, Episodes, Songs, Dresses, Music Videos, and Trends That Entertained Us Over the Past 10 Years'. *Entertainment Weekly*, 11 December. Issue 1079/1080, 74–84.

George, Nelson. 2010. *Thriller: The Musical Life of Michael Jackson*. New York: Da Capo Press.

Gilroy, Paul. 1993. *The Black Atlantic: Modernity and Double Consciousness*. London: Verso.

Go, Julian and Anne L. Foster, eds. 2003. *The American Colonial State in the Philippines: Global Perspectives*. Durham, NC: Duke University Press.

Goffman, Erving. 1959. *The Presentation of Self in Everyday Life*. Garden City, NY: Doubleday.

Gonzales, J. R. Lopez. 2014. 'Why Filipinos Love to Sing'. *GMA News Online*. 25 March. http://www.gmanetwork.com/news/story/347475/opinion/why-filipinos-love-to-sing.

Goodman, Steve. 2010. *Sonic Warfare: Sound, Affect, and the Ecology of Fear*. Massachusetts: Massachusetts Institute of Technology.

Goodwin, Andrew. 1992. *Dancing in the Distraction Factory: Music Television and Popular Culture*. Minneapolis: University of Minnesota Press.

Gov.ph. 2003. 'Thomasites: An Army Like No Other'. *The Official Website of the Republic of the Philippines*. 12 October. http://archive.today/6HbZJ.

Gov.ph. 2012. 'Philippine Madrigal Singers to Perform in Malaysia'. *Philippine Government Official Gazette*. 29 June. http://www.officialgazette.gov.ph/2012/06/29/philippine-madrigal-singers-to-perform-in-malaysia/.

Governor's Profile. 2012. 'The Governor: Governor Gwendolyn Garcia.' *Ato Ni Bay!* http://atnibay.blogspot.com/2012/03/governor.html

Grusin, Richard. 2009. 'YouTube at the End of New Media'. In *The YouTube Reader*, edited by Pelle Snickars and Patrick Vonderau, 60–67. Stockholm: National Library of Sweden.

Gutierrez, Maria Colina. 1961. *The Cebuano Balitao and How It Mirrors Visayan Culture and Folklife*. Cebu City: University of San Carlos.

Hall, Stuart. 1997. 'The Local and the Global: Globalization and Ethnicity'. In *Culture, Globalization and the World-System*, edited by Anthony D. King, 19–40. Minneapolis: University of Minnesota Press.

Hall, Þorbjörg Daphne, Nicola Dibben, Árni Ingólfsson and Tony Mitchell. 2019. *Sounds Icelandic - Essays on Icelandic Music in the 20th and 21st Centuries*. London: Equinox.

Hanson, Gary and Paul Haridakis. 2008. 'YouTube Users Watching and Sharing the News: A Uses and Gratifications Approach'. *Journal of Electronic Publishing*, 11 (3), Fall. https://quod.lib.umich.edu/j/jep/3336451.0011.305?view=text;rgn=main

Harmon, Amy. 2003. 'Ideas & Trends: Flash Mobs; Guess Some People Don't Have Anything Better to Do.' *New York Times*, August 17 (Online) https://www.nytimes.com/2003/08/17/weekinreview/ideas-trends-flash-mobs-guess-some-people-don-t

Harris Interactive. 2013. 'More Employers Finding Reasons Not to Hire Candidates on Social Media'. *Career Builder*. (Online) http://www.careerbuilder.com/share/aboutus/pressreleasesdetail.aspx?sd=6/26/2013&id=pr766&ed=12/31/2013.

Hatkoff, Craig. 2011. 'Tribeca Disruptive Innovation Awards'. *Tribeca Film Official Website*. 26 April. https://www.tribecafilm.com/stories/51b608b8f52704afc200000b-moment-of-invention-4sog.

Hawkins, Stan. 2009. *The British Pop Dandy: Masculinity, Popular Music and Culture*. Farnham: Ashgate.

Hawkins, Stan. 2015. *Queerness in Pop Music: Aesthetics, Gender Norms, and Temporality*. New York: Routledge.

Hegarty, Paul. 2008. *Noise/Music: A History*. London: Continuum.

Herzfeld-Schild, Marie Louise. 2013. '"He Plays on the Pillory." The Use of Musical Instruments for Punishment in the Middle Ages and the Early Modern Era'. *TORTURE Journal: Thematic Issue on Music in Detention*, 23 (2), 14–23.

Hopkirk, James. 2005 'Checking into the Bangkok Hilton'. *The Observer*. (Online) 23 October. https://www.theguardian.com/travel/2005/oct/23/thailand.darktourism.observerescapesection.

House of Representatives. 2016. House Bill 1035: An act prohibiting the use of videoke/karaoke systems. (July 5, 2016). Quezon City: Republic of the Philippines.

Hunte, Tracie. 2007. 'Prisoners' Dance: Celebration or Human Rights Violation?'. *ABC News*. (Online) 14 August. https://abcnews.go.com/icaught/story?id=3478161&page=1.

Hutcheon, Linda. 2000. *A Theory of Parody: The Teachings of Twentieth-Century Art Forms*. Urbana: University of Illinois Press.

ICDP. 2013. 'How States Abolish the Death Penalty'. *International Commission Against Death Penalty White Paper*. Accessed 18 January 2014. http://www.icomdp.org/cms/wp-content/uploads/2013/04/Report-How-States-abolition-the-death-penalty.pdf.

Inglis, Ian and Paula Hearsum. 2013. 'The Emancipation of Music Video: YouTube and the Cultural Politics of Supply and Demand'. In *The Oxford Handbook of New Audiovisual Aesthetics*, edited by John Richardson, Claudia Gorbman and Carol Vernallis. Oxford: Oxford University Press.

Irving, D. R. M. 2010. *Colonial Counterpoint: Music in Early Modern Manila*. Oxford: Oxford University Press.

Israel, Dale G. 2010a. 'Cebu Inmates Can Dance but Half Won't'. *Global Nation Inquirer.net*. (Website) 3 March. http://globalnation.inquirer.net/cebudailynews/news/view/20100303-256400/Cebu-inmates-can-dance-but-half-wont.

Israel, Dale G. 2010b. 'Net Users' Call: Let CPDRC Inmates Dance'. *Global Nation Inquirer.net*. (Website) 2 February. http://globalnation.inquirer.net/cebudailynews/news/view/20100223-254828/Net-users-call-Let-CPDRC-inmates-dance.

Ivey, Bill and Steven J. Tepper. 2006. 'Cultural Renaissance or Cultural Divide?' *The Chronicle of Higher Education*, 52 (37). http://chronicle.com/weekly/v52/i37/37b00601.htm.

Jackson, Michael. 1982. *Thriller*. (LP) Epic Records.

Jackson, Michael. 2014. 'Michael Jackson – Slave To The Rhythm'. YouTube video. 19 May. https://youtu.be/jDRTghGZ7XU.

Jackson, Naomi and Toni Shapiro-Phim, eds. 2008. *Dance, Human Rights, and Social Justice: Dignity in Motion*. Scarecrow Press.

Jacob, Paul (PaulJacob). 2010. 'ABBA Medley – Philippine Madrigal Singers'. YouTube video. 6 February. https://youtu.be/6PbHl3vcc90.

Jarboe, Greg. 2011. *YouTube and Video Marketing: An Hour a Day* (2nd Edition). Hoboken, NJ: Wiley.

Jarrett, Kylie. 2008. 'Interactivity is Evil! A Critical investigation of Web 2.0'. *First Monday*, 13(3). https://firstmonday.org/article/view/2140/1947

Jenkins, Henry. 2006a. *Convergence Culture: Where Old and New Media Collide*. Cambridge, MA: MIT Press.

Jenkins, Henry. 2006b. *Fans, Bloggers, and Gamers: Exploring Participatory Culture*. New York: New York University Press.

Jenkins, Henry. 2013. *Spreadable Media Creating Value and Meaning in a Networked Culture*. New York: New York University Press.

Jenkins, Henry, Katie Clinton, Ravi Purushotma, Alice Robison and Margaret Weigel. 2006. *Confronting the Challenges of Participatory Culture: Media Education for the 21st Century*. An occasional paper on digital media and learning. Chicago: MacArthur Foundation.

Jenkins, Henry, Xiaochang Li, Aba Domb Krauskopf and Joshua Green. 2008. *If It Doesn't Spread, It's Dead: Creating Value in a Spreadble Marketplace*. Cambridge, MA: Convergence Culture Consortium.

Johansson, Mats. 2012. 'Michael Jackson and the Expressive Power of Voice-produced Sound'. *Popular Music and Society*, 35 (2), 261–279.

Johnson, Bruce and Martin Cloonan. 2009. *Dark Side of the Tune: Popular Music and Violence*. Farnham: Ashgate.

Journeyman Pictures. 2007. *Jailhouse Rock – Philippines*. Accessed 12 November. http://youtube.com/watch?v=wAjItY7X0Yc.

Kagen, Melissa. 2013. 'Controlling Sound: Musical Torture from the Shoah to Guantánamo'. *The Appendix*, 1 (3). (Online) 20 August.

Kant, Immanuel. 1996 [1797]. *The Metaphysics of Morals: Immanuel Kant*. Translated by Mary J. Gregor. Cambridge: Cambridge University Press.

Karnow, Stanley. 1989. *In Our Image: America's Empire in the Philippines*. New York: Random House.

Kay, Aaron C., Martin V. Day, Martin P. Zanna and A. David Nussbaum. 2013. 'The Insidious (And Ironic) Effects of Positive Stereotypes'. *Journal of Experimental Social Psychology*, 49 (2), 287–291.

Keen, Andrew. 2007. *The Cult of the Amateur: How Blogs, Myspace, Youtube, and the Rest of Today's User-Generated Media are Destroying Our Economy, Our Culture, and Our Values*. New York: Crown Publishing Group.

Kelly, Philip F. 2000. *Landscapes of Globalization: Human Geographies of Economic Change in the Philippines*. London: Routledge.

Kielyl, Julia and George Hodgson. 1990. 'Stress in the Prison Service: The Benefits of Exercise Programs'. *Human Relations*, 43 (6), 551–572.

Kipling, Rudyard. 1929 [1899]. 'The White Man's Burden: The United States and The Philippine Islands'. In *Rudyard Kipling's Verse: Definitive Collection*. New York: Doubleday.

Kjus, Yngvar and Anne Danielsen. 2016. 'Live Mediation: Performing Concerts Using Studio Technology'. *Popular Music*, 35 (3), 320–337.

Kofahl, Randy (RandyKofahl). 2008. 'NEW-Inmates at CPDRC Dance to "Electric Dreams" 08/30/08'. YouTube video. 1 September. https://www.youtube.com/watch?v=cDvI1M7hNa4.

Korsgaard, Mathias Bonde. 2017. *Music Video After MTV: Audiovisual Studies, New Media, and Popular Music*. London: Routledge.

Kramer, Jerry. dir. 1983. *The Making of 'Thriller'*. (VHS) USA: Vestron Video.

Kramer, Paul A. 2006. *The Blood of Government: Race, Empire, the United States, and the Philippines*. Chapel Hill: University of North Carolina Press.

Kravets, David. 2014. 'Minutes-Long Michael Jackson Hologram Show Cost "Multiple Millions"'. *Ars Technica*. (Website) 29 May. https://arstechnica.com/information-technology/2014/05/minutes-long-michael-jackson-hologram-show-cost-multiple-millions/.

Landis, John. dir. 1983. *Thriller*. Short film/Music Video.

Lange, Patricia G. 2007. 'Publicly Private and Privately Public: Social Networking on YouTube'. *Journal of Computer-Mediated Communication*, 13 (1), 361–380.

Lange, Patricia G. 2014. 'Commenting on YouTube Rants: Perceptions of Appropriateness or Civic Engagement?'. *Journal of Pragmatics*, 73, 53–65.

Lazaredes, Nick. 2007. 'Jailhouse Rock Cebu's Youtube Celebrities.' *SBS Dateline*. (Online) 10 October. http://www.sbs.com.au/dateline/story/transcript/id/131759/n/Jailhouse-Rock-Cebu-s-Youtube-celebrities.

Lévy, Pierre. 1995. *Collective Intelligence: Mankind's Emerging World in Cyberspace*. New York: Plenum Press.

Lipsitz, George. 1994. *Dangerous Crossroads: Popular Music, Postmodernism, and the Poetics of Place*. New York: Verso.

Livingstone, Sonia. 2004. 'The Challenge of Changing Audiences'. *European Journal of Communication*, 19 (1), 75–86.

Lockard, Craig A. 1996. 'Popular Music and Politics in Modern Southeast Asia: A Compartive Analysis'. *Asian Music*, 27 (2), Spring–Summer, 149–199.

Lockard, Craig A. 1998. *Dance of Life: Popular Music and Politics in Southeast Asia*. University of Hawaii Press.

Lovink, Geert and Sabine Niederer, eds. 2008. *Video Vortex Reader: Responses to YouTube*. Amsterdam: Institute of Network Cultures.

Lowe, Lisa. 1996. *Immigrant Acts: On Asian American Cultural Politics*. Durham, NC: Duke University Press.

Madianou, Mirca and Daniel Miller. 2012. 'Polymedia: Towards a New Theory of Digital Media in Interpersonal Communication'. *International Journal of Cultural Studies*, 16 (2), 169–187.

Madianou, Mirca, Liezel Longboan and Jonathan Corpus Ong. 2015. 'Finding a Voice Through Humanitarian Technologies? Communication Technologies and Participation in Disaster Recovery'. *International Journal of Communication*, 9, 3020–3038.

Mangaoang, Áine. 2019. '"Here Lies Love" and the Politics of Disco-Opera'. In *The Routledge Companion to Popular Music Analysis: Expanding Approaches*,

edited by Ciro Scotto, Kenneth Smith and John Brackett. New York: Routledge, 347–363.
Mannocci, Alice, Daniele Masala, Daniele Mipatrini, Jenny Rizzo, Sara Meggiolaro, Domitilla Di Thiene and Giuseppe La Torre. 2015. 'The Relationship between Physical Activity and Quality of Life in Prisoners: A Pilot Study'. *Journal of Preventative Medicine and Hygiene*, 56(4), E172–E175.
Manovich, Lev. 2001. *The Language of New Media*. Cambridge MA: MIT Press.
McCarthy, Sarah, dir. 2008. *Murderers on the Dance Floor*. (Documentary) Channel 4.
McClintock, Anne. 1995. *Imperial Leather: Race, Gender and Sexuality in the Colonial Contest*. New York: Routledge.
McKay, Deirdre. 2007. '"Sending Dollars Shows Feeling:" Emotions and Economies in Filipino Migration'. *Mobilities*, 2 (2), 175–194.
McKay, Deirdre. 2016. *An Archipelago of Care: Filipino Migrants and Global Networks*. Bloomington: Indiana University Press.
McLaughlin, Noel and Martin McLoone. 2000. 'Hybridity and National Musics: The Case of Irish Rock Music'. *Popular Music*, 19 (2), 181–199.
McLuhan, Marshall. 1994 [1964]. *Understanding Media: The Extensions of Man*. Cambridge, MA: MIT Press.
McNeill, William H. 1995. *Keeping Together in Time: Dance and Drill in Human History*. Cambridge: Harvard University Press.
Mercer, Kobena. 1986. 'Monster Metaphors: Notes on Michael Jackson's Thriller'. In *Welcome to the Jungle: New Positions in Black Cultural Studies*, edited by Kobena Mercer, 33–51. New York: Routledge.
Michaels, Sean. 2010. 'Did Karaoke Versions of Sinatra's My Way Provoke Killings in the Philippines?' *The Guardian*. (Online) 9 February. https://www.theguardian.com/music/2010/feb/09/sinatra-my-way-killings-philippines.
Miethe, Terance D. and Hong Lu. 2005. *Punishment: A Comparative Historical Perspective*. Cambridge: Cambridge University Press.
Miller, Daniel and Mirca Madianou. 2012. *Migration and New Media: Transnational Families and Polymedia*. London: Routledge.
Miller, Daniel and Jolyanna Sinanan. 2012. 'Webcam and the Theory of Attainment'. *Working Paper for the EASA Media Anthropology Network e-Seminar Series*.
Miller, Kiri. 2014. 'Dance Like the Xbox is Watching'. Paper presented at the *Creativity, Circulation and Copyright: Sonic and Visual Media in the Digital Age Conference*, the Centre for Research in the Arts, Social Sciences and Humanities, University of Cambridge, 28 March.
Mkrdichian, Joy. 2009. 'Copyright and Choreography: What Constitutes Fixation?'. *Entertainment Law Seminar*, Chicago-Kent College of Law, December 18.
Moor, Peter J., Ard Heuvelman and Ria Verleur. 2010. 'Flaming on YouTube'. *Computers in Human Behavior*, 26 (6), 1536–1546.
Murphy, Peter, Michael A. Peters and Simon Marginson. 2010. *Imagination: Three Models of Imagination in the Age of the Knowledge Economy*. New York: Peter Lang.
Ness, Sally A. 1992. *Body, Movement, and Culture: Kinesthetic and Visual Symbolism in a Philippine Community*. Philadelphia: University of Pennsylvania Press.

Nicholson, Judith A. 2005. 'FCJ-030 Flash! Mobs in the Age of Mobile Connectivity'. *The Fibreculture Journal*, (6). (Online) http://six.fibreculturejournal.org/fcj-030-flash-mobs-in-the-age-of-mobile-connectivity/.

Nielsen, Jakub. 2006. *Participation Inequality: Encouraging More Users to Contribute*. Nielsen Norman Group. (Online) 9 October.

Novek, Eleanor. 2009. 'Mass Culture and the American Taste for Prisons'. *Peace Review: A Journal of Social Justice*, 21 (3), 376–384.

NPR. 2007. 'Filipino Inmates' Video Is a "Thriller" on the Web'. *National Public Radio*. 9 August. http://www.npr.org/templates/story/story.php?storyId=12643181.

O'Connell, John Morgan and Salwa El-Shawan Castelo-Branco. 2010. *Music and Conflict*. Chicago: University of Illinois Press.

O'Flynn, John and Áine Mangaoang. 2019. 'Sounding Dublin: Mapping Popular Music Experience in the City'. *Journal of World Popular Music*, 6 (1), 32–62.

Ong, Jonathan Corpus. 2009. 'Watching the Nation, Singing the Nation: London-based Filipino Migrants' Identity Constructions in News and Karaoke Practices'. *Communication, Culture & Critique*, 2, 160–181.

Ong, Jonathan Corpus. 2017. *The Poverty of Television: The Mediation of Suffering in Class-Divided Philippines*. London: Anthem Press.

Ortigas, Marga 2007. 'Philippine Prisoners Thrill the Web'. *Al Jazeera*. (Online) 1 August. http://www.aljazeera.com/news/asia-pacific/2007/07/2008525173610939949.html.

Papaeti, Anna and Morag J. Grant. 2013. 'Introduction'. *Torture Journal: Thematic Issue on Music in Detention*, 23 (2), 1–3.

Patajo-Legasto, Priscelina. 2008. *Philippine Studies: Have We Gone Beyond St. Louis?* Quezon City: University of the Philippines Press.

Perillo, J. Lorenzo. 2011. '"If I Was not in Prison, I Would not Be Famous:" Discipline, Choreography, and Mimicry in the Philippines.' *Theatre Journal*, 63 (4), 607–621.

Perrott, Lisa. 2017. 'Bowie the Cultural Alchemist: Performing Gender, Synthesizing Gesture and Liberating Identity'. *Continuum*, 31 (4), 528–541.

Peters, Kathrin and Andrea Seier. 2009 'Home Dance: Mediacy and Aesthetics of the Self on YouTube'. In *The YouTube Reader*, edited by Pelle Snickars and Patrick Vonderau, 187–203. Stockholm: National Library of Sweden.

Piech, Dan. 2013. 'Online Video: A Statistical Review'. *Com Score, Inc.* (Online) 28 March. http://www.comscore.com/Request/Presentations/2013/Online-Video-A-Statistical-Review.

Pinches, Michael, ed. 2005. *Culture and Privilege in Capitalist Asia*. London: Routeledge.

Pini, Maria. 2009. 'Inside the Home Mode'. In *Video Cultures: Media Technology and Everyday Creativity*, edited by David Buckingham and Rebekah Willett, 71–92. London: Palgrave Macmillan.

Pisares, Elizabeth H. 2006. 'Do You Mis(recognize) Me: Filipina Americans in Popular Music and the Problem of Invisibility'. In *Positively No Filipinos Allowed: Building Communities and Discourse*, edited by Antonio T. Tiongson, Jr., Edgardo V. Gutierrez, and Ricardo Valencia Gutierrez. Philadelphia: Temple University Press.

Prior, Nick. 2013. 'Vox Pop: Exploring Electronic and Digital Vocalities.' Paper presented at the *Music, Digitisation, Mediation: Towards Interdisciplinary Music Studies Conference*, University of Oxford.

Prison Dancer. 2012 'The Interactive Web Musical'. (Website) Accessed 5 July 2013 http://www.prisondancer.com.

Racelis, Mary and Judy Celine Ick. 2001. *Bearers of Benevolence: The Thomasites and Public Education in the Philippines*. Pasig City: Anvil.

Rafael, Vicente L. 2000 [1997]. '"Your Grief is Our Gossip": Overseas Filipinos and Other Spectral Presences'. In *White Love and Other Events in Filipino History*. Durham NC: Duke University Press.

Reid, Shaheem. 2009. 'Michael Jackson's Life & Legacy: Global Superstar (1982–86)'. *MTV News*. (Online) 2 July. http://www.mtv.com/news/1615220/michael-jacksons-life-legacy-global-superstar-1982-86/.

Richardson, John. 2012. *An Eye for Music: Popular Music and the Audiovisual Surreal*. Oxford: Oxford University Press.

Riminton, Hugh. 2007. '"Thriller" Prisoners Prepare to Make "Electric Dreams" Come True'. *CNN.com*. (Online) 5 September. http://edition.cnn.com/2007/WORLD/asiapcf/09/04/dancing.prisoners/#cnnSTCText.

Rodell, Paul A. 2002. *Culture and Customs of the Philippines*. Westport, CT: Greenwood Publishing Group.

Rogers, Holly. 2013. *Sounding the Gallery: Video and the Rise of Art-Music*. Oxford: Oxford University Press.

Roma-Sianturi, Dinah. 2009. '"Pedagogic Invasion": The Thomasites in Occupied Philippines'. *Kritika Kultura*, 12, 005–026.

Rosaldo, Renato. 1998. 'Ideology, Place, and People without Culture'. *Cultural Anthropology*, 3 (1), 77–87.

Rosales, Mellanie Joy C. 2010. 'Former Inmates Continue to Dance Outside CPDRC'. Retrieved http://www.philstar.com/cebu-news/587526/former-inmates-continue-dance-outside-cpdrc.

Roth, Mitchel P. 2010. *Crime and Punishment: A History of the Criminal Justice System*. Belmont, CA: Wadsworth, Cengage Learning.

Rushkoff, Douglas. 1994. *Media Virus: Hidden Agendas in Popular Culture*. New York: Ballantine.

Salois, Kendra. 2015. 'Connection and Complicity in the Global South: Hip Hop Musicians and US Cultural Diplomacy'. *Journal of Popular Music Studies*, 27, 408–423.

Schechner, Richard. 1988. *Performance Theory*. New York: Routledge.

Schechner, Richard. 2006. *Performance Studies: An Introduction*. New York: Routledge.

Schoop, Monika E. 2017. *Independent Music and Digital Technology in the Philippines*. New York: Routledge.

Schopenhauer, Arthur. 1819. *Die Welt als Wille und Vorstellung (The World as Will and Idea)*. Reproduced in *Music and Aesthetics in the Eighteenth and Early-Nineteenth Centuries*, edited by James Day and Peter le Huray, 1981. Cambridge: Cambridge University Press.

Scott, William H. 1994. *Barangay: Sixteenth-Century Philippine Culture and Society* (5th Edition 2004). Quezon City: Ateneo University Press.

Seno, Alexandra A. 2008 'Dance Is Part of Rehabilitation at Philippine Prison'. *The New York Times*. (Online) 15 January. https://www.nytimes.com/2008/01/15/world/asia/15iht-inmates.1.9223130.html?pagewanted=all&_r.

Short, Sean. 2013. 'Thriller Flash Mob, Norwegian Gem 2013'. YouTube video. 20 June. https://youtu.be/ocltxlOr33k.

Shuker, Roy. 2008. *Understanding Popular Music Culture*. New York: Routledge.

Silverman, Kaja. 1992. *Male Subjectivity at the Margins*. New York: Routledge.

Simons, Jan. 2011. 'Between iPhone and YouTube: Movies on the Move?' In *Video Vortex Reader II: Moving Images Beyond YouTube*, edited by Geert Lovink and Rachel Somers Miles, 95–105. Amsterdam: Institute of Networked Cultures.

Sinnreich, Aram. 2007. *Configurable Culture: Mainstreaming the Remix, Remixing the Mainstream*. PhD Dissertation: University of Southern California.

Small, Christopher. 1998. *Musicking: The Meanings of Performing and Listening*. Middletown, CT: Wesleyan University Press.

Snickars, Pelle and Patrick Vonderau, eds. 2009. *The YouTube Reader*. Stockholm: National Library of Sweden.

Sontag, Susan. 2003. *Regarding the Pain of Others*. New York: Picador.

Sony Pictures (SonyPicturesDVD). 2010. 'Michael Jackson's This Is It – They Don't Care About Us – Dancing Inmates HD'. YouTube video. 22 January. https://www.youtube.com/watch?v=mKtdTJP_GUI.

Sparke, Matthew. 2005. *In the Space of Theory: Postfoundational Geographies of the Nation-State*. Minneapolis: University of Minnesota Press.

Stanyek, Jason and Benjamin Piekut. 2010. 'Deadness: Technologies of the Intermundane'. *TDR: The Drama Review*, 54 (1), 14–38.

Sterne, Jonathan, ed., 2012. *The Sound Studies Reader*. New York: Routledge.

Stone, Philip R. 2006. 'A Dark Tourism Spectrum: Towards a Typology of Death and Macabre Related Tourist Sites, Attractions and Exhibitions'. *TOURISM: An Interdisciplinary International Journal*, 52 (2), 145–160.

Strangelove, Michael. 2010. *Watching Youtube: Extraordinary Videos by Ordinary People*. Toronto, ON: University of Toronto Press.

Subaihi, Thamer Al. 2013. 'Emirati Life: We Can All Learn from the Happy Folks of the Philippines'. *The National*. http://www.thenational.ae/lifestyle/emirati-life-we-can-all-learn-from-the-happy-folks-of-the-philippines/.

Tadiar, Neferti Xina M. 2004. *Fantasy Production: Sexual Economies and Other Philippine Consequences for the New World Order*. Hong Kong: Hong Kong University Press.

Thelwall, Mike, Pardeep Sud and Farida Vis. 2011. 'Commenting on YouTube Videos: From Guatemalan Rock to El Big Bang'. *Journal of the American Society for Information Science & Technology*, 63 (3), 616–629.

Thompson, Marie. 2012. 'Productive Parasites: Thinking of Noise as Affect'. *Cultural Studies Review*, 18 (3), 13–35.

Thrill the World ABQ. n.d. (Website) http://www.thrilltheworldabq.com.

Tiongson, Antonio T., Gutierrez, Edgardo V. and Ricardo V. Gutierrez. 2006. *Positively No Filipinos Allowed: Building Communities and Discourse*. Philadelphia: Temple University Press.

Tolentino, Rolando B. 2008. 'Dogeating/Dogeaters: Abjection in Philippine Colonial and Neocolonial Discourse'. In *Philippine Studies: Have We Gone Beyond St. Louis?*, edited by Priscelina Patajo-Legasto, 665–682. Quezon City: University of the Philippines Press.

Tolson, Andrew. 2010. 'A New Authenticity? Communicative Practices on YouTube'. *Critical Discourse Studies*, 7 (4), 277–289.
Travel Film Archive (travelfilmarchive). 2008. 'Manila - Castillian [sic] Memoirs 1930s'. YouTube video. 19 April 2008. https://youtu.be/ZOI6rc38Qic.
Turner, Graeme. 2004. *Understanding Celebrity*. London: Sage.
Turner, Graeme. 2006. 'The Mass Production of Celebrity: "Celetoids," Reality TV and the "demotic turn"'. *International Journal of Cultural Studies*, 9 (2): 153–165.
UCA News. 1993. 'Death Penalty Approved, Ramos Expected to Sign before Christmas'. *UCA News*. 1 December.
UNESCO. 2009. 'Philippine Madrigal Singers group will be named UNESCO Artist for Peace'. *UNESCO*. (Website) http://www.unesco.org/new/en/member-states/single-view/news/philippine_madrigal_singers_group_will_be_named_unesco_artis/.
United Nations. 1987. *Convention Against Torture and Other Cruel, Inhuman, or Degrading Treatment or Punishment*. Treaty Series, vol. 1465.
Urry, John and Jonas Larsen. 2011. *The Tourist Gaze 3.0*. London: Sage.
Van Dijck, José. 2009. 'Users Like You? Theorizing Agency in User-Generated Content'. *Media, Culture & Society*, 31, 41–58.
Van Leeuwen, Theo and Ruth Wodak. 1999. 'Legitimizing Immigration Control: A Discourse-Historical Approach. *Discourse Studies*, 1(1), 83–118.
Vernallis, Carol. 2004. *Experiencing Music Video: Aesthetics and Cultural Context*. New York: Columbia University Press.
Vernallis, Carol. 2013. *Unruly Media: YouTube, Music Video, and the New Digital Cinema*. Oxford: Oxford University Press.
Vestil, Justin K. 2017. 'Inmates Traumatized by Strip Search: CHR 7'. *Sun Star Philippines*. (Online) 7 March. http://www.sunstar.com.ph/article/129830/.
Villaruz, Basilio Esteban S. 2006. *Treading Through: 45 Years of Philippine Dance*. Quezon City: University of the Philippines Press.
Vogel, Joseph. 2012. 'The Misunderstood Power of Michael Jackson's Music'. *The Atlantic*. (Online) 8 February. https://www.theatlantic.com/entertainment/archive/2012/02/the-misunderstood-power-of-michael-jacksons-music/252751/.
Waldron, Janice. 2013. 'User-Generated Content, YouTube and Participatory Culture on the Web: Music Learning and Teaching in Two Contrasting Online Communities'. *Music Education Research*, 15 (3), 257–274.
Wasik, Bill. 2011. '#Riot: Self-Organized, Hyper-Networked Revolts – Coming to a City Near You'. *Wired*. (Online) 16 December. http://www.wired.com/2011/12/ff_riots/all/1.
Way, Lyndon C. S. 2015. 'YouTube as a Site of Debate through Populist Politics: The Case of a Turkish Protest Pop Video. *Journal of Multicultural Discourses*, 10(2), 180–196.
Wiley, Christopher. 2012. 'Putting the Music Back into Michael Jackson Studies'. *Michael Jackson: Grasping the Spectacle*, edited by Christopher R. Smit, 101–116. Farnham: Ashgate.
Williams, Fleur Cathrael. 2013. 'The Embodiment of Social Dynamics: A Phenomenon of Western Pop Dance within a Filipino Prison'. *Research in Dance Education*, 14 (1), 39–56.
Wilson, Chris. 2014. 'The Selfiest Cities in the World: TIME's Definitive Ranking'. *TIME*. (Online) 10 March. http://time.com/selfies-cities-world-rankings/.

Wilson, Jacqueline Z. 2008. *Prison: Cultural Memory and Dark Tourism*. New York: Peter Lang.
Wisdom, Stephen. 2001. *Gladiators: 100 BC–AD* New York: Bloomsbury.
Wodak, Ruth. 2001. 'The discourse-historical approach.' In *Methods of Critical Discourse Analysis*, edited by Ruth Wodak and Michael Meyer, 63–94. London: Sage.
World Bank. 2013. 'Philippine Economic Update: Accelerating Reforms to Meet the Jobs Challenge'. http://www.worldbank.org/content/dam/Worldbank/document/EAP/Philippines/Philippine_Economic_Update_May2013.pdf
YouTube. 2007a. 'YouTube Elevates Most Popular Users to Partners'. *YouTube Official Blog: What's happening on YouTube*. Accessed 13 June 2013. http://youtube-global.blogspot.ie/2007/05/youtube-elevates-most-popular-users-to.html.
YouTube. 2007b. 'You Drive the YouTube Experience'. *YouTube Official Blog: What's happening on YouTube*. Accessed 13 June 2013. http://youtube-global.blogspot.ie/2007/08/you-drive-youtube-experience.html.
YouTube. n.d. 'Statistics'. (Website) Accessed 20 August 2013. http://www.youtube.com/yt/press/statistics.html.
Žižek, Slavoj. 1989. 'Looking Awry'. *October*, 50 (Fall), 30–55.
Žižek, Slavoj. 1992. *Looking Awry: An Introduction to Jacques Lacan Through Popular Culture*. Cambridge, MA: MIT Press.

INDEX

ABBA 2, 155, 211 n.10
Abu Ghraib 97
advertisements, advertising 8, 21, 29, 32–4, 82, 88, 127–8
affect 21, 27–8, 77, 118, 129, 131, 145, 150, 182–5, 190
   affective memories 148
   affective processes 162, 171, 192
   noise as affect 109
African-American 124, 130, 209 n.10
amateur, amateurs 13, 31–5, 39, 133, 163. *See also* pro-ams
ambassador 173–4. *See also* cultural diplomacy
'Ambassadors of Goodwill' 145, 150, 175–6, 194
American popular culture 41, 48, 56, 63, 142–3
An American Werewolf in London (film) 128, 209 n.9
Appadurai, Arjun 45, 141–3, 209 n.3
archive, archives 26, 84, 91, 125, 181
   digital archives 24–6, 32, 65, 84, 125, 148, 166, 170
Attali, Jacques 3, 19, 97, 108–9, 199
audience 1, 8–10, 23–4, 27, 64, 72–3, 84, 88, 117, 124, 128–30, 144, 182, 190
   audience response 42, 68, 100–3, 112–14, 141
   film and television audiences 128–9, 144–5, 150
audiovisual 11–13, 33, 65–6, 84, 89, 145–6, 168, 184, 193
   aesthetics 1, 19–20, 23, 38, 114
   culture 9–10, 26, 30–1, 158, 163, 170, 181
   technologies 108, 192

Thriller as audiovisual text 5, 16, 72, 125–7, 130–1
auditions 40, 80
Auslander, Philip 118, 135, 165, 177

bakla 41, 47, 68, 161, 197
balikbayan 53–4, 166. *See also* OFW
bass 16–17, 108, 126
battle 3, 5, 58, 60, 121–2, 204 n.14
Bentham, Jeremy 105–7
Bernstein, Elmer 42, 71, 127–8, 209 n.9
Beyoncé 128
Bhabha, Homi 68, 88, 147, 199 n.2, 204 n.14
Bieber, Justin 36–8, 68
BJMP (Bureau of Jail Management and Penology) 150
blackness 130, 208 n.2
body, bodies 4, 29–30, 94, 96, 110–11, 190
   body language 42, 71
   criminal bodies 17, 87–8, 97, 100–6, 146, 151, 186
   dancing bodies 43, 110–11, 113, 126, 132, 135, 148, 172–3
   Filipino bodies 53, 166, 186, 190
   male bodies 39–40 (*see also* 'docile bodies')
Born, Georgina 19–20
Boym, Svetlana 148
brown 17, 49, 188
Brown, Michelle 6, 84, 87, 97, 157
Buenconsejo, José Semblante 147
Burgess, Jean 21, 27, 30, 35–6, 38, 132, 158, 163
Butler, Judith 6, 42, 111–12, 165, 199 n.2

calisthenics 65, 92–3, 109
camera 84, 88, 108, 121, 130, 134–5, 141, 144, 165, 169
   angle 15, 17, 41–3, 71–4, 78, 95, 117, 149
   surveillance 73, 105
   video 16, 21, 80, 114, 133
capitalism 40, 142, 163
   global capitalism 40, 144, 147
   late capitalism 118, 143, 144, 191
Castro, Christi-Anne 8, 48, 146–7, 173, 177–8, 204 n.10
Catholicism 45, 57, 59, 62, 77, 122–3, 188. See also Christianity; nuns
Cebuano culture 47, 58–9, 64, 77, 80, 84, 188
Cebu Provincial Government 77, 82–3, 114, 186, 204 n.1, 207 n.9. See also Garcia, Gwendolyn
celebrity 143, 146
children 3, 7, 49, 57–8, 62, 134, 137, 144, 199 n.5
choreographer 65, 104, 108, 111, 118, 129, 168–9, 207 n.7
   CPDRC choreographer Vince Rosales 80–1
choreography 23, 60, 76, 79–81, 87, 114, 118, 139, 146, 151, 174, 178–9, 189
   choreography as discipline 87, 104, 108, 111–13
   Thriller choreography 43, 74, 121–4, 129–33, 135–6, 149
Christianity 7, 58–9, 99, 207 n.8, 210 n.5
church 7, 56, 77, 188, 202 n.3
cinema 21–2, 39, 52, 56, 78, 149, 201 n.13
civilize, civilizing 48–9, 66, 97, 101, 106
class (social) 27, 34, 51, 92, 145, 164
classical music 78–9, 94
Cloonan, Martin 4–5, 97, 199 n.5
colonialism 10–12, 45–9, 51–6, 63–5, 147, 151, 172, 193
   American 8, 45, 47–9, 51–6, 63–4, 91, 94, 144

colonial stereotypes 7, 45–6, 57–8, 64–8, 83, 151, 178–9, 191–2
   Japanese 52–3, 202 n.1
   Spanish 45, 54, 56, 77, 91 (*see also* neocolonial; Orientalism; postcolonial)
communication 12, 19, 25–30, 104, 107, 141, 165–8, 177, 191
communicative performance 19, 38, 72, 135
community 6–7, 30, 98–9, 121, 124, 126, 135, 151, 171, 178, 191
   Filipino communities 8, 62, 166, 172, 174
   online communities 88, 160, 201 n.11
   YouTube and 24, 26, 31–2, 39, 81, 83, 141–2, 158, 162, 164, 166, 183 (*see also* OFW; fandom)
competition 57, 60–1, 121, 137
computer 21, 22, 35, 157, 188
   monitor/screen 16, 21, 22, 105
Constantino, Renato 51–2, 63
control 6, 9, 54–5, 66, 146, 157
   penal 64, 100–8, 110–14
   programmatic 68–9, 173
Cook, Nicholas 24, 165–6
copyright 40, 161, 168–9
corporal punishment. *See* death penalty
corporeality 104, 110, 123, 145
covers 35, 143, 165
CPDRC live (public performances) 66, 82f, 86, 94, 108, 113, 115, 139–41, 178, 190
'CPDRC Song, The' (song) 83, 199 n.1, 205 n.3
cultural diplomacy 173, 211 n.9. *See also* ambassador
cultures 5, 12, 34, 40, 45, 56, 108, 148, 170
   convergence 27
   global 148
   hybrid 68, 147
   media 2, 73, 184
   popular music 1–2, 88, 124–5, 179, 181

INDEX

prison 6, 84, 86, 88, 92, 103, 187 (*see also* American popular culture; celebrity; Cebuano culture; Filipino culture; internet)
Cusick, Suzanne 5, 97, 199 n.5
cyber 89, 118, 146

dance 6, 23, 118, 131–6, 144, 155, 164–6, 187, 189, 192
   American 53, 56, 63, 123, 143
   communal 121, 129, 149, 181
   dance-off 122, 144
   as discipline 102, 109–13, 143, 146, 148–50, 171
   national 123
   Philippine 11, 55–65, 80, 84
   Spanish colonial 64
   videos 10, 178 (*see also* choreographer; choreography; dance therapy; Jackson, Michael; rehabilitation)
dancers 43, 60, 65, 74, 108–9, 129, 133–6, 164, 188
   backing 117, 169
   lead 66, 80, 102–3, 176
Dance of the Steel Bars (film) 149
dance therapy, dance/movement therapy 64–5, 83, 87, 112, 150, 175–6
Dancing Inmates 102–3, 113, 143, 164–5, 178
   accolades 175
   commercialization of 115, 150, 169
   merchandise 84, 153
   payment 86 (*see also* 'Ambassadors of Goodwill')
Dawkins, Richard 29–30, 108, 150
death 51, 58, 74, 86, 118–19, 185
   Michael Jackson's 1, 117, 119, 124, 148, 169, 171
   social 119, 208 n.1
death penalty 75, 77
Deleuze, Gilles 104, 107
diaspora 7–8, 46, 48, 62, 147, 161, 166

disco 47, 95–6, 102, 114, 144, 203 n.5, 210 n.5
discourse 4, 6, 10, 25, 30, 47, 55, 124, 131, 145–6, 166
   colonial discourse 49, 94
   discourse analysis 9, 158–9, 165, 167, 170–2
DIY (Do It Yourself) 9, 31, 33–4, 39, 183
'docile bodies' 95, 101–5, 109
drag 143–4, 161
drag queen 42, 47, 164. See also *bakla*; gender; trans
drugs 77, 113, 176, 185–7
drum, drums 61, 83, 112, 141, 169
Duran Duran 23
Duterte, Rodrigo (16th President of the Philippines 2016) 185
DVD 169, 182–3

education 27, 65, 81, 133–4
   colonial 47–8, 51–4, 63, 144
   prison 87, 115, 207 n.12 (*see also* school; YouTube and education)
Elequin, Eleanor T. 63
embodiment 5, 62–3, 125, 130–1, 136, 143–6, 183
   embodied discipline 104, 111–14, 171–2, 178
emotional contagion 103, 113, 163
emotional disorder 110
emotional distance 87
emotional labour 190
emotions 103, 111, 112, 139, 161, 171
empire 45, 48–9, 56, 179, 203 n.4
empowerment 25, 31, 147, 163
endorphins 111
entrainment 108
essentialism 47, 55, 68, 152, 174. See *also* stereotypes
experience 22, 49, 81, 88, 89, 94, 112, 142, 144–5, 147, 150, 152, 189
   Filipino experience 46–7, 57
   music experience 3, 12, 20, 57, 78, 126, 135

INDEX

music video experience 23–4, 131, 134, 165, 169–71, 192
prison experience 2, 78–9, 83–4, 87, 98, 108–9, 145, 185–6
Web 2.0 experience 24, 25, 28, 31, 36–9, 103, 178

Facebook 8, 26, 150, 160, 178, 187, 188
fandom 10, 35–6, 39, 40, 122–4, 139, 141, 160, 169. *See also* Jackson, Michael, fandom
femininity 15, 29, 41–2, 55–6
Filipino culture 9, 41, 45, 47, 52–3, 58–9, 64, 77, 88, 142, 178, 188, 192
Filipino music 45–7, 52, 55–9, 61–5, 147, 173–4
film music 42, 71, 127–8
flash mob 132–4, 209 n.11
Foucault, Michel 3, 6–7, 97, 106–7, 110, 199 n.2
   Discipline and Punishment (book), 99–104
Frith, Simon 22, 36, 132, 200 n.5
fun 58, 83, 86, 137–8

'Gangnam Style' (song) 37 168, 182, 210 n.1
Garcia, Byron F. (CPDRC Warden 2005–10) 74, 140, 146, 154
   family 12, 66, 75–7
   inmate's relationship with 66, 68, 103
   interviews and public statements 78, 83, 102–3, 113–14, 148, 175–7, 187
   in the media 79, 82, 86, 92–4, 109–10, 112, 139, 141, 145, 172–3
   YouTube account 10, 16, 33, 78, 80, 184 (*see also* legislation; Garcia, Gwendolyn; Garcia, Pablo)
Garcia, Gwendolyn (Governor) 75–7, 113–14, 139, 143, 186, 204 n.1, 207 n.9, 207 n.11
Garcia, Pablo P. (Representative) 75

gaze 15, 80, 107, 114, 143, 150–2
gender 7, 42, 121, 124, 165, 197.
   See also bakla; drag; trans
Goodman, Steve 3–4
Google 21, 26, 31–3, 88, 137, 162, 201 n.8, 210 n.3
governmentality 6
Guantánamo Bay 97
guitar 72, 101, 155, 204 n.12

Happy Jail (film) 150
harmony 47, 57, 63, 152
hataw sayaw 84
health 2, 88, 94, 111, 114, 146, 190, 205 n.3
Hegarty, Paul 109
heritage 12, 48, 130–1
   Philippine 61–2, 77, 81, 124
   (*see also* tourism)
Hollywood: film aesthetics 45, 72, 78–9, 96, 127–8, 131, 143, 149, 169, 182
   actor 183
   musicals 23
hologram 118
human rights 12, 75, 77, 144, 185–7
humiliation 4, 5, 89, 96, 98, 99, 115, 131, 145, 206 n.4
humour 148, 161, 163, 166–7, 169, 171
hybridity 9, 11–12, 19, 68, 82, 146, 148–9, 172
   Philippine 147, 189

identity 6, 27–29, 36, 39, 54, 64, 68, 124, 146, 152, 166
   national 62, 167, 172, 174, 203 n.8
   Philippine 47, 52, 54, 58, 63, 147, 151, 172, 174, 178
   self-identity 31, 38, 183
   social 36, 45, 58
ideology 2, 26, 28, 51–2, 94–5, 99, 102
   dance rehabilitation ideology 4, 87, 111
'I Love Cebu' (song) 189
imagination 12, 141–3, 151, 179
immediacy 125, 130, 157, 179, 192

imperialism 5, 7, 48–9, 51, 54, 63–5, 68, 92, 144, 147, 151, 202 n.1, 203 n.4. *See also* colonialism; neocolonialism; postcolonialism; racism)
independent 1, 9, 39, 149
independence 7, 54, 61, 63, 68, 151, 202 n.1
individualism 6, 36, 104, 110–11, 113, 131, 160, 185
industry 56, 192
    media 29, 39–40
    music 124, 126, 184, 210 n.1
    prison 87, 149
Instagram 26, 84–5, 134, 167, 178
internet 7, 21, 25, 34, 81, 88, 105, 115, 125, 142, 162, 167, 171, 183
    internet content 26, 33, 114, 175
    internet fame 1, 82, 103, 115, 139, 141, 145
    internet motives 163, 170 (*see also* cyber; Web 2.0)
internet culture 1, 11, 21–2, 24, 26, 28–38, 88, 132, 150, 160–3, 183
intimacy 9, 36, 41, 72, 133, 135, 172

Jackson, Michael 1, 66, 102, 146, 162, 194–6
    dance moves 19, 117–18, 121
    death 1, 83, 117–19, 124, 148, 169, 171
    fandom 121–4, 161, 164, 168–9, 171
    'Heal the World' (song) 176
    legacy 9, 83, 124, 150
    music videos (other than *Thriller*) 23, 103
    Off the Wall (album) 125
    This Is It (film) 169
    voice 19, 43, 117, 130 (*see also*, 'Thriller')
jail 80, 87, 92, 103, 110, 148, 172, 175–6, 187. *See also* prison
James, Rick 126
Japanese 52, 80, 81, 85, 202 n.1
Jarrett, Kylie 28
jazz 8, 56, 64, 125, 129, 173

Jenkins, Henry 20, 26–7, 29–32, 39, 160, 163
Jones, Quincy 125–6, 129–30
jukebox 35, 168

karaoke 7, 141, 155, 168, 185, 203 n.9

labour 13, 53, 57, 77, 88, 108, 142, 163, 169, 190, 206 n.4
    co-labour 118, 163
Landis, John 23, 72, 127, 128, 130, 208 n.5
language 33, 51, 55, 59, 63, 77, 81, 94, 148, 185
    body 42
    Cebuano 59, 113, 159
    cinematic 22
    colonial 47, 92, 144
    English 52–3, 57, 83, 144, 159
    musical 136
    music as 'universal' 94, 151, 177
    of new media 21, 29, 168, 170
    Taglish 159
legislation 77, 175, 185
leisure 52, 79, 82, 103, 115, 143, 171, 191. *See also* time, leisure
Lipsitz, George 190–1
Lonely Planet Philippines (book) 81
lyrics 83, 95–6, 141, 155, 189, 205 n.4
    discussion of 'Thriller,' 17, 103, 130, 165

Macapagal-Arroyo, Gloria (14th President of the Philippines 2001–10) 53, 77, 197
Madonna 23
Madrigals, The (Philippine Madrigal Singers) 173–4
Manovich, Lev 21–2, 135
Marcos, Ferdinand (10th President of the Philippines 1965–86), 53–4, 58, 143, 202 n.1
Marcos, Imelda Romualdez (10th First Lady of the Philippines 1965–86) 58, 143, 203 n.5
Mars, Bruno 38, 68, 81
mash-up 24, 83, 160
McClintock, Anne 148, 151, 199 n.2

McLuhan, Marshall 20, 139–41, 209 n.2
McNeill, William 112, 178
meaning 3, 72, 74, 94, 103, 131
   cultural 63, 68
   extra-musical 173
   production of 109, 130, 135–6, 165, 192
   social 147, 165, 183, 211 n.7
   (*see also* symbolism)
mediate 35, 192
melody 63, 153–5
   countermelody 130
meme 29–30, 150
mental health 2, 4, 110, 111
Mercer, Kobena 124–5, 128, 130–1, 208 n.2
metal (genre) 95–6
military 51, 55, 105, 109, 186
   US 95–7, 199 n.4, 202 n.3 (*see also* soldier; War on Terror; World War II)
mimicry 38, 41–2, 68, 142–3, 179
   musical-mimicry stereotype 64, 142–3
mood 111
morality 89, 102
morals 2, 5, 84, 98, 100, 168, 191
movement 59, 101, 104, 112, 123
   American Civil Rights 131, 209 n.10
   dance 43, 61, 71, 110, 123
   music 33, 111
Mozart, Wolfgang Amadeus 78–9
MTV (music television network) 1, 23–4, 38–40, 125, 129–30, 132, 151, 201 n.13, 208 n.3, 208 n.5
music industries 11, 32, 34, 125–6, 128, 184, 210 n.1
musicking 35, 149, 165, 173
music video 1–2, 68, 128–9, 132, 159
   digital experience of 11, 109, 183, 192
   DIY 9, 34, 132–4
   history of 22–4, 200 n.3, 200 n.4, 200 n.5
   music video game 134
   on YouTube 26, 35–6, 38–40, 46 (*see also specific songs*; *Thriller* (short film))

'My Little Grass Shack in Kealakekua, Hawaii' (song) 189
myth 55, 57, 118, 144, 150, 172, 204 n.10
   YouTube myths 34 (*see also* stereotype)

narrative 11, 80, 147, 167
   cinematic 96, 128, 149
   historical 3, 20, 59
   music video 73–4
   in *Thriller* 42, 128, 131, 204 n.2
   of transformation 144–6 (*see also* music video; YouTube)
neocolonialism 12, 46, 53, 63, 68, 151–2, 172. *See also* colonialism; imperialism; postcolonialism
neoliberalism 6, 26, 28, 40
new media communication 25–6, 88, 132, 158, 162, 165–8, 170, 181, 184, 191
Niere, Crisanto 42–3, 66–7, 149, 176
noise 25, 107–9, 185
noontime TV 144–5, 176
nostalgia 45, 150–2
   globalized 148, 149
   history of 148
   hybridity and 11–12, 139, 143, 172
   and music 87, 111
   'neocolonial nostalgia' 151
   YouTube and 158
nuns 188–190. *See also* Catholicism

ocular 79, 107, 114
OFW (Overseas Filipino Workers) 8, 53–4, 57. *See also balikbayan*
Orange is the New Black (TV series) 84, 205 n.4
Orientalism 49, 55, 68, 151. *See also* colonialism; imperialism; neocolonialism; postcolonialism
Oz (TV series) 84, 205 n.4

pain 5, 98–9, 102
panoptic 3, 84, 105, 108, 199 n.2
   Bentham's panopticon 105–7
   digital panopticon 12, 95, 105, 191
   surveillance 106, 109, 114

Papaeti, Anna 3–4
parody 129, 131
participatory culture 40, 68, 150,
    160–3, 183
  online 10, 24–8
  YouTube 21, 33, 68, 88, 132, 161–2
Patajo-Legasto, Priscelina 46, 49
'Pavlov's Dogs' (song) 95–6
performance 104, 107, 174
  domestic 133–5
  private 133–4, 136, 189–90
  and punishment 100, 124
  recorded 107, 113, 131–3, 176–7,
    181, 183
  theory 111, 164–5 (see also CPDRC
    live; posthumous)
Philippine Exhibition. See St. Louis
    World Fair
Philippines 9, 13, 45–9, 55–66, 82, 114,
    121–4, 141, 144, 150, 173–9
  and digital culture 8, 138, 166, 171
  education 51–3
  Philippine-American War 48, 51,
    202 n.3
  Philippine studies 8, 46–7, 54, 59
  politics 47, 77, 185–6, 203 n.5
  postcolonial 7, 11, 51, 54, 143–4,
    172, 191 (see also Filipino
    culture; Filipino music;
    legislation; postcolonial;
    pre-Hispanic; tourism)
philosophy 40, 83, 94, 110, 187
photographer, photographers 81
photograph, photographs 1, 23, 69, 76,
    83–5, 97, 136, 153, 167, 186
pleasure 29, 49, 87, 148, 183
  activators 42, 111, 150, 171–2
  audience 172
  guilty 131
  music and 21, 56, 68, 78
  sonic 19
popular music charts 125, 127, 149,
    205 n.4, 210 n.1
postcolonial 2–3, 7, 9, 11, 46, 54, 68,
    146, 151, 172, 191–3
  postcolonial performance 12,
    45, 68 (see also colonialism;
    neocolonialism)

posthumous 117–19
pre-Hispanic 47, 55, 56, 64
Price, Vincent 17, 72–3, 128, 130,
    200 n.1
Prison Break (TV series) 84, 205 n.4
Prison Dancer (musical) 149
prisoner health 88, 94, 111, 114, 146,
    205 n.3
prison industry 87, 149
pro-ams (professional-amateurs) 27,
    32. See also amateurs
producer 26, 27, 39, 83, 125, 141, 163
punishment 4, 79, 84, 108, 191
  capital 75, 77
  historical accounts of 10, 92,
    98–102, 104
  modern 6, 97, 104, 157
  in popular media 84–6, 157
  punitive 64, 107 (see also death
    penalty; humiliation; torture)

Queen (band) 109, 184, 194–6

Race 7–8, 125, 181, 203 n.8
racism 7, 65, 68, 166
radio 27, 52, 57, 79, 125, 182, 208 n.6
Ray, Ola 17, 41–2, 71
recidivism 110, 114, 175
record industry. See music industry
recording 16, 34, 43, 124, 144, 149, 178
  artists 118
  bootleg 35, 40
  equipment 84, 108, 202 n.1
  gramophone 52, 206 n.2
  as surveillance 109
rehabilitation 65, 115, 148
  cyber 89
  legislature 150
  music/dance as 9, 64, 80, 83, 87,
    92–4, 111, 175
  programme 82, 114, 144, 153–4
  punishment and 98, 101, 103, 151,
    171
  'responsive rehabilitation' 92, 94,
    187
  US colonial practices of 91–4
religion 113, 161, 168, 188
  and colonialism 52–4

in the Philippines 45–6, 62, 64 (*see also* Catholicism; Christianity; nuns)
and punishment 99, 111, 206 n.2
remediation 12, 16–17, 33, 129, 148, 158, 183, 192
  Michael Jackson and 72, 124, 118
  Thriller remediations 30, 125–7, 130, 132, 135–6, 165
remix 10, 16, 28, 30, 39, 42, 83, 127
repetition 4, 32, 165, 178
Resane, Wenjiel 42, 47, 66, 68, 71, 103, 176, 183
response 5, 7, 86, 98, 170
  emotional 100, 160, 167 (*see also* audience response)
retribution 86, 98–9, 101
rhythm 17, 42, 63, 111–12, 117–18, 126, 129, 139
riot 100
Rogers, Holly 20, 200 n.3
Rorschach (band) 95–6
Rosaldo, Renato 45, 148, 151

St. Louis World Fair 11, 47, 49–50, 65–8
school 51, 63, 65, 133, 157, 164, 210 n.2. *See also* education
Schopenhauer, Arthur 94
scream 71, 96, 130
screen 17, 19, 73, 79, 85, 96
  computer 16, 21, 22, 105
  culture 21–2
  digital 152, 158, 177, 192
  media 21, 25, 74, 130–1, 142, 158, 192, 203 n.5
  surveillance 105
  television 22, 135
Shawshank Redemption, The (film) 78–80
Sinulog 60, 62, 80, 113, 155, 189
'Slave to the Rhythm' (song) 117
slavery 208 n.1
sleep 35, 58, 206 n.2
social media 158, 177, 187, 192
  and attention 132
  in the Philippines 7–8, 138, 167
  and prison 84, 97

social networking sites 7, 8, 24, 34, 88, 134, 160, 167, 178, 205 n.8, 209 n.2 (*see also* Facebook; Instagram; screens; Twitter; YouTube)
soldier 51, 53, 92, 96, 110–12, 148. *See also* military
sonic warfare 96
Sony 40, 161, 169, 211 n.8
speakers 16–17, 20, 155
  prison loudspeakers 1, 16, 72, 78–9, 102, 108–9
spectators 11, 87, 111, 150
  historical accounts of punishment and 92, 100, 211 n.6
  ideal 97, 100
  penal spectators 12, 157–9, 191
Sprechgesang 17, 128, 130
Stanyek, Jason 118
stereotypes 81
  colonial 7, 68, 151
  Filipino 45–6, 58, 83, 178–9, 191–2
  musical 57, 64–5, 203 n.8 (*see also* colonialism; Orientalism; racism)
subaltern 13, 68, 145, 147, 151
subjectivity 5–6, 11, 28, 34, 68, 142, 191
  distributed 183
surveillance 6, 73, 102, 104–9, 114, 136
symbolism 188
  cultural 5, 45–6, 140, 173
  Philippine 62, 147, 172
  punishment and 99
  YouTube and 167
synch 15, 45, 143, 160
syncopation 8

Tadiar, Neferti 47, 143–4
technology 3, 19, 27, 30, 88, 114, 177, 202 n.1
  digital 8, 22, 33, 133, 181
  DIY 39
  media 118, 139, 179, 183, 208 n.3
  mobile 136
  music 83, 190, 200 n.1
  personal 125, 132

Web 2.0 25–6, 28, 141 (*see also* internet)
television 21–3, 31, 34, 39, 57, 74, 84, 86, 125, 132, 135, 141, 145–6, 155, 163, 175–6
Temperton, Rodney L. 125–6, 130
terror 97, 131, 192, 199 n.4, 212 n.1
'Thank You for the Music' (song) 153, 155
therapy, therapeutic 2, 4, 64–5, 87, 110–12, 144, 150, 171, 175–6
third world 47, 53, 143–4
Thompson, Marie 109
Thriller
  (album) 124
  as audiovisual text 5, 16, 72, 125–7, 130–1
  choreography 43, 74, 121–4, 129–33, 135–6, 149
  making of 125–31, 208 n.5
  (music video, short film) 9, 16–17, 42, 72, 123–31, 148, 200 n.1, 204 n.2
  (single) 125–8, 208 n.4, 208 n.6
time
  leisure 39, 79, 108, 188
  passing of 87, 111, 115
  (sentence) 102
  and new media 27, 36–7, 118, 135, 139, 141, 183
'Together in Electric Dreams' (song) 139, 141–2, 209 n.1
torture 86, 199 n.4, 202 n.3, 206 n.3
  forms of 95–7
  music as 3–5, 199 n.5
  no touch/white-collar 5, 96, 206 n.2
  public 101
tourism 7, 81, 86, 88, 115
  Cebu Provincial Tourism and Heritage Council 77, 81, 204 n.1
  dark 86
  destination 12, 82, 86, 149, 157, 204 n.1
  international 45–6, 84, 138
  music 64, 81, 88
  penal 12, 66, 80, 84, 86–7, 178, 191
transformation 12, 92, 101, 113, 130, 144–6

trans (gender/sexuality) 40, 163, 175
transgression 96, 103
Twitter 138, 167, 178

universal 24, 35, 42, 68, 81, 98, 147, 151
  media machines 22
  universality 94, 157 (*see also* language, music as 'universal')

Vernallis, Carol 2, 13, 22, 25, 38, 40, 46, 158–9
Vertov, Dziga 21 133
Vevo 34, 36, 103, 117
VH1 129, 200 n.4
Village People, The 68, 83, 109, 144, 210 n.5
Villaruz, Basilio Esteban S. 63–4
Vimeo 35, 134, 209 n.4
violence 51, 113, 131, 151
  aesthetics of 72, 96
  music and 3–5
  prison 65, 77, 79, 114
  punishment and 99–101, 103, 206 n.4
viral 1, 11, 115, 169, 172
  features of viral media 29–30, 108
  phenomena 47, 123, 158, 167, 181, 207 n.9
  success 81, 86, 139, 158, 174, 192
  video 10, 12–13, 29–30, 114, 124, 150, 170
voice 68, 107, 112–13, 168
  double-voiced 131
  mediated 19, 130, 151
  and significance 36
  singing 78, 141, 155 (*see also* Jackson, Michael, voice)

war 63, 95–6, 112, 208 n.5
  Cold War 173
  on drugs 185
  music and 2–4, 58
  on Terror 97, 199 n.4 (*see also* Philippine-American War; sonic warfare; World War II)
Web 2.0 28–30, 89, 201 n.11
  platforms 24–26
  users 33, 163. *See also* internet

Western 49, 65–6
  art 4
  civilization 63
  culture 142, 147, 178
  hegemony 46
  music 5, 20, 56, 68, 96, 146–7, 179
'White Man's Burden, The' (poem) 48–9
World War II 48, 57, 202 n.1

YouTube
  audience 12, 31, 39, 81, 107–8, 135, 139, 151, 158–65, 170–7
  comments 7, 12, 73, 83, 88, 146, 158–62, 166–74, 210 n.2, 210 n.5
  and copyright 161, 168–9, 210 n.4
  cultures 1, 38, 80, 88, 172
  and education 21, 35, 40, 74
  and participatory culture 21, 68, 88, 132, 161–2
  screen 16, 21, 136, 157, 191
  videos 6, 9, 21, 31, 33, 46, 80, 91, 102, 152, 158, 164, 176 (see also screen)
YouTuber 31–2, 88, 141, 158–60, 162–8, 170, 174

Zižek, Slavoj 150
zombies 17, 42–3, 65–7, 71–3, 121, 123, 125, 129–30, 204 n.2

www.ingramcontent.com/pod-product-compliance
Lightning Source LLC
Chambersburg PA
CBHW052032300426
44117CB00012B/1793